THE
CHOPSTICKS-FORK
PRINCIPLE

A MEMOIR AND MANUAL

First Edition, ©2002 Cathy Bao Bean
Second Edition, ©2003 Cathy Bao Bean
Third Edition, ©2008 Cathy Bao Bean
Fourth Edition, ©2011 Cathy Bao Bean

Printed in the United States of America
Cataloging-in-Publication Data
     1. Biography, Bao Bean, Cathy; Bean, Bennett
     2. United States, Chinese American Cultural History
     3. Family Life
     4. Title

Bao Bean, Cathy, 1942-
     The Chopsticks-Fork Principle, A Memoir and Manual.

Non-fiction
ISBN 0-9725663-0-9

Front cover design by Bennett Bean
Book design by Marty Blake

We Press, P. O. Box 436
Allamuchy N.J. 07820
www.wepress.org

THE
CHOPSTICKS-FORK
PRINCIPLE

A MEMOIR AND MANUAL

BY

CATHY BAO BEAN

Year of The Word Dragon

Cathy Bai B

WE PRESS

NEW JERSEY

2002

ACKNOWLEDGMENTS

This can only be a starting line for thanking those who acknowledged me with their kind attention. To further signify how each sustained and substantiated me with their perceptions and gifts would be akin to deciding which was more nourishing during a time of need—the vitamin pill or feast. I therefore take the simplest and hardest route by listing the people who informed me and this book with their generosity, interest and caring.

Maria-Victoria Abricka	Sieglinde Anderson
Adrianne Aron	Jean Bao
John Perrin Bean	Maria G. Bolton
Judith Campbell	Judy Consentino
Julia Yuen-Heung To Dutka	Joanna Shaw Eagle
Leslie Ferrin	Herb Ferris
Christopher Funkhouser	Kate & Jack Gallagher
Monie Hardwick	Shelby Hearon
Amy Hufnagel	WinWin Kyi
Roger A. Johnson	Stephen M. Johnson
June Kapp	Amy Kossow
Lynda Cornell Lindner	Adele McCollum
Margaret McGarrity	Mark McGarrity
Ellen & Bill Mickelsen	Michelin & Marty Miller
Chan Moore	Celia Morris
Ralph V. Norman	Carol R. & Michael Ochs
Joan O'Mara	Emily & Tony Pantaleoni
Darlene M. Payne	Ursula Perrin
Jayne Pettit	Nancy Picchi
Merrill Maguire Skaggs	Carlos Torre
Kate Warwick	Adrienne Davis Whitehead
Bruce Wilshire	Donna Wilshire

Linda Noel, Carol Lambert & our fellow aerobicizers
Marianne Gilbert Finnegan and the participants
in the **Society for Values in Higher Education**
Forms of Autobiography Morning Group

DEDICATION

TO

BENNETT

OUR PARENTS

and

WILLIAM

FOR THE WORLDS OF

SIMILARITY AND DIFFERENCE

THEY CREATED

PREFACE: GOING AROUND

We had stories and we gave them to our son, William. Heavy with intent, they were the ballast for our shared and separate journeys, steadying us through the surprises and arguments, the differences and similarities. As reminders of our own rebellion and conformity, the stories helped us explore places where parents fear to tread and children will. As portents of our own future, they centered a couple from the Age of Aquarius and Confucius for a voyage with a kid who introduced us to *Calvin and Hobbes* cartoons and thinks Wall Street is the hub of the universe.

Using the stories, we talked ourselves into a relationship with our selves and a child who would not only think it's okay that his parents do this sort of thing, but would also revel in telling them back. The going around and coming around was possible because the stories were more than "just the facts" about more than the "strictly personal." As such, they gained the power to shape our lives and influence how others perceive us and the worlds we live in. This book is the result of believing that such empowerment can be shared.

The writing, however, was a problem. To my linear American mind, the story-telling process could be explained with step-by-step directness, taking the reader from my birth to his adulthood, proceeding from left to right, from the top of the first page to the bottom of the last. But my Chinese mind balked. It wanted to give William, and you, images or "characters" that would start from the traditional right of a wise Asian elder and end on the "left" side of most matters, including the page.

So I selected facts, attached stories to them, then played with their chronology. Just as I did with William. In putting more than one mind and voice into them, I hoped to increase their dimensions with points that he, and you, could think up. Like the stars, these can form constellations—constant yet moving, able to mark places and ideas that are beyond what is immediate and local, capable of tantalizing us with the unseen even as they are visible from wherever we happen to be standing at the time.

THE FACTS

I was born in China as *Bao Kwei-yee*, a native of *Ningpo* by virtue of my father's ancestry, in the Year of the Water Horse, during the 77th or 78th Cycle (depending on which book you consult).

Four years later, my parents, older sister Bette, and I arrived in Brooklyn. As a result, I became "Cathy Bao," born about 800 miles southwest of those same forefathers, on August 27, 1942, in *Kweilin/Kuei-lin/Guilin* (depending on which atlas you consult). In the process, I also became a Virgo and Dodgers fan. My younger sister, *SanSan*, stayed in China.

One day later, Bette and I were enrolled in Public School #8. I spoke no English. Bette could say "Lucky Strike" and "Shut up." The Principal let her skip 2 grades and made me do kindergarten twice. Bette also skipped pneumonia, mumps, measles, chicken pox and lice. I did them twice too (except the pox).

In 1949, we moved to Elmwood Park, NJ. I started to think in English and forget in Chinese.

In 1951, we bought our first house half a block from Teaneck High School, reputed to be the best on the East Coast.

In 1953, I went to summer camp and got "scalped."

Four years later, I was in 10th grade and got "scalped" again.

In 1958, I received my first birthday cake.

The next year, I received the Junior Citizen of the Month Award. The following night I was summoned to court.

In 1960, I went to college where I majored in History, Government and screaming. (The latter didn't help me become the Jew I wanted to be, but it did get me on the cheerleading squad and, from there, on to a full page of *Sports Illustrated*...clothed!)

In 1962, I heard Malcolm X tell my roommate she was no longer a Negro, she was a Black Woman. That same year, *SanSan* got out of

China and drank the contents of her finger bowl.

The next year Bette wrote a worldwide best seller about *SanSan*.

In 1964, I went to graduate school in California and learned how to Philosophize and be a Matchmaker.

One month later, I met Bennett Bean, a Caucasian male who didn't wear socks and wanted to make art. He thought I was Japanese.

Two days after he found out I wasn't, he was declared psychologically unfit to serve in the army.

Two weeks later, he proposed. I accepted.

In 1965, I received a Kent Fellowship from the Danforth Foundation after a 5-minute interview. I enrolled at the University of California in Berkeley. There I met several of Bennett's friends. Mostly they lived in communes and nudist colonies. I became a Democrat.

The next year, Bennett started teaching at a private college. After he shaved his beard and cut his hair, we got married. My mother said the word "sex" to me for the first time.

In 1967, the Whitney Museum bought Bennett's sculpture even though it was upside-down, and I was accused of being a prostitute by the concierge in a big hotel (probably because I escaped a third scalping by the Bag Lady on the Staten Island Ferry and he didn't know women with long Chinese hair might use their brains for a living).

The next year, I started teaching at a state college for less money than I made as a waitress and helped start the Black Studies Program.

One year later, we were both fired. The students protested and we were both re-hired. Soon thereafter, I developed my Menopausal Theory of Cooking.

In 1970, we met Billie Burke. Once the Good Witch Glinda in *The Wizard of Oz*, she had since become a Real Estate agent. She pointed us toward the eastern equivalent of Kansas, northwestern New Jersey, where we bought an old farmhouse. The neighbors thought I was the maid.

One year later, I got tenure. When the chairperson asked me to make curtains for the office, I resigned and became a feminist before I became a "Chinese-American."

In 1973, I became a US citizen—that's when the mayor asked me to be a Lenape Indian in the town's Bicentennial Parade and I gained 70 pounds.

In early 1974, our son, William, was born. He weighed only 7 pounds, 14 ounces. 24 hours later, I decided Santa Claus and the Tooth Fairy didn't exist, Cinderella was a wimp, and Pinocchio had extraordinarily poor taste in friends.

The next year, Bennett got fired again. A few months later, the National Labor Relations Board ordered the school to give him back his job.

In 1976, *SanSan* got divorced. She thought she was Japanese.

In 1977, William took off his diaper and I started teaching at another state college.

Two years later, Bennett was fired again. This time, when the N.L.R.B. told the college to give him back his job, he declined the honor and became a full-time artist. When the Internal Revenue Service told me we owed them taxes as a result, I declined that honor.

In 1986, William turned 12 and had his first birthday party. I turned 44 and didn't stop smoking because the hypnotist couldn't find my subconscious. So I incorporated and opened up an aerobics studio. Around this time, my college roommate became an African-American.

In 1990, William got his first tattoo.

One year after that, I slept next to some of my teeth and started to write my memoir. William got a second tattoo.

In 1993, Bennett was invited to the White House. He wore pink socks.

That same year, William, at 19, decided he would marry at the age of 27. I made a few suggestions. He said, "No thank you," indicating that I would get my chance at making "confusion among the cutlery" *after* a few dates.

In 2002, once again the Year of the Water Horse, after 59 years of constructing a home to have a wedding, I began the second cycle of my life by urging the newlyweds, William and Lisa, to make another life and, thereby, make me a grandparent. After 35 anniversaries, Bennett continues to have too many lives.

6

PART ONE

DOUBLE VISIONS, TWICE REMOVED

We pass on legacies, hoping our children can and do accept them. We also eliminate what we don't want to be remembered or repeated.

The children who are thereby endowed—and bereft—don't always agree with their parents which is the legacy and which should be forgotten or not experienced again.

For some, the giving and receiving engender more gratitude than dread because the process means continuity. For others, because disruption is promised.

CHAPTER 1

THE CUSTOMS EXCHANGE: COMING IN, GOING OUT

THE CUSTOMS EXCHANGE: COMING IN...

Families traveling together may make a joint declaration to customs, a procedure that permits one member to exceed his or her duty-free exemption
to the extent that another falls short.
> —*Birnbaum, America's Favorite Travel Guides*

I know the sun was shining that day in June, 1951, though I can only
suppose how the four of us got to Teaneck, NJ—probably in the old
'47 dark blue Chevy. The other clear memory I have was hearing the
doorbell ring and, then, my mother calling me. Stepping aside, she
pointed outside. There might have been a moving van parked by the
curb, but I can't picture it now. Maybe it was still at the apartment in
Elmwood Park, loading up the furniture that I also can't recollect.
What I can bring back, standing against the background of our very
own front lawn, were two big girls. Now more shy than when they
mistakenly asked my mother if she could come out and play, they were
waiting to see what size I would be. When seeing didn't help, one
asked what grade I was in.

I said the magic word, "Fourth."

It couldn't have been better. Claire lived across the street from our
first house, a compact split-level, with brick front and shutters, each
flap decorated with a cutout in the shape of a shamrock. And Jan lived
behind Claire, so their yards touched cater-corner. I'm sure Jan had a
front door, but it was the back one I got to know. During the warmer
days, we'd careen in and out of the screened entryway. If it got too
cool, we'd take a little longer to turn the handle of the solid inner
door. By the end of that first summer, if someone had locked either, I
would have landed in the hospital with a dislocated shoulder.

In Jan's house, we sprawled all over. We did what wasn't an option
at mine—move chairs to build forts, cover the dining room table with
paper dolls, dress up in curtains. Her parents, now Aunt Dorie and
Uncle Herb to me, seemed to accept this sort of behavior as an
inevitable consequence of having children. Except for my sister's and
my rooms, our house was always neat, ready for guests. On the other
hand, there was at Jan's house, something that didn't exist at mine:
places that were off-limits.

"See that?"

"What?"

"The box."

Looking on the floor of her father's closet, I saw too many, "Which one?"

"*That* one."

"I see. What about it?"

"IT's in there." she whispered.

Cued, I lowered my voice and body to match hers, "Really?"

"Yeaah."

"Wow."

This was important. Used to playing hide-and-seek throughout her house, we generally stayed out of Uncle Herb and Aunt Dorie's room. So being there at all demanded a respectful pause. But I could tell from my friend's manner that she expected more. So, in silent reverence, we knelt before the shoe box.

As great as my awe was, I soon needed more of a reason to spend my time in an otherwise ordinary closet.

"Jan?"

"Yeah?"

"*What's* in the box?"

The tips of her fingers reached out and carefully lifted the lid. Looking inside, I saw a gun. In this house-of-no-locks, in a town of no violence, in a country where *If I Knew You Were Comin' I'd've Baked A Cake* was a popular song, we watched the gun as we would observe creatures in the snake house at the zoo. The thing itself kept us from reaching out. The shoe box was more inviolate than the thick glass, the weapon even less susceptible to tampering than the giant python.

"Jan, *why* does your father have a gun?"

"He works for the F.B.I."

That capped it. Not only did I have the best friend in the world but her father had fought Al Capone single-handed. Or close to.

Once again we crouched in silence, enveloping the revelation in an aura of quiet. That done, we tiptoed out of the room. Then hid our trail by thundering down the stairs and crashing out the door.

In the backyard, we flopped down on a patch of grass—evidence that it must have been a windy day when her neighbor sowed his seeds. If I was to take my turn, it had to be soon. A lot of being Best Friends is in the timing.

"Guess what?" I began.

"What, Cath?"

"I've got a sister."

"Yeah, I know." Too polite to say, "Big deal, so do I," I knew Jan was thinking just that.

"I don't mean Bette. I have another one."

More interested, Jan looked up, "You mean a baby?" How else could she have missed seeing another Bao. Had it been the walking variety, we would have used it by now—to divert her younger brother, Chuckie, from tagging along after us all the time.

"No, not a baby. At least not any more, I don't think."

"Whaddaya mean, 'You don't think'? Don't you know?" Her look told me she might be having second thoughts about being best friends with an idiot.

"I mean she's not a baby. But the last time I saw her, she was."

Jan sat up. I'd gotten her. I rose too, and we sat, facing each other, in the cross-legged position of a serious conversation.

"Where is she? Why haven't you seen her? What's her name?"

"Jean. But we call her *SanSan*. That means "three-three," because she's the third daughter. She's in China."

"What's she doing there? You didn't *forget* her, did you?"

Jan knew I had been born in China. And she knew from her own experience that, in the excitement of going on a trip, it's possible to leave something important behind and not realize until you've been in the car an hour. But it's not so easy to leave a baby

And so I told her my secret. As we idly pulled up the remaining patch of lawn, I told her that, when we came to America in 1946, we were only supposed to stay a year, so *SanSan* was left in the care of my Aunt.

"Uh?"

My "explanation" was making less sense to her with every word. Normal people get baby-sitters. But for a year?! I could see her wondering if her best friend's whole family didn't have a problem with reality. I started to panic. I had to make her understand.

"*SanSan* was only fifteen months. My mother would've had trouble taking care of three kids all by herself in a strange country. I wasn't supposed to come either. But I packed my doll suitcase, stood by the front door with it, and threw a tantrum. She gave in. I guess she figured, at four, I might be old enough to learn a little something from the trip."

"'Trip'?! Cath, it's *1951*." Stopping to calculate on her fingers,

"You've been here five years!"

Letting up a little, Jan must have realized that her interrogation was too insistent. Her new neighbors might be forgetful, maybe crazy, possibly criminal, but that was no excuse for being impolite. On the other hand, five years was an awful long time to leave a kid just 'cause you didn't want to change a few diapers. And what about the poor aunt? Family is family, yet Jan's most favorite relative had a limit of about two weeks for the three of them. It could go to a month if there was only one.

My "secret" was unraveling. I hadn't meant for her to pull out this much. Actually, it wasn't a secret. But it was "family business." And there were rules about family business. I wasn't always clear exactly what those rules were. I knew age didn't matter that much. Bette and I heard Grown-up Talk all the time. And I knew it wasn't limited to blood relatives. Or maybe it was just that we had to make do with family friends, since most of the Baos and Fangs were still in China. I knew that if there was a "lesson" to the story, just about anybody could hear it. On the other hand, if the gossip revealed an abiding character flaw or gross failing that could reflect badly on the whole family, it was hardly ever discussed. In some cases, like this one, the silence had to do with the Communists and the Nationalists.

"Jan, she lives in *Red* China."

"Ooooh." Now we were getting somewhere. All Americans, even fourth-graders, knew that it was better to be dead than Red.

"After we arrived here, there was a Civil War back home."

"Yeaaah." This, too, made sense. Jan never went to the Deep South on vacation.

"And the Communists fought the Nationalists, the *Kuomintang*."

"The Who?" Oops. I was losing her again.

"The good guys."

"Got it."

"So when the Communists took over The Mainland...."

"Where's that?"

"It's China. Sort of. It's where the Chinese live. But it's not 'China'. That's on Taiwan."

"Where's that?"

"Near the Mainland. It's an island. Some call it Formosa."

"For-Who?"

"Never mind. The point is: The Communists won't let my sister out. That's why she's not here with us."

"Oh, Cath. How sad. What a bunch of meanies."

Finally. She said what I wanted to hear.

But it wasn't the truth. Not really. How could I explain that it's hard to be sad about someone I didn't know? Or even admit that I'd never seen my parents cry over their loss? Yet for the sake of everyone's future, we lived as part, apart. Bonded by something more immediate than feeling, more urgent than tears, we lived like so many Chinese before us: with separation but not distance. We were each with many selves—mothers, fathers, sons, and daughters—who daily, yearly, lived without spouses, siblings, and parents.

Long before "broken home" became a household word, trying to describe to the average American how good and real people could, for reasons other than military or religious duty, be "married" without seeing each other, or "loving" without helping their child take a first step, was too difficult to attempt. Without a lot of explaining and so little comparable experience, it's no wonder people on this side of the ocean thought of Chinese as "heartless," "emotionless," "inscrutable." And without a lot of realities to compare and appreciate, it's no wonder people from across the ocean can think of Americans as "soft," "undisciplined," "without subtlety." Sitting in Jan's backyard, between Cranford and Werner Place, the idea that a Mainland bureaucrat might read my parents' letters before they arrived in my aunt's hands, or plot to kidnap my father in order to boast his "happy repatriation," was a *fact* of my life but had little to do with it. Although everything about it.

Aunt Dorie called. I was saved from having to give more details. It was five o'clock and time to help get dinner ready. With a handshake, we signaled our confidence in each other and our agreement to return to the world of ordinary mortals. Jan never asked more about *SanSan*. Nor did I ask if Uncle Herb ever took the gun out of the box.

Back at my house, I knew that if I hurried, I could finish up my chores in time to be on Teaneck Road when my father stepped off the bus. I loved to watch when he did, looking so dapper in his suit and hat. Giving me a smile, he would keep hold of the newspaper, but let me carry his brief case. That was the same as holding hands—which is what Jan did with her father.

I always asked if he had a good day at the office. He always did. I hardly ever told him how I had spent the day, unless it had to do with

Mommy, in which case I would get another smile and maybe a light thwack with the newspaper to show how much he appreciated having such a dutiful daughter. We spoke English. He was very good at it—better than most Americans. He enjoyed making conversations and being the Master of Ceremonies.

The walk from the bus stop was a short one, up the tree-lined street of one-family houses. Every few steps, we would pass a grassy lawn, sometimes greeting a neighbor working on a flower bed or removing a tricycle from the driveway. Whatever the condition of the back yard, the front view was a presentation of the house, not at all like the pictures I'd seen in books of Chinese homes where high walls made it impossible for insiders and outsiders to exchange casual glances.

As much as I loved walking with my father, I was glad we lived in the middle of the block and not further up Cranford Place. I never seemed to have enough things to say—important stuff that would capture his interest. I could always get his attention. But that wasn't the same.

When we stepped into the house, my mother would be waiting. She too would ask if he had a good day at the office. Now speaking mostly Chinese—which I sort of understood—his response sometimes took all of dinnertime, even the rest of the evening. They never pecked cheeks like Jan's parents, or even hugged. In our house, the public gesture would have been redundant; in our universe, a red flag to gods who tended to look at close proximity as only chemical, never magical. The difference was what I expected—the same as if Jan and I each brought home extra homework to be done over a weekend. Aunt Dorie would, likely as not, express some sympathy, even help ease the burden by reading a story with her, whereas my mother would look at an armload of books as a natural extension of my student's body. As to chancing a discussion with me about some girl osculating a slimy Frog-Prince, let alone a young man kissing an unchaperoned Beauty sleeping with a bunch of wild animals in the woods? No way.

As my father, Bette and I took our places at the kitchen table, my mother would be at the stove nearby, a bowl in hand, asking how much rice we each wanted. I never asked for more than half. Too many times, American mothers would look at my short, skinny body and serve me a fully loaded plate to "fatten me up" or "put meat on my bones." These Fork Dinners meant I had "to clean my plate" or be considered rude or forgetful of "the starving Armenians." With not enough time to grow between the salad and dessert, I learned to swallow very hard, so my esophagus could act as a compressor, jamming out all extraneous air from the food. The result was a mass of incredible density and weight. And a very strong stomach.

At home, however, I could choose how much to take. But once received, I had to eat every grain or dishonor the farmer whose labor produced it. We thought it odd that Americans seemed to plan a meal so that every diner got equal portions, no matter what size or how hungry they were. Afterward, helping to clear the table, it killed us to see the uneaten portions thrown out. On the other hand, our American guests would look at what my mother cooked for them and wonder if an army was going to join us for dinner. They didn't understand that we were honoring them (and making sure the gods only associated our house with plenitude). Oddly, they also were uncomfortable about wrapping the leftovers for another day (or for live burials if we didn't get to them before something else did). In those days, because "doggy bags" were only available in Chinese restaurants, we tried to clear the table as quickly as possible and forestall their wondering where our nonexistent pet was.

Absorbing the two styles of dining eventually evolved into my Chopsticks-Fork Principle: a way to get a handle on our cultural differences and similarities. The Chopsticks table is round with a lazy Susan in the middle to deliver the various dishes within reach of every diner. At an extra large table, standing is permitted as when the hostess searches for a special morsel to give an honored guest. There is no other centerpiece so everyone present, including children of all ages, can make eye contact—which is all one requires to start, interrupt, continue, override, or repeat and repeat and repeat the thought, report, description, gossip, judgment, event, etc. that will become part of the oral-aural history of the speaker, listener, group. A "quiet Chinese dinner" is an oxymoron. Being part of the group partaking of the meal is primary; all forms follow this binary function. Hot tea is served before, during and after the meal to aid digestion. Cold water is a Western invention. While special sauces are served alongside certain dishes, having salt, pepper, soy and mustard sauce on the table to cater to individual preferences is another Western invention. To make these available as a matter of course is to announce that the chef doesn't know how to complete the recipe or the diner doesn't know when to leave well enough alone.

Weapons are inappropriate when dining with family and friends, so knives aren't part of the usual place setting. It is therefore the chef's job to prepare most ingredients in bite-size pieces. Exceptions—like a whole fish or shrimp, beef stew, noodles—must be so "done" that chopsticks, sometimes with the help of lips, teeth and tongue, are sufficient to rip, stab, probe, bone, or shell. That is, to achieve whatever remains to be done to the item before swallowing can take place. While more proactive, there are rules. I hadn't thought of them until I first saw Bennett, my future (Caucasian) husband, eat with chopsticks. Pleased that his skill with utensils was already as multicultural as mine, I couldn't believe what he did with them. First, he picked up his rice bowl to his lips. Okay. Then he proceeded to shovel nonstop until the bowl was practically empty. Not okay. Horrified, I suggested to the barbarian that two delicate sweeps was the limit. Somewhat sheepishly, he allowed as how he acquired his technique by watching Toshiro Mifune and Blind Samurai movies.

At a Chopsticks table, I automatically put both arms on the table and lean in toward the center to signal my joining in. Then, like a spider, our conversations weave a web by crisscrossing in tangents, diameters and radii. Periodically, one person or topic attracts everyone's attention and the unity is strengthened. At family gatherings, rarely was I the one—neither my Chinese nor my opinions were to be trusted. Though the last time I did manage both to the delight of all, including my parents, was when I initiated a discussion on the designs of bathrooms around the world.

In contrast, the Fork table is usually rectangular with one or more centerpieces bifurcating it longitudinally. The effect of having flowers, candles, and/or sculptural objects is to emphasize the aesthetics, not just the function of the dining experience. When tall, the display can also discourage talking across the table. While this means extra care must be taken to create a good seating plan (by alternating gender, volubility, common interests, etc.), it does tend to keep the noise level down. (So does the practice of feeding young children earlier or elsewhere.) Apropos to a democracy, the more that is individualized, the more splendidly formal the occasion. In the extreme, this means each diner is allocated salt cellars and pepper shakers, different forks and (sets of) plates for each course, knives for each texture, glasses shaped for each type of liquid.

At a Fork table, I right away place the hand that's not in use in my lap. It doesn't matter that I like *wontons* better than filet mignon, or think it's inefficient to put the fork first in the left hand for cutting and then in the right for delivering. Preference is irrelevant, being proficient in both ways means I can chew with confidence, without making anybody feel ill at ease—including me—about which of the four forks, three knives, and one spoon to use for which course (not counting the utensils which come with and after dessert). Maintaining a little distance, physically and conversationally, the Americans know I'm both respectable and respectful because I can sit, unpropped, juggle silverware without violating my neighbors' air space, and pace myself so I don't begin before everybody else is served or end after others are sated. With the exception of folks who have dementia or imbibed too many cocktails, one isn't supposed to repeat the same story over and over, but is expected to be a good enough talker and listener that reruns are kept to a minimum.

While both Chopsticks and Fork people hope it's all delicious, the former say so by not making too many recommendations on how it could have been better (based on their experience tasting some renowned cook's version) while the latter pay their compliments to the chef by saying it was the best they ever tasted. When eating with forks, we wait for everyone to be seated. At a Chopsticks Dinner, the hostess might spend more than half the evening cooking so each dish is piping hot when first tasted. This was one reason we used to linger after every meal, picking at this or that morsel, to keep my mother company as she ate.

Even when she started to work outside the house and there were many dinners we couldn't share, our self-image was of a family that did. Similarly, I continued to feel like a daughter who meets her father at the bus stop even when I didn't because school had started and there were so many friends to distract my filial heart. But when I did meet him, I had more to say. Mostly about arithmetic. Never about the twins next door. Jan used to kid me that if I married one of them, my name would be Cathy Cathie. That would have been fun, but I didn't think it was worth the uncertainty of not knowing who was my husband, Ricky or Walter. Besides, chitchatting to one's father about boyfriends was not appropriate for college kids, let alone a fourth-grader.

I told my father about the play I was producing, but not about the fights I had. They never resulted in any visible wounds except the time I retaliated by putting chewing gum in Stephen Miceli's hair after he pelted us with popcorn at the movies. That was scary. His mother had to cut it out. That meant he had to come to school with an almost bald spot. For days, I expected her to show up at my doorstep, towing her evidence by the hand, pleading her case before my mother. At the time I didn't know most American parents indulgently wrote off this sort of thing as an example of how "boys will be boys." As for my mother, one look at his head, and she'd have ruled against me, however much popcorn he'd thrown. Having incited the disorderly conduct of Stephen's hair, I had forced his family into a terrible choice: either they endanger his educational viability by keeping him home from school or they lose face by sending out a son who couldn't appear "normal" in public.

Sometimes I was tempted to tell my father about the fights. I wanted him to know that Daughter #2 might be a bit undergrown, but she was no pushover. If a boy went after my pencil or scarf, I didn't run away. By the end of November, I had Scheduled Bouts before and after school, two or three times a week. (Maybe they did know. For years, I thought their Chinese nickname for me referred to the "Little Fatty" I was when a baby. It turns out that *Shao Tüfei* means "Little Bandit.")

The flirting—for that's what my friends called it—had to stop. I was running out of pencils and my mother was starting to wonder how I could lose so much of my wardrobe just walking to school. After the chewing gum incident, I made a deal with Stephen (he was still growing back his hair and ready to negotiate). For a couple of pieces of candy, he would get his best friend, Fred, to be my official body guard. It worked out great. Fred was monstrously big and almost as tough as I was.

None of the other girls fought the way I did. Part of it was because I was the new kid in school; part of it was the fun in proving that looks can be deceiving—like at that first recess. Biding my time, I stood around while the captains picked everybody else before me. For half the game, I sat against the fence until the rules demanded that they give me a turn regardless of the two outs and a man on base. Making my way to the bats, I saw the outfield closing in, and the infield taking the opportunity to tie a shoelace or start a conversation. Selecting the heavier bat, I heard the snickering. Then, top-heavy, I assumed my Jackie Robinson stance. Since most girls—and some

21

guys—would wait for the pitch with the bat resting on their shoulders, this cued a couple of the kids to back up to their former positions. Willing the ball into my range, I smashed the sucker over all their heads.

Daddy would have enjoyed it had he been there. Too bad I couldn't just tell him. That would have been bragging, and that was more than "impolite." When I credited my homer to good fortune or took full blame for striking out, it was because the gods might be listening in. Capable of anger, even jealousy, they might be provoked into teaching me a lesson. Or worse, taking my lack of humility out on my father. If all they heard from a household were disclaimers like, "My wife? Pretty? Her toenails are ingrown and her ankles are too fat." then they wouldn't think the family was getting too proud. On the other hand, to tell my father (and the gods) after something good happened might suggest that success wasn't routine. People and gods are supposed to bring about the best possible under the circumstances. That's a given. If the effort yields better results than they or we anticipated, the astonishment is a bonus (but no excuse to rest on one's laurels). This is how we *behaved*, not how we "believed." We acted as if the gods existed but we didn't worship them. What we knew about their attitudes came through stories, not "commandments."

Still, I would have liked my father to have been a witness to my victory, to have him invisibly at my side. Just once. Expecting or needing more would have been too much for both of us. To secure my future and his senior years, no one could afford immoderate or immodest demands on the other's time. This was assumed, never discussed. If he preferred playing tennis to commuting, or wondered how a bat and ball would get me from the sandlot to Istanbul, I never heard it. Nor did I hear talk about "following in his footsteps" or "leaving the nest," or "having a better life." My parents never said, "Why can't you be like so-and-so?" or "Remember, we're counting on you," as if I needed the reminder or could fail to grow up, go to college, have a career, and be available to them in their old age as they were to me in my childhood. What they did do was tell me stories about far-fetched people—like the one about the filial daughter who chopped off a piece of her arm to feed her starving parent. Talk about intense! Intents?

How and what they taught us contrasted with another game we used to play at recess, *Mother, May I?*

I remember the first time I was the Leader. Confronting my classmates, I said, "Take two giant steps forward."

Almost as one, they asked, "Mother, May I?"

Magnanimous, I responded, "Yes, you may."

They did. Except one, who took three. I spotted him. In this game, as in others, the strategy is to end up ahead of the pack, but not to stand out too much—being too different raises fear and attracts suspicion. Pointing, I named him and his offense, then ordered him back to the starting line. My look could do that. He obeyed. What power!

Meanwhile, the rest weren't so neatly lined up. Those with long legs or the ability to make a great leap forward from a standing start were now in front. I decided to face the other way and lure the daring ones with false security. Many would stay put, taking a step only with permission, but others would take the dare and chance a quick run before I could whip around and catch them in the act. Calculating that none were close enough to make a dash and tag me while my back was turned, I waited an extra second, turned quickly, and caught several on the move. Satisfied, I repeated the ploy. But the rest were closing in. I got anxious, "Take one baby step forward."

"Mother, May I?"

"No, you may not."

With that unexpected call, a few were tricked. I was sure there were others, but they got away with it because they hid behind the ones in front—who were now too close for me to look at all at once. I could sense their growing impatience, their impending rush. No matter how clever I was, my gambits could only change the end game, not the outcome. I got panicky. And decided this wasn't fun anymore.

I also decided it was a lousy way to raise kids.

Not that I stood on the playground, as prescient about my future as I was wise to Little Steve using Big Fred as a blind. Rather, I was beginning to detect the patterns: about the hierarchy in "May I?"; the competition in "Scrimmage," the strategy in "Stealing second base," the grit in "Facing off," the safety in numbers, the risk in being ahead.

In the process, I was becoming more bicultural, more like everybody else. A lot of people don't think of themselves that way, but they are—it comes with the territory of spending half the time at home or with memories, the other half elsewhere, like tourists. But immigrants do it more. It can be exhausting—which is why there are those who prefer to stay in Little Italy or Soho, Little Tokyo or Germantown, to eat at the same table or live in the same dorm, where they can relax, and just twirl or slurp the noodles with no thought about whether to ladle or stab them instead. My great fortune was having parents who balanced the fascination of touring with the desire to return home, the excitement of emigrating with the comfort of nesting. They encouraged me to "get along" in Teaneck. And I did.

I absorbed the differences between our not holding hands and my friends not holding hands, between my not telling my parents, and their not telling theirs, between saying it and meaning it, between their asking for permission and my hardly ever doing so. I thought I knew how my parents felt from what they told me people, real and imagined, *should* feel. For a long time, it didn't occur to me that there was much discrepancy. Or maybe it was the asking about feelings that was of no use—like standing in the sunshine during a picnic and saying, "Aren't you glad it didn't rain after all?" Or maybe it was just the times. In those days, *Movietone* and televised news might show people hugging or weeping but reporters didn't bother interviewing the lone survivor of a family crash with a "How do you feel?" Anyway, we didn't ask the question in public or private. If I felt some inexpressible confusion, then I probably hadn't paid good attention; if I needed my parents' permission, then I probably shouldn't be doing it; if we needed "to talk it over," it was probably out of the question. What my parents acknowledged of my conduct was what was supposed to be. The rest went into limbo. Some emerged when shared with friends who also didn't tell their parents everything, but most remained incognito.

Maybe that's why it took as long as it did to find the words to express the different patterns. As a suburban American, I could have a First and Second Childhood, a Subconscious, Love, Individuality, Justice and Rights. As a Confucian[1] Chinese, I could expand into an ever larger web of Human Relationships made proper by degrees of obedience, authority, trust, labor, modesty and, sometimes, affection. As a Bao and Fang living in New Jersey, I was to accomplish the "all" of the All-American, but weave only with the larger Chinese web in mind. It seemed to be that simple—until the day I wrote the letter to the *Reader's Digest* and showed it to my father.

"Cathy, I know you've spent a lot of time on it. But I don't think

---

[1] Although I do quote scholars in this book, I use this term not as a scholarly reference so much as a catch-all for the ideas I thought my parents were attributing to the philosopher when they said things like, "Confucius says...."

you need to mail it."

"But Daddy, it's so unfair. Kids aren't like that. We're not a bunch of hoodlums."

"They know that."

"Then why don't they say so?"

"It's a magazine."

"That everybody reads."

"Yes."

"People should know the truth."

"Yes, but what truth will they get from reading your letter?"

"That we're not all bad."

"Maybe what they'll think is only that you are praising yourself."

"Oh."

At the time, writing it was extraordinary. The letter was an indictment, a public airing of a private grievance, an outright criticism of people who had nothing to do with me, who weren't related to me, but who had somehow injured me. It was my first collision with an institution and my experience with riding a "high horse."

And it was boastful. In the Confucian and Buddhist scheme of things, each individual is responsible for strengthening the moral fiber of the universe while simultaneously obliterating the ego. Thus everything depends on everyone. Since the "they"s of the world had not yet crystallized in my mind as "the media," "the government," "the police," "the church," "the system," for me to redress one journalist's error by publicizing my (self) righteousness wouldn't tilt the balance for the better. And so the letter remained unstamped.

What was ordinary then, and since then, was my father asking me how I spent the day, and my thinking ahead so as to prioritize the list and call attention to the exemplary deeds: "playing ball with Jan," "reading," "collecting dead bumblebees," "polishing shoes." I liked to put in a little something from each category to assure him, Chopsticks-Forks style, that I was developing the range of skills needed to harmonize my life with the family's as well as an assortment of people. I included nothing that might disturb our domestic tranquility or the human world as Confucius would have it.

If I had been playing with dolls, I avoided saying so, or stressed the "who with" rather than the "what." Pretending a "thing" could talk like a human was difficult. I did it. Not to would have been unsociable, even snotty. But I found the make-believe part hard to do and report. Chit-chatting about what hasn't really happened when there is no moral lesson involved or no spinning needed to explain what a god might have overheard and misinterpreted was not much more acceptable than talking about boyfriends and kissing.

So I learned to knit and sew for my doll, concentrating on the creation of tiny outfits rather than fantasies. They had the added advantage of being something I could actually display to my parents. I didn't know how much they impressed my father until, one weekend, he took out some wire cutters and pliers, and made a set of miniature hangers.

That was the closest he ever came to entering my child's world. We did a lot of stuff together, but it was "real" stuff like cleaning out the garage or washing the car. He never joined in a board game or asked about characters that didn't exist, the way Aunt Dorie or Uncle Herb might. Once, he had to take my doll to the hospital, but that wasn't "playing." It happened because one of his associates from the office had to do some weekend work at our house. The man brought his daughter along. Closer to my age than Bette's, she became my responsibility. If she had a reason for hurting me, I can't remember it. All I can recall is how she maliciously tore out the doll's hair—a Victorian coiffure of honey-colored elegance. I didn't stop her because that would have embarrassed the father who couldn't stop her without mentioning the unmentionable: his daughter's (and, therefore, his) failure to be a Good Guest. Had we both not ignored her vandalism, it would have caused a whole chain of events and admissions that shouldn't happen if my father and he had to work in the same office together, if we had to live in the world we created.

After they left, my father took out the telephone book, made a call, handed me the hairless doll, and drove me for many miles. The trip was his paternal recognition that I'd done my filial duty by not altering that girl's face on the spot. And by not crying my heart out until after their car turned the corner. In doing this, he taught me that hearts can break, but that there are remedies.

I'd never heard of such a place as a Doll Hospital. It smelled of musty wood and had no furniture except a long counter. There were no walls, just shelves, filled with cubbyholes and boxes. A man, wearing an apron, came out of the back room. He looked exactly the way I imagined Master Cherry did when he tried to make Pinocchio into a table leg. My father told me to explain what I wanted—which wasn't easy since I wasn't sure what we were doing in this strange shop. Running out of words, I carefully laid my doll before him, letting him see for himself. Except for its hard rosy surface reflecting the light from the bare bulb overhead, it looked quite dead, its eyes wide open.

"Mmm, I see."

Not saying more, he went to a shelf and took down a box. It was covered with dust and not very awe-inspiring. But inside! Wigs. All colors and styles. One by one, Master Cherry took them out and held each type on my doll for me to see. None were Victorian; my doll would never be the same. Swallowing my disappointment, I looked at the array on the counter and got caught up in the old man's patter. He lured me with his discussion of each wig's virtues, real qualities—color, length, hairstyle. I had never heard a grown person talk about a doll as if it mattered. On the other hand, he wasn't pretending. He wasn't trying to make my doll into a "person," just a better doll.

"Now these. These you can comb. If you do it carefully."

That did it. I examined this last batch, combing each with my mind—Victorian, Chinese, whatever my fingers could manage. Finally, I pointed at a lump of gleaming auburn redness, nodding my decision.

My father didn't ask "Are you sure?" or "Don't you think it's awfully bright?" He simply added his nod to mine, and stood by me as Master Cherry disappeared into the back with my doll and wig. The minutes passed and I got worried. What was he doing back there? I had picked out what I wanted. Why weren't we in the car by now?

Taking my cue from my father, who didn't seem impatient, I kept my questions to myself, and waited. When the old man finally emerged, holding forth my doll, I remained speechless. The ringlets didn't slide off! My doll had "hair," not just a wig.

I didn't thank my father. We often said "please," but rarely a "thank you." Some words are more for guests than family. Family members are supposed to be a certain way. Thanking each other for it could insinuate that either might have done otherwise, and that meant we didn't understand our respective roles or could really be "free" not to fulfill them. However, the longer we stayed in this country, the harder it got for me to figure out which "thank you" ritual was operative: the one that is right for the universe governed by Confucius' Five Relationships or the one that is suitable under The Bill of Rights.

In the car, I nevertheless felt the need to say something. "Daddy, I picked this color because it's like Maureen O'Hara's." My father nodded his acceptance of my gratitude and, thereby, gave his approval. I had chosen well.

I don't know who started it or when but, for as long as I can remember, Daddy was Humphrey Bogart and Mommy was Maureen O'Hara. I guess it was my father's mouth, the assured way he carried himself, his newspaper, that led people to see the similarity in the jaunty hat, the manner that all good gangsters or adventurers should have. And my mother was the sparkling O'Hara. We would stand on Fifth Avenue, watching the Easter Day Parade—she never wore a fancy hat, she didn't need one—and photographers would stop to take a picture of her open, perfectly shaped smile on an utterly beautiful face. But they always asked permission before raising their cameras. Instinctively, they knew not to take any liberties with my mother.

At home, my father must have told my mother because, after the initial cursory glance, she returned to my room for a better second look. I then reinforced their interest in my doll by making clothes as glamorous as her hair—a bright yellow taffeta skirt bordered in black velvet, a sweeping cape with red accents, and a fitted, slitted, Chinese dress just like the ones my mother wore. It had been Daddy's "business" to buy the wig. Making the hangers was for me alone, for my pleasure alone; a reward for and worth my waiting.

When they were done, each exactly contoured, he came up to my room and amazed me more by drilling holes in my perfectly smooth closet door just to attach a tiny pole. He stayed to watch me arrange the doll clothing on the hangers, and then hook them over the newly installed rod. As we stood back to admire the effect of the miniature wardrobe within the regulation-sized one, we were commending each other on the fine job we had both done, on the patience. It was hard to keep a matter-of-fact tone in my voice when there was so much pride and love trying to escape the pressure of being in so insignificant a body.

I showed the hangers to all my friends. They were impressed, but not overwhelmed. Used to parents who helped with a drawing or sipped "tea" out of "play" cups, they couldn't seem to appreciate the magnitude of the hangers and the esteem my father bestowed on me in making them. I didn't know I needed Chinese friends, ones who lived up the block or went to the same school. Most of my parents' friends lived in New York. Of those who had children, most kids weren't my age, or were back in China. Visits with the few who could have filled the void were so infrequent that we hardly recognized each other for having grown so much in-between them. Unable to see them in action on a daily basis, I got the impression that they probably didn't dress up and go trick-or-treating on Halloween. Or if they did, their parents wouldn't have tolerated them playing touch football in the street with the Cathie twins.

Sometimes what I gathered about their lives was pretty unimaginable—like when one girl who was already in high school asked her mother, in as formal Chinese as I'd ever heard, if she could buy a blue umbrella. I mean, *really*! I could understand needing permission to buy something that expensive but getting an okay on the color?! I started to giggle, like "This is a good joke, eh?" when her mother said she'd go to the shop herself and check out if the shade was really dark enough because she didn't want people to get the wrong idea about her daughter. Realizing she was serious, my jaw dropped too far from my upper teeth to finish the laugh. Detecting a tiny shake of the head from my mother, I eased my mouth back in time to have it nailed in place with a look from her mother that was designed to keep it shut until I was old enough to have kids of my own. That done, she proceeded to tell my mother some story about some other girl. I didn't catch the details, but the gist of it was that kids get hurt or go wild if they speak too much English and walk around in bright colors.

My mother stiffened. Making a quick decision, I interrupted, and asked, in Chinese, if either wanted another cup of tea. They both said "No." She as if the word was a piece of dry ice, my mother as if to the youngest bride of the youngest son whose zero status makes her one hundred percent subject to the whim of just about everybody except the dog. Accepting the instant transition to Old China, I followed up by asking, again in Chinese, for permission to go outside and play. Dismissing me, my mother quickly returned my conspiratorial grin before facing her critic with a "Now, what were you saying, my Dear?" kind of look.

This was definitely not a Chopsticks-Fork family. I'm sure they thought that setting the table with sharp instruments was barbaric.

Later, my parents said there were too many Overseas Chinese who tried to raise their children as if they were still in the China of their grandparents. Although we didn't yet know any who went to the other extreme—total Americanization—I knew my parents would have disapproved of that too. Part of Bao lore was the tradition, but it also included stories of my parents' rebellion, of whatever it took to venture so far from home. Our motto was "[Have the courage and know-how to] take the best from East and West." The Umbrella Woman must have had the same gumption once. So how could she be unafraid to cross an ocean and yet be so afraid of a medium blue? How could she want something new for herself but perpetuate the old in and on her daughter?

"Hrumph, no more *shuai*."

"What's that?"

My mother demonstrated. With her feet firmly planted, she rotated her upper torso several times. Her arms, hanging loose, followed her shoulders and did wrap-arounds about her body.

"Swing."

Thereafter, about once every year or two, she would swing for me. She wanted me to know about versatility and flexibility, about how being well placed meant being able to move in any direction at a moment's notice. Each time she did it, she enjoyed her ingenuity more and the delight made her a little girl, arms swirling, as pleased with the feel of it as the lesson being performed. I thought it was a tradition. I grew up believing every Chinese child learned how to swing. Now I think she made it up. Maybe just for me. When I asked her, so I could explain the concept to my son, she couldn't understand my sloppy pronunciation. When I demonstrated, she shook her head and told me *shua*i is a to-and-fro or forward-and-back motion. When I insisted on the version she taught me and repeated the word, she mimicked my intonation and said, "*Shuài*? Like fall down? Lose one's balance?"

"No, Mommy. *Shuai*. Like this." And once again twisted gaily.

"Never heard of it."

Oh well. This, like so much that was important in our household, had a *MaMa-HuHu* quality about it. Literally, "HorseHorse-TigerTiger," it connotes "neither one way nor the other," or "either way." But there's also an element of *comme çi, comme ça*, or "so-so" in the phrase. The *MaMa-HuHu* meant my parents were casual, but never careless. Their ideas were weather balloons to my mind's eye, fascinating me with their staying power amidst the crosswinds, then astonishing me with their deft mobility in a breeze.

They ruled by proclamation of simple rules but governed with complex examples. Sixteen years after we arrived in the U.S., they did the same with *SanSan*.[2] Reminiscent of what happened with Bette and me, on the next available school day after my little sister arrived, my parents sent her to Teaneck High to watch kids learn about Huckleberry Finn. Nearly two decades after that, when my uncle arrived in America, he was enrolled at City University of New York. At a time when "multiculturalism" had no meaning, good or bad, my parents invented the concept for us. When my mother saw my uncle doing his early morning *taijiquan* exercises by the front door, she pulled him inside, remonstrating, "Not in the front. This isn't China. Do you see anybody else on the block doing that? In America, the front is where you put out the garbage and pick up the newspaper. Do it in the backyard, like barbecues." When her "don't stick out like a sore thumb" and "look/see" lessons weren't enough, my father patiently compared cultures to explain how the differences were reflected in the everyday jargon that never appeared in grammar books. And throughout, we watched them make forays into the world and return with a variety of imports: the virtues of laughing at oneself, permanents, American breakfasts, Halloween and Christmas. Sometimes the timing got mixed up as when we wore costumes to decorate the tree, but our enthusiasm more than made up for any confusion this may have caused our friends. Once my mother came back from the store with four pairs of mukluks, each exactly the same as the other. Unaware of their Eskimo origins, she appreciated their comfort and warmth. I asked her, "Why four?" She shrugged. Without pointy toes and slim high heels, not one of the Bao females ever wore them. And since they were our size, my father couldn't (for which he was very thankful). These occasional flops didn't matter. We still got the idea.

Though they sometimes forgot what they said, or lamented where my ideas took me, they were, nonetheless, the instigators. If their grandchild grew up in a world where the extraordinary and ordinary were made into each other, it was because I could say to the clerk, "Please, I would like to buy an umbrella. No, not that one. The red one."

[2] For details, please read *Eighth Moon* by SanSan as told to Bette Lord. When there was no further need to "disguise"/protect our family remaining in China, later editions were published under "Bette Bao Lord" to capitalize on her other successes.

THE CUSTOMS EXCHANGE:...GOING OUT

The three stages of culture shock are: Enrapture, Disillusionment, Adaptation.
                    —*Robert Storey, Lonely Planet Travel Survival Kit*

Twenty-three years later, during the month of Aquarius, two years before the American Bicentennial, William Bao Bean was born—clueless at 7 pounds, 14 ounces.

"The one with the blindfold. Under the Bili Light. That's your grandson, Mr. Bao."

Watching my father while he squinted his already small eyes to find the human form amidst the medical artifacts, the nurse explained, "He's under the ultraviolet because of the jaundice. Nothing serious. A lot of babies are born with the condition. It's temporary. It doesn't hurt; it just makes the skin appear yellow."

With a totally straight face, my father responded, "He looks perfectly normal to me."

The nurse started to explain again. And then stopped abruptly as my father's words penetrated. She looked to Bennett for a clue. He was dead pan. Veteran of a thousand maternity ward introductions, nothing had prepared this woman from a small New Jersey town for the playful man from *Ningpo* and the roguish straight man from Iowa. Her "Yes, but the yellow isn't..." sounded almost impolite, under the circumstances.

My father smiled her to an understanding that the jest was intended though her discomfort was not. She returned it with one that gradually warmed to the situation. He had exposed her to a different way of looking and she had let it flash quickly on her embarrassment before letting its illumination reveal a larger stage. The nurse was a pushover.

While William was absorbing the ultraviolet, my parents were soaking up the details of his delivery by emergency Cesarean section. Bennett and I each described the events from our respective viewpoints. Then we told it from each other's viewpoint. Then my parents each told the other all four versions. And then they told it back to us. With each telling, it became, gradually, a "story." Part of the past. Part of family lore. With each telling, the fortunate outcome was stressed. The story, complete with happy ending, was thus finalized in their minds and the minds of the gods. Done, there could be no different epilogue, no additional chapter, no untold misfortune.

But not everything is worth repeating. During the rest of my hospital stay, I started to sort through the kinds of experiences William would have and what we would or wouldn't make of them. Remembering Mr. Gunnar, my high school biology teacher, I recalled his lecture on Hybrid Vigor. The idea was that when two different strains of corn were crossed, the result was greater than was normal for either parent type. The idea was powerful—and not just botanically. And William would be the proof. We wouldn't just throw him into The Great Melting Pot, vaguely hoping he'd emerge able to do more than grunt in two languages or co-exist in the vicinity of his grandparents without grossing them out. If he was to converse while dining— not just eating—and be interesting to people who didn't *have* to love him, we had to be much more careful and deliberate about his cultural nurturing. Lying in my arms, looking like Winston Churchill gone Asian, it was obvious that, physically, we had the makings for such an experiment. And that, intellectually, we had the wealth of his Bao and Bean heritage—from "The Middle Kingdom" to its American equivalent, "The Lawn" at the University of Virginia. Practically, however, I did, every so often, wonder how much difference it would make that William wasn't an ear of corn.

Brushing aside this detail, I proceeded to my first idea: I would inform him, "This is a rose" or "That is a skunk," but I wouldn't characterize the odor as "good" or "bad." One day, he could decide for himself. Thinking it over, I was unable to foresee any difficulty with this resolution. Leaving out my two cents on odors couldn't be crucial. As far as I knew, there was no philosophical point that rested solely on knowing whether someone likes or dislikes a particular smell. My second idea: I would never tell William stories with Wicked Mothers— "step-" or otherwise. The role I had just taken on would be tough enough to play without panning myself in a preview. (I thought about but didn't dwell on the possibility of my own demise and that, one day, he might have to love one.)

But mere omission wouldn't be enough. For if Confucius was right and what people really need are models of excellence, William would have to learn something positive. I couldn't just say, "Cinderella was a weakling for accepting the bad behavior of her step relations, and Pinocchio an inveterate liar with extraordinarily poor taste in friends, so don't be like them." Or just avoid declaring, "You ought to know better," as if the human condition was self-evident or cultural foundations self-revealing. The whole project was starting to resemble what I did for school: a course outline but for a very long term. As with my students, I wanted to teach how to care deeply yet think critically, to be pragmatic yet honor certain ideals; to anticipate—even relish— challenges yet be serene. But unlike most of them, William would be, from the beginning, made conscious of his Double Major, of his learning how to live in America and how to draw sustenance from Chinese roots—to be at least bicultural. Actually, so were my students, they just didn't know it. Instead, most believed themselves to be culturally neutral, even "normal" so that every other way of being was "different" and, by implication, "abnormal." An increasing number have even thought it's unpatriotic to encourage self-examination, especially among immigrants, not realizing that it is the art of critical thinking that best portrays the strength of democracies.

As I waited for the nurse to bring in William, I envisioned different colored kernels, all on the same cob—the kind that appear in Halloween and Thanksgiving Day displays, each ear boldly exhibiting its variegated heritage. It didn't take much to go from that image to a mental collage of William, like a Picasso—one Chinese and one Caucasian eye on a half yellow half white face, his mother's ankles, shoulders and underarms,[3] his father's immune system, hands and, of course, teeth. Even when Bennett informed me that the colorful variety is Indian corn, not hybrid corn, I wasn't deterred from planning our son's entire future. The kid didn't have a chance.

As he nursed and I thought, I looked more carefully at my newborn's coloring, somewhere in-between Bennett's and mine. Going to the Nurse's Station, I checked *The Random House Dictionary* under Mendel's laws.

> Genetics, the basic principles of heredity discovered by
> Gregor Mendel, showing that alternative hereditary factors
> of hybrids exhibit a clean-cut separation or segregation
> from one another and that different pairs of hereditary

---

[3] Keep an eye out for research on "olfactory perception" by Dr. John Pierce. I alerted him to "racial" differences and that the only information in the popular press that I recall which mentions the "underarm phenomenon" was during the Vietnam War when water buffalo would charge Caucasians, presumably detecting their pungent/acrid/offensive odor as an enemy.

traits are independently sorted from each other.

He was wrong. William and, I hoped, human cultures were the proof.

In the meantime, our son's agenda was less theoretical so my life took on the same pattern that parents the world over develop when there is a newborn: feed, diaper, and launder. Part of me was grateful that William didn't do much because he couldn't do much. The prospect of what his eventual mobility would do to my chore list was mind-boggling. The other part of me was anxious for something news-worthy. When he slept through the night at four weeks, we were joyful and told the family. When he smiled at five weeks, we were ecstatic and made him perform for our friends. When he cooed at six weeks, we tried to figure out in which class he would graduate from Harvard. When he cried for no good reason at seven weeks, we were highly sus-picious and came to understand the existential meaning of free will.

Looking forward to a quiet evening of retrospective musing on the day of smiles and gurglings, we heard William crying in a different key. Clip-clopping toward his room in my wooden sandals, the crying stopped. I stopped. The screeching started. I took a noisy step. The screeching stopped. After a few more halting paces—each one followed by another round of silence and shrieking—I figured out the score. It was *Fantasia*. The Sorcerer's Apprentice, a.k.a. Mickey Mouse, a.k.a. William, was using his vocal cords as the baton to conduct the orches-tra, a.k.a. broom serfs, a.k.a., us. I went back to our room and announced to Bennett, "Steel yourself. We're in for a long night. He's crying for no reason except to see if he can make us appear at will."

Now I grant that a child his age has limited resources by which to control his world. But William was using tears to get sympathy and manipulate. There would be no Bili Light for this kind of "jaundice." We wanted him to know that people, including himself, are not to be used, that healthy emotional commitment is a matter of mutual trust, not easy opportunity. Throughout the first hour, we repeated this belief like an incantation against his spell. By the second hour, William was caterwauling—beyond a play for sympathy, this was extortion. We held hands for comfort, clip-clopped periodically to check whether he still stopped at will, and turned up the volume on the television set. Toward the third hour, the din was almost unbearable. Then he sud-denly stopped. Tiptoeing in stockinged feet, we listened outside the door. William was happily babbling to himself. Waiting another minute just to be sure his shift in mood was permanent, we went in and greeted him as if we just happened to stop by. He cooed his "Hello" as if to unexpected, but welcome, callers. Swooping him to our room, we gave him all the attention he could possibly want.

Positive and negative reinforcement—worked on the dog, why not the baby?

From then on, if he cried for no acceptable reason, we simply explained our preference that he do so by himself and put him in another room. As soon as he stopped crying, we picked him up. Our American friends approved of the fact that we explained the reason for his exile and then let him cry until he chose to stop. Americans fear repression, reduction of individuality, restriction of freedom and self-expression. They believe that the person who can stand above the maddening crowd must draw strength and conviction from within, independent of others. Until recently, Kipling's poem was taught to every school child, "If you can keep your head when all about you are losing theirs...you'll be a Man, my son!"

Our Chinese relatives praised William's general good behavior and sociability. Chinese fear isolation, being set apart. The Confucian social ideal defines individuals not as separate entities but, rather, as persons only in orderly relationship to others. If William wanted company and enjoy its full benefit, he shouldn't be a detraction or too different from those around him. Thus if Kipling had been Asian, his poem might have been, "If you can keep your head when all about you are losing theirs...then there is probably something very wrong with you, your family, your village, your ruler, and your ancestors!"

First crying. Next The United Nations. The need for more detailed guidance than a dog-training manual was evident. Maybe, somewhere, someone had written a book on how to achieve a balance between different, seemingly opposing, cultural forces. Maybe it would tell us how to create magic for the young, but prepare for the reality of the old. Maybe it would explain how to make distinctions like "right" and "wrong" clearly enough so the immature can grasp them yet not so categorically that they prevent the mature from considering degrees of difference. Maybe it could advise us about what to do with Santa Claus and the Tooth Fairy.

Still satisfied that what I'd decided about smells and children's stories was valid, I came up against a more formidable duo than Cinderella and Pinocchio: the jolly man in the red suit and the woman with a dental fixation. These two were not just a matter of omitting stories about weaklings and liars. These two required the collusion of parents and society. These two made me face the heavy-handed question: Did I want to take a chance that, one day, William might say "Yes," when I asked, "Have I ever lied to you?"

Part of me said, "Get real! We're talking about 'Ho-Ho-Ho' and shiny quarters under the pillow, not philosophy." And the other part of me kept thinking about the parents of my students. Many had indulged themselves and their children with a Lollipop World for eighteen years and then expected their kids to be fully equipped to enter some Real World. During the formative years, they preferred the simplicity of Walt Disney's "...happily ever after," to the complexity of Grimm's ending:

> When the marriage day came, the two step-sisters, wish-
> ing to share Cinderella's fortune, contrived to be present.
> As the bridal party walked to church, they placed them-
> selves, one on the right and the other on the left of the
> bride. On the way, the doves picked out one eye from
> each of them. When returning, they changed places, and
> the doves picked out the other eye of each, so they were
> for their wickedness and falsehood both punished with
> blindness during the rest of their lives.

The upshot was: I told our son all about the **Imaginary** Tooth Fairy and **Make-Believe** Santa Claus. By dubbing the two with qualifiers, I hoped to give our son fantasy and reality simultaneously. Having decided how to prep William's brain for Philosophy 101, I then faced the fact that Harvard expects its students to be toilet-trained.

The month before William was born, I had received several packages from my mother-in-law. One contained Bennett's childhood treasures: marbles, Lincoln Logs, lead soldiers, Tinker Toys—all in their original boxes. Another held the storybooks with illustrations so powerful that their images continue to surface in his artwork. The last was full of diapers: triplicate forms of pure white cotton softness.

I unpacked all of it. Arrayed on the bed, they were a means by which I could conjure memories that weren't mine. As I touched each keepsake from Bennett's earlier world, The Wife in me shared his mother's nostalgia. And The Child in me was saddened by the absence of anything comparable—what was not left in China, was stored in memories I couldn't access. As I scanned it all, The Manager in me was horrified. How would I keep track of it all? One solution would be to store them in the attic: souvenirs to be fondled every ten years or so, not objects to be used or abused. But the dutiful and frugal Daughter-in-law in me prevailed and William's life began with the same accouterments his father had, down to the diapers. The changing detail wasn't so bad at first. Used milk is pretty innocuous stuff. Thus, the first time the pediatrician said the baby could start solid food, I inquired if there were any health benefits in doing so. He said, "No, but some parents prefer to start early."

I asked, "Why?"

"It gives them a feeling of involvement."

I thought, "More 'involvement'?!? William and I are *Homo sapiens* of the Asian variety, we've got our hands full with how to cope with a mutual dependence network that extends back to our ancestors and forward to our descendants.

Besides, being Chinese—or Cathy—I don't take kindly to sudden changes. So William remained on a liquid diet while Bennett tried to ease me into the process of American parenting by systematically making "how-to" books appear wherever I was in the habit of sitting. Looking at one, I had seen 18 pages filled with a six-column table of the changes that would take place during a child's first four years. If this was supposed to reassure me, it didn't. According to Francis L. K. Hsu, noted cultural anthropologist,

> American parents are...so determined to do the right
> thing, that they handsomely support a huge number of
> child specialists...I know of no piece of traditional litera-
> ture aimed at making the Chinese better parents,...

Nevertheless, being Chinese—or Cathy—I tend to revere the written word. What I saw in the six-column table was an interminable progression of "stages," each one exponentially more complex than the previous one. Considering how long it took to master the first two pages, I figured that, at the rate we were going, it was possible William could reach page 18 before I did. According to the experts, such an outcome was to be avoided. For while the books differed on some details, they seemed to be unanimous in telling me that William's happiness in this life and, probably, the next, would depend upon us being one stage more well-adjusted than he was. On the other hand, already in charge of nursing, washing, and left-brain education (Bennett was responsible for the bathing, furnishings, and right-brain learning), I was in no hurry.

But one day William did need cereal. The effect was awesome. The most imaginative alchemist couldn't have predicted the result of adding so simple an ingredient to a baby's recycling system. Laundering, never much fun, became a daily struggle of mind over matter. By the end of the thirtieth bowl of cereal, the diapers were dis-reputable two-ply versions of their former fluff. Whenever I felt the urge to buy the non-recyclable disposables so temptingly displayed at the supermarket, I fortified myself with the thought that I was doing my part in saving Planet Earth. But clearly, it was time for William to begin his formal education. So, with William ensconced in the shop-ping cart, I started to linger at the rack of children's briefs and discuss with him the marvels of *duankuzi* or "short pants." And I consulted Spock.

> During the first year there is a small amount of readiness
> for partial training in some babies....

I concluded that our son must be one of the "some." After all, if he was to win a Nobel Prize in the same year he had a retrospective at the Museum of Modern Art, it could never be too early for a precocious nature to reveal itself. While The Manager was mentally allocating half the diapers for use in the studio and half for household dusting, The Wife sent Bennett out to buy a child's toilet. The Husband returned with a wooden contraption, circa 1920. Another "good deal" from the flea market.

It was wondrous indeed. Depending upon how you organized its various parts, it could serve as high chair, desk or toilet. I strategically placed it in my office and, per the good Doctor Spock's prescription, intermittently peered at William's face for signs of "movement." The moment I saw the telltale look of bemused concentration that always preceded a *big convenience*,[4] I scooped him out of the desk and, with my free hand, tried to make the potty materialize.

All I got was something resembling a Chinese puzzle after its clutch piece has been disengaged. Releasing William, I put my whole body and mind into finding the correct alignment of its gears. Muttering, I alternately invoked calm logic to inform my efforts, and excruciating

---

[4] For years I thought the translation of *xiao bian* and *da bian* was "little change" and "big change." This made so much biological sense that it never occurred to me that this was my sort-of Chinese speaking. Now that I know otherwise, I've taken the liber-ty of changing history and using the correct translation.

pain to descend upon the (misogynous male) #!*!!#! who contrived this instrument of torture to punish women who were so short-sighted as to grow only two hands. William, nearby on the floor and seemingly oblivious, was absorbed in drawing yet another Self-Portrait(-in-Dirty-Diaper). Cleaning up both messes, I grumbled; he chortled.

Convinced that I could do better with less versatile equipment, I immediately purchased a small chamber pot of molded plastic. This uni-body model, neither aesthetically interesting nor double-jointed, did simplify procedures. Whenever I requested, William would amenably oblige me with a perfunctory session on the seat. We played this game for over two years. The stockpile of "short pants," acquired in a gesture of atonement for finally succumbing to Pampers, remained pristine. William's approach to personal hygiene remained otherwise. Our son was now so developmentally behind, we would have to settle for a Pulitzer and The Whitney.

Then I heard about **Toilet Training In Less Than A Day**.

The theory, according to my friend, appealed to my left brain. The method was to transform the process into a joint venture: The child trains a lifelike doll while the parent trains the child. Thus the child can get the conceptual hang of it even as he or she learns to anticipate and imitate the doll's behavior. In the jargon of her psychology course, she told me that the discipline of the superego would take place if the id's pleasure principle could be sublimated into a desire for cleanliness by transference and ego-identification with the doll.

I took her word for it and, without bothering to read the book, forayed into my things-to-sort room and found the Betsy Wetsy my niece had bequeathed to William when she outgrew it. Finding that it looked too unlike my son for him to readily identify with it, I:
- Cut its orange hair;
- Quieted the resultant Mohawk with brown shoe polish;
- Scoured all remaining evidence of its previous persona; and
- Named it Fred.

Reinforcing my friend's advice, I reread Dr. Spock:

> Training may sometimes be aided greatly...by the child's passion to imitate everything he sees done by others...
> Your main cue is to remain friendly, encouraging, and optimistic.

Calling William, I explained the agenda to him in my most friendly, encouraging and optimistic voice:

1. Feed Fred with the smaller bottle of water while I feed you from the larger one;
2. Place Fred in the cereal bowl at the same time you sit on the John;
3. You will both undergo a *little convenience.*

Three bottles of water later, *no convenience* came from either. Nonplused, I firmly instructed William to stay put, picked up the doll and, with a twist of the wrist, yanked its head off. Enthralled, William watched wide-eyed as I rearranged tubing. Evidently one had come loose and misdirected the fluid into Fred's right leg.

Once again I placed the adopted, coiffured, baptized, and now reassembled doll on William's lap. Once again I explained, in my most friendly, encouraging and optimistic voice, the Three-Step Procedure. Once again we administered the water. Once again, *no convenience.*

William, expectant but ever patient, sat. At this point, despite my increasing agitation, I did stop to wonder whether decapitating the doll a second time would lead William to draw the wrong conclusion about some unspoken "Step Four." My concern became moot as we noticed water forthrightly exiting Fred's neck, rippling down the back, and into the bowl.

The following week, William interrupted his Tinker Toy project and my tax return calculations to inquire, "If I wear *duankuzi*, can I go to school?"

More involved with the I.R.S. questions, I distractedly nodded.

He got up, took off the diaper, put on his underwear, tugged on my sleeve, and announced, with prophetic finality, "Ready."

I got up and, carrying a supply of one-ply cotton dust rags to the studio, tried to remember all the different Nobel Prize categories. The next week we entered Miss Glusa's classroom.

The sun must have been shining when our son first emigrated. The day, the story, required clear visibility and so I've deduced it. From the fact. From being able to look around.

Seeing no one else in the parking lot, I hummed one of those waltz tunes that everybody knows, and danced toward the old '71 Subaru. Opening the door, I again checked for spectators. There were none. So I did a Gene Kelly "ta-da" with an imaginary umbrella, clicked my heels, added a "Free at last," and bowed myself in behind the wheel.

As I shifted into first, the other parents started to appear. Most looked like they'd just been pronounced "guilty" of some terrible crime. A few walked part of the way backwards, trying not to lose sight of where they had been, of where I had left them, maneuvering for a peek through the small window in the door that separated them from their children gathered on the other side.

Popping the clutch, I peeled out onto the road. Pushing the speed limit, I rushed past the orchard and horse farm, the creamery and Chrusz's General Store, back to my home office and the list of all the philosophy departments in northern New Jersey that were about to learn that my maternal retirement had just ended and that I would consider it an honor to teach at their college.

Later, licking the last envelope, I gathered all the scrap paper that held the discarded punctuation of my career or the misaligned columns of my academic background and put them on the little desk/potty/high chair near mine. William would color them in. Or use his typewriter to write his version on the back. He much preferred his small Smith-Corona to my newer Olympia. An early electric model, his carriage moved back and forth when you hit the "return," and his keys clicked more resolutely than mine. (Except the "J." He didn't mind. He couldn't spell. Still can't.)

After lunch, I took my usual nap, dressed, and returned to the site of my liberation. There was only one parent at the classroom door now, mashing her cheek bone into the glass so that the eye above it moved up and down, up and down—the way children do when they demonstrate, "This is Chinese. This is Japanese. Chinese. Japanese." Her other eye went from side to side, pulled by an invisible apron string attached to her offspring inside. I wondered if she had stood vigil since the morning. Edging my way through the door (it was that or realign the woman's nose), I went into the large room to retrieve my three-year old from a most marvelous invention: Day Care.

Waiting for a break in the conversation that William was having with no one in particular, I asked, "*Wo men hui jia, hao bu hao?*"

Looking up, he stated, rather than asked, "Yes, MaMa. But I come back tomorrow...yes?"

It was the first time. Up until that moment, he spoke English only to his father.

He seemed to have paused before forming the last word. At first, I couldn't tell if it was because he was hesitant about leaving. Or how to talk to me.

Looking at him, I could see the overhead light reflected among the dozen or so cowlicks that he had inherited from my father, and my father's father, and all the fathers before him. The strands were not as stubborn on William. When kept long, their ability to stand out like oases against the horizon was minimized by gravity. What never failed to startle me about them was not their capacity to go every which way, but their color: medium brown, even golden in the sun. My hair could only go from black to red when scorched. And his eyes. Though brown, they were flecked with the hazel of his father. Neither was at all what I expected from Mendel's Laws. I was supposed to be dominant, not subdued.

As I surveyed his upturned face and wondered how he managed to defy Nature, to be so unlike all those fruit flies and peas we had grown in the school laboratory, William had ended his sentence with a "yes?" Without the query, it would have been a political statement, pure and simple, an Emancipation Proclamation by a child who had just been toilet-trained. Yet his "yes?" was not for my permission. Having addressed me in English, he had taken his stand. As the philosopher J. L. Austin explains about performative words like "I promise," just to voice it is to do it. But in William's question was an invitation: "Will you join me?" And an admission: "Your approval is important." At least that's what I decided he meant.

I replied in Chinese, "*Yes. Oh, yes, indeed. Tomorrow!*" while graciously accepting the applause I heard from Dr. Spock and John Dewey.

Holding hands, we went out to the car. Securing his seat belt, I thought about the pile of job inquiries I'd dropped into the mailbox, hearing, feeling, once more, the satisfactory thud they'd made upon landing. Driving home, William, reverting to the language of my early childhood, expressed complete satisfaction with "*going to school.*" And so did I. We continued to talk about what we'd done that day; anything more complicated would have required my using English. The Chinese words I (and therefore he) knew were good enough to discuss what could happen to an eight-year old who was born in China but who grew up in New Jersey during the '50s. Thus "crawling up a tree," simple arithmetic, and body parts from the neck up or thigh down were no problem. If I could keep it going until William needed to talk about algebra or sex, he would be bilingual.

But that night, sitting at the table in our country kitchen, I heard my son announce, in the language of his new peers, what I had never thought to say as a child and certainly not to my mother in so pre-emptory a tone, "I speak English."

Quietly I responded, in Chinese, "*Yes, and you speak Chinese.*"

Even more emphatically, he declared, "I speak **English**."

Not content with Emancipation, he wanted Independence as well. Was this how it would start? After only one day in school? Was this why those parents lingered at the Day Care door? Should I continue in Chinese the way my mother did? Should I, like her, seem to ignore the linguistic line in the cultural sand? Or should I deliver some cut-down version (which was all I could manage in Chinese) of the lecture I had subjected myself to since college, the one that starts out with "I wish I'd paid better attention when I was a child, then I could speak my native language more fluently now that I realize the importance of...."? A second later, without having to explain a lifetime of reasons, I told his father, "Bennett, take him to New York after school tomorrow."

The next day, once again confident, I escorted William down the hall to his classroom. Giving him a hug and kiss, I told him to have a good time and that I would see him later. Turning, I started to make my way through the phalanx of parents and children huddling and sobbing near the door. Feeling rather smug that we didn't have *their* problem, I was only a few steps out the door when I heard William cry out, "MaMa." Going back through the crowd, I saw him standing by himself, arms at his side, tears rolling down his face.

"*What's the matter, William?*"

"Nothing," he replied in his being-at-school language.

"*Then why are you crying?*"

"I'm supposed to."

"*What do you mean, you're 'supposed' to?*"

"Children cry when parents leave them at school."

"Well," I thought to myself, "The kid's observant." With no Chinese vocabulary for "kid" or "observant," all I could have managed out loud was the usual "*It is good, you are able to see/look.*" Somehow he had gotten a rudimentary version of The Chopsticks-Fork Principle from that. Once I had tried to be more specific, but "Don't stick out like a sore thumb," came out, "*Don't lift a(ny) finger.*"

So I relied on the "see/look" formula. Although he was too young to have had the experiences that would deepen his grasp of the Principle that took me half a lifetime to gather, his dutiful crying did exhibit an important aspect of the idea, that is, not to join his tears with the others' might be construed as criticism of them. As he continued to cry, I asked, "*Why do you think they cry?*"

"Because they're going to miss their mothers."

Happy he also understood enough about their First Day at School ritual to be concerned that I might need the reassurance of his tearful good-bye, I nevertheless didn't want common sense to get overrun by oversensitivity. "*How can you miss me, William? I was just here.*"

"But I might. Later."

While his "later" gave me pause, I said, "*Not likely, you'll be too busy. Anyway, you should stop crying because you'll get a stuffy nose. And you know how you hate* snorfling." ("Snorfling" was one of those words peculiar to our household.)

"Okay, MaMa." ("Okay" is universal.)

But it was said with less than wholehearted belief. Asking him to wait a minute, I rummaged in my purse for the envelope that my mother had recently given to me. In it was a set of pictures that she had taken during two years' worth of visits. Going through the pile, I found one that showed the lower part of Bennett's face—actually his beard—a view of my back, and pieces of William's upper left and lower right limbs, circa fifteen months. For once I was sorry that my mother wasn't better at aiming the camera; this snapshot of our truncated household was the best of the batch.

"*Here, William. Put this in your pocket. If you think you miss me or BaBa, then look at the picture. Okay?*"

By giving him the picture, I conveyed a complex of yeses: "Yes, you are right not to shame others unnecessarily," and a "Yes, you are kind to think about me," and a "Yes, we both have needs." But I also gave him the message," "Be strong," and "For goodness sake, let's not overdo it."

Holding it, he studied it first, then put it in his breast pocket, instinctively treating it like an Asian handles a business card. Giving me a nod of firm conviction, his second "Okay" closed the subject.

Waving good-bye, I left. No more hugs or kisses. I didn't want him to think his serious decision needed reinforcement or that he was being consoled for a loss, imminent or eventual. The parents who had been watching looked at us in horror—I must be heartless. Unloving. Without emotions. Another inscrutable Chinese raising an inscrutable child.

Miss Glusa seemed noncommittal. Of the two teachers available, I had chosen her over the bubbly, cuddly one. From Europe, older, and more matter of fact, she was a solid—but not stolid—presence in her room. When shopping for a school, she was the only one who didn't overwhelm me with gushing promises and cheery forecasts. While she introduced herself, the children didn't stop what they were doing, hungry for distraction. The preliminaries done and without invitation or direction to William, she had set a deliberate pace back into the class, creating a slipstream that drew the potential student after her. She did the same on his second day. Whether or not she understood my motives, her style reinforced them. At that moment, she could have done what I hadn't. She could have created a space in some corner of his psyche, a place of yearning, a breeding ground for homesickness. She didn't. And I was grateful.

Sure there was a part of me that wanted to stay and hover, to enfold William, to make myself indispensable to him. Even to cry with him. He was so little, so vulnerable. So "cute." It was the same kind of urge I felt when checking on him at night. Beautiful in his sleep, it was such a temptation to pick him up, to appropriate his warmth, to nudge him into consciousness and indelibly impress him with my loving, invulnerable arms. It was such a temptation to take away his rest and make him my plaything.

I resisted so he would be vulnerable, to the world outside, to school. At three, he was old enough to learn that our family couldn't be "left" somewhere else or "missed;" that family is part of the self, and as long as he's in touch with himself, he is with his family. And the converse is true—when he is in school, so are we. As he gathers new experiences, he is adding to our storehouse. Those experiences are what can be missed, not family. That's what I learned as a child when my parents left SanSan in China. William would too.

The picture was my idea, but the impetus came from long ago, another urge as old as parenthood, one I did not resist. Like his forebears, I would go back and forth, back and forth, weaving into this child the stories, intertwining his lifeline with threads I have brought out of the past and returned with the present. But the texture of his future—our immortality—would be in words and deeds that can always mean more than they seem at one time, so I had to develop a way of joining them, without enjoining him. For while every culture abounds with wisdom about the best pattern and instruction for the surest stitch, and every generation passes on to the next the tales and games, songs and images, plays and books that define the hierarchy among colors, the value of tried and true methods, this wouldn't be enough for what I had in mind: a fabric of Chinese silk and American cotton.

Although I derived my raw materials from countries who knew how to add a bit of trim from foreign ways, neither had taught me the technique for creating a multicultural mesh. They had no advice on how to combine such different filaments to make something that could endure my wash-and-wear pace, or be appropriate for the fashion of William's age. Something with a pattern recognizable to my parents—relationships conceived by Confucius, rituals designed by Buddha—yet not so unfamiliar that the people in our town couldn't detect the stars and stripes. Something with vivid colors, but not so contrasting that the scheme had no subtlety. Something with structure, neither so soft it had no shape, nor so stiff it had no give. To make it, I would have to cut and bind, disrupting some lines but obliterating none. To dye and bleach, highlighting some hues but muting none altogether.

Driving home, I went more slowly than usual. In William's absence, I gave the time to him, to the hope that, one day, he would be pleased with what we had created and tell me so, in English and in Chinese.

Past the orchard and horse farm, the creamery and general store, I tried to see in the landscape what William would have seen: trees and fences to climb, old buildings to explore, a counter full of penny candy. The moment I felt the allure of each, I immediately thought of the risks: broken legs, cave-ins, and a patchwork of teeth that would convince him, as it did me, that the Marquis de Sade had been cloned a hundred times over and each one lived under a "Dentist" sign. Shuddering, I thought about another wonderful invention instead— fluoride. Rounding the blind curve near our house, I startled a deer crossing the road. As I braked, so did he. Uncertain whether to go back or forward, he looked through the windshield. Deciding I was more likely to cut off his retreat than progress, he turned and bounded in the direction he had been heading. Quickly disappearing into the underbrush, I could tell from the noises that he was well on his way.

THE CUSTOMS EXCHANGE:
COMING IN, GOING OUT

Seventeen years later when William was almost a college senior and I was almost spending what had not existed since he first entered Day Care—discretionary income—I tried to detect if he was well on his way from the noises he made. With a EuroPass in one hand and a list of youth hostels in the other, he spent the summer touring places I had only read about.

"How was France, William? Did you get to Chartres? to Notre Dame?"

"No, but I saw a lot of good cheeses in Paris."

Since then, he's accumulated more frequent flyer miles than I could endure in a lifetime. He doesn't seem to hesitate before sending his fancy suits and shirts to the cleaners, buying an impromptu red-eye flight on the internet, and filling a backpack with the basics: tees, jeans, jacket, shoes, and a cap. If he's lucky, he finds a guide as good as Miss Glusa.

> Hi All:
>
> I'm back in Cuzco after four days of slogging up and down mountain paths known as the Inka Trail, carrying a 30 pound pack, and living in a tent. Watching the sunrise hitting the ruins of Machu Picchu was amazing as was walking through the ancient town without a horde of grotesque tourists marring the serenity. But waking up in a tent at 3:40 in the morning to hike the last two hours to do it was painful. I hadn't done a hiking-camping trip since I was 13 and now I remember why. Great experience but next time I'll give the alpha male bit a rest and spend the $10 for a porter to carry my bag that one 3000 vertical foot stretch the morning of the second day. Did I mention it's hard to breath at 12,600 feet (just below the snow line).
>
> I think the best part was being surrounded by absolutely nothing but blue sky and clouds, no cars, people, noise, pollution, CNBC, venture capitalists or clients....

Or umbrellas of any color. But enough bottled water to make Fred need a doll hospital.

CHAPTER 2

COMMONWEALTH, COMMON TOUCH

COMMONWEALTH...

We do not have solitary beings. Every creature is, in some sense, connected to and dependent on the rest.

—Lewis Thomas, The Lives of a Cell

Because my parents exported as well as imported, encouraging Bette and me to go wherever there might be something handy to learn, we landed at many of the sites that were considered "must see" places by the typical American of the early '50s.

"Where're we going, Mommy?"

"Shopping."

"Great! What's on the list?"

"Name tags."

"Name tags? For what?

"Your clothes."

"My clothes? Mommy, I haven't lost anything since last year."

"They say you have to or it'll get lost in the laundry."

"Laundry? The washing machine's in the basement. How far can it go? Then, cautiously, "*Who* says?"

"Camp Rotomac."

"I'm going to *camp?*"

Satisfied that her surprise had elicited the awe it deserved, my mother smiled and said, "Yes. It's too hot. I don't want you in the water here...." Her lips faded to a line, giving voice to what she would not put into words for the gods to hear. I was just finishing the fifth grade. Without much of a spring, throughout the world schools and houses were already filling up with the heat of an early summer and fear of polio. If an American president could get it, no one was immune.

In my case, fear of polio twice. Not that I'd gotten it the first time that anyone knew but, given the gods' track record, my mother wasn't taking any chances. It seemed like the deities could see there were two kids in the house and so there should be, eventually, two check marks under each childhood disease. But every time they noticed a single check, they'd look down to correct the oversight, hear the younger sister badgering the older with a "Me too, me too!" and zap, give me Bette's turn by mistake. This had already resulted in my fighting two bouts of measles (we didn't know the second time was Rubella) and two of mumps (first on both sides, then on the right). At this rate (not counting rematches with measles), I would be hit for another go-around with chicken pox and, maybe, the left mump thrown in for balance. Add to that, the stuff I didn't need to get, but did—whooping cough, pneumonia, and lice—it wasn't surprising that my mother was worried about polio. What did surprise her Chinese friends was her solution: to send us *further* afield, beyond their experience to a different norm. What surprised me was the extravagance.

"Gee, that's great! When?"

"July 1st."

"For how long?"

"Two months."

"I can't believe it! Where's Rotomac?"

"In Vermont. Here, Cathy, you take the list."

"Look at all this. Foot locker, Flashlight, Rubber boots, Canteen, *two* Bathing Suits! Wow!"

"Rotomac will teach you how to swim properly, sing American songs, and play games according to the rules."

Bette and I were going to be Regular Campers. And safe.

As it turned out, nothing is 100% risk-free and the only thing "regular" at Rotomac was the letter-to-home sessions. There were other rules though I can't remember one that wasn't set aside if this seemed the better thing to do. The owner, Dr. Forrest, a pebbly woman with lots of eyebrows, was no dictator so I wanted to obey her every word. And I would have followed her son, the almost-doctor Tommy, to the ends of the earth. Within a week, all 24 campers could imitate his giant sheep dog lope, elbows crooked above his waist, hands flip-flopping each barefoot step. By the second, we could reproduce his toothy grin at Cook and wheedle another helping of ice cream.

For a while, I mailed pages to Teaneck (Bette never was much of a letter-writer and long-distance telephoning was for emergencies only). I wrote about how we went after frogs in the swimming hole and filled our canteens in the brook, about when we visited Lettie's tarpaper shack and drew messages in the dirt and in the air so her brother could see what his ears and throat wouldn't or couldn't hear and say. I sent snapshots of our counselors on the ball field—Christine pitching to Norman with Bette at first, wearing jeans and a bra, ready to tag him if he got that far. Unconcerned with explaining that it was super hot and that someone had forgotten the bases and markers, I only mentioned how we all had gladly sacrificed our shirts to make a diamond and how neat it was that my 15-year old sister was a match for the older Norman and so she always captained the one team while he headed the other. I scribbled out whole songs from the African Veldt:

> Old Tantekoba she is so dumb,
> She stirs her coffee with her big fat thumb.
> Old Tantekoba she ought to know,
> She ought to stir it with her great big toe.

By the time my parents got them, I was so happy with Rotomac that safety wasn't an issue. If all this wonderfulness had its attendant risks, then so be it. At ten, I knew everybody, except Bette, got sick. That a few, including Bette, were crazy. What I didn't do was connect that information with brothers who were deaf and mute, or counselors who played softball.

It happened in the middle of the night while I was asleep in the dormitory. Like The Hole, it wasn't very fancy—just a long, single-story building with an entryway in the middle that divided the boys' sections from the girls'. Most of the beds were double structures of metal tubing and springs that creaked every time someone climbed in or out. Maybe it wouldn't have happened had I slept in a top bunk, out of reach. But Dr. Forrest had assigned those to the older kids. The counselors had single cots, near the door. That's what makes my picture of what happened so weird. For the recollection I have now came from the dreamy one I got as I meandered in and out of consciousness, of being in a bed, isolated by a glow of light that put the rest of the room in darkness. There was no bunk above me, nothing but a vague awareness of sounds I should not be hearing.

> Dear Mommy and Daddy,
>
> Last night I woke up 'cause Julie (she's the really pretty counselor I told you about) was cutting my hair. It was all over my pillow. She's been complaining that it goes in my soup. But that's not true. Ask Bette.
>
> Love, Cathy

I must have heard the scissors snap together when they sheared through each handful. I don't remember getting Bette but I know she was by my bed when I dozed off. Too sleepy to help my sister clean up, I lay back down and was enveloped by my inexperience, by the space and time between action and reaction. Some call it shock. Maybe it was, but it was more a biding, as William would one day wait until I came to his classroom and know, from my response, whether he had been a victim of attack or circumstance, and decide whether he would retaliate, isolate, or ameliorate. For me, the sound of a broom and hushed words allowed me to brush aside the issue of why she cut my hair and wonder, instead, about how Julie could have seen what she was doing, using only a flashlight. She had been so strict about whittling—telling us always to aim the knife *away* from the body.

The next morning, my friend, Marion Marx, told me she had kind of woken up too, because of all the whispering. She thought she heard Bette say something to Julie that made her cry, and that's why our counselor left camp the next day. We never did get that straight since no one talked about it much. Without the brouhaha, it was a mishap. Not a disaster.

> Dear Mommy and Daddy,
>
> Florrie taught us new songs today. Somebody said Dr. Forrest gave all the counselors a big talk about camps in Germany so maybe these songs are from there. My hair looks a little funny but, don't worry, I can still make a braid to one side.
>
> Love, You know Who
>
> p.s. Too bad I wasn't around to get your call.

What I did get was the impression that my parents weren't as ecstatic about Rotomac as I was. I didn't want to rub it in so, by the third week, my letters were shorter—with more detail about the food and fewer about when Tommy told us how babies were made. Or when the salamanders I had collected got out of the huge jar. For days after the Great Escape, the desiccated bodies of the ones who couldn't find their way out showed up in our beds, towels, shoes—everywhere. Of the original hundred or so, more than half were accounted for. We thought that was pretty good. Dr. Forrest was less sanguine.

Nor did I mention how I would get up early, scramble into my cold clothes under the covers, and then run over to the Mess, set the long boardinghouse reach table, and sit by the wood stove to keep Mac from going up in smoke. He was the camp dog. At first I was afraid of the terrier. He would stand square in front of people and bare his teeth while his whole body trembled. It turned out he was grinning. Too ancient to keep himself warm, he would lie as close to the stove as possible without having to move when Lettie added wood and reminded me, in her twanging vernacular, that poor Mac was numbed by age, so

I must be sure to flick off the embers that fell on what was left of his short hair. It was like being in the Wild West, and I loved it.

Except writing home. It became such a chore that, one day, out of desperation, I wrote something about, "Wasn't it nice the Korean War ended?" My father wrote a dissertation back about the fact that I had neglected to date the letter, that such laxity and inattention to detail, whatever the circumstances, could open the way to many disasters. He closed by urging me to affix the month, day, and year atop each piece of correspondence. He never mentioned the war I don't think. But he did say he talked to Marion's Mom. How in the world did he find Marion's Mom? I showed his letter to my friend.

"What do you think it means?"

"I dunno. I wonder what they talked about."

"Hard to tell from here."

"Yeah."

You know what, Marion?"

"What, Cath?"

"I think we're not coming back next summer."

"I think so."

Yet expecting it to end as a once-in-a-lifetime experience didn't make it any the less so, or us greedier for more. Accepting the inevitable void, we didn't try to fill it with frantic gathering—with more birch bark or salamanders, with more good times than could fit in the remaining month. If the bark from a fallen branch was not as large or white as what could be stripped from a standing tree, or the dead salamander not as fascinating as a live one, we didn't contrive to make up the difference. We accepted Rotomac as our good fortune, not our right. Whether from China or Germany, neither Bao nor Marx had been in this country so long that we spoke of "rights" lightly.

The feeling stayed with me into the future, into my first appointment at a beauty parlor. I was there to have my once-again long hair piled into a crown of glory for the most important event of my tenth grade life: The Dance. With my new image snipped from a movie magazine, I handed it to the beautician when I mounted the leathery chair as if it were a throne. Then, uncomfortable with the outright vanity, I toned down my aspirations with mention that my split ends might need trimming.

With no warning, the woman laid the shears flat against one side of my head and cut, grinning maniacally as she crowed, "Too late now!" I didn't scream or run out. I sat stunned that, once again, someone had decided my hair was an offense. Within seconds, her eyes lost the telltale gleam and she asked me what I wanted done. Maybe I was an idiot for telling her and, then, letting her. But I felt in her the same woe I saw in Julie the morning after. It was a pleading to keep still, to let it be, to help her surround the incident with silence so it could be an isolated one. At fifteen, in the beauty parlor, I had the power to do what I couldn't do at eleven. Seated in front of the mirror, looking once again lopsided, I recalled the last day of camp, our pledge to remember Rotomac forever. The leave-taking ritual had evoked sounds from Lettie's reclusive brother, soothing sounds that no one had heard before. Remembering, I let the beautician do the best she could to salvage the damage done. Had Julie stayed on, she would have done the same—so strong was my faith in the healing powers of Rotomac and community, so habituated was my belief in the efficacy of expecting the desired outcome. Crying wouldn't have done it. Though I did that too before wrapping my head in a scarf to dance in the school gym, acting as if it was the latest fashion, and then willing my hair to grow back. Fast.

My mother seemed to ignore most of it: the lonely braid, Julie's picture, the scarf. Without the brouhaha, it was a mishap, not a disaster. Yet this time, I was older. And though I took the Chinese initiative in wordlessly concluding that I had not upset the order of things by putting hair in the soup or chewing gum in the hair, I wasn't entirely clear whether my submission made me submissive. Nor was I clear whether this made me a "good girl" or "bad" in someone's eyes.

Living with my mother's blind eye to fragile hearts and my father's seeing into doll hospitals for curing broken ones, I felt the power of the family circle at the same time I felt how it separated us. From their vantage point I saw the world filled with all sorts of people who cannot or will not learn, and that "teaching them a lesson" or writing the *Reader's Digest* was either beneath or beyond us. From the perspective of a tenth grader in the '50s, I saw America filled with people endowed with inalienable rights and obligations to teach everyone lessons about equality (though men do it publicly and women at home). The subtleties of both were lost on me because I went to Rotomac.

Though more "camp" and less "regular" than my parents condoned, I could see the Forrest's world because my family opened the doors and encouraged me to step outside. However, once there, I had to hold my own where solitary families are not enough and words must be exchanged so that people can drink or swim in water that won't poison frogs. If, one day, this would mean I could gladly hear war protesters and feminists chant "Hell no, we won't go" and "equal pay for equal work," it also meant I had to be sensitive to nuances if I wanted to feel hopeful about going back through those doors to find parents who could find pleasure in my company.

I've heard parents vow, "I'll never make the same mistakes with my kids that my parents made with me." My standard response is, "Probably not. You'll think up new ones." And then we laugh—a nervous incantation to quell the fear that our children will say the same about us. In the case of the Americanized, this is often followed by an enumeration of grievances, the short list of woes written with too many tears to be forgiven or forgotten. The still-Chinese tend not to put these into words which the deities can hear for injustice, however grave, is no excuse for ingratitude—one could have remained in oblivion and never been born. This silence is sometimes construed as filial piety.

Silence would play a great part. As with the later letters from Rotomac, I learned that, by omission, I could isolate thoughts and feelings, separating them from one context, placing them in another, sometimes to reflect on how they changed in the process. By not always giving them voice, I became more private and, eventually, more dependent on a configuration of non-family members to know me. I became more American. Other campers' parents got anxious if their children failed to make "good" friends who would, in turn, be trustworthy confidantes. My own warned me against such a breach by "aliens"—and that included spouses—with tips on how best to form a tight circle of the family's wagons. I knew both cultures regarded a sibling confidante to be a blessing though Americans would agonize before invading their united privacy while Chinese would worry if all their kids didn't tattle on each other. In the absence of reliable peers and siblings, American parents would try to be best friends to their children, while Chinese acted as if any social needs that couldn't be best provided by family members were not really relevant in the larger, longer scheme. And if you thought they were, this probably indicated a weakness in your character.

Unable to translate American hopes and fears into Chinese or the Chinese ones into English, with one sister in China and the other in a grade too high to be interested, I gradually transformed the use of silence and talk to communicate with myself and, eventually, my son. Not all the conversations have been smashing successes but each failure did provide room for improvement if I would only do what neither culture does enough of: listen. This is what I did when, once again, my coiffure was an issue.

"God bless your hair."

Hearing her at the same time I became aware she was stroking my head, I turned and saw an unkempt woman standing among several grimy bags. In the one from Bloomingdale's, I spotted a large pair of scissors.

"Aren't you afraid someone might cut it off? It's quite lovely you know."

Smiling to keep us both calm, I sidled away along the railing. Not wanting to take any chances with the nine years' worth of growth I had acquired since the Tenth Grade Dance, I said, "Thank you," before putting half the Staten Island ferry between us. Then, with my back to the cabin wall, I kept my eye on her until the rush of tourists eager to admire the Statue of Liberty made it impossible. Out of sight but not out of mind, she became more memorable for having disappeared. Adrenaline pumping, I pictured her joining Julie and the beautician in a long line of maladjusted people hell-bent on scalping me. Why hair? Some catholic urge to put me in a nunnery where shorn heads are holier ones? Or some Philistine dread of Samson-like locks? Or a way to show disrespect or gain control that was foreign to me?

Why *my* hair?

Was it because it was on a Chinese head? Too shiny to be deprived? Or too shiny not to be depraved? Would they have let me alone had I been in Chinatown instead of a summer camp, or in front of the beauty parlor carrying cast-off bags instead of a purse? Or was I so obviously un-American that everyone had the right to teach me a lesson about having too much personal style and carrying uppity red umbrellas? After two successes and one near miss, paranoia was an easy option. I could interpret all situations by the one dim light, and be absolved of any further obligation to delve more deeply into root causes, let alone seek more adroit solutions than getting a bowl cut and melting into the "normal" landscape for the likes of me.

But would that be enough? I had parents and sisters, a husband and several friends, a few neighbors and many students. And what I heard myself telling them, over and over, about being a dysfunctional victim simply would not jibe with the kid who went to Rotomac. So I would have to change that story too.

Asking all the questions but not fixating on the truth of these answers, I used the silence of my mother to let the fear go flaccid, and imparted to The Bag Lady no more malicious intent than her action, even her words, implied. After all, she had done nothing but touch me. In doing so, she could appear in my mind along with Lettie's brother, without foreboding, then reappear in William's mind so he could greet the children in the classroom down the hall from Miss Glusa's and think nothing of playing near the Boy with the Box.

...COMMON TOUCH

It appears that America, the melting pot of human races, has also become the melting pot of lice....the louse adapts its color to that of the host, so that we have the black louse of Africa, the smoky louse of the Hindu, the yellowish-brown louse of the Japanese, the dark brown one of the North American Indian, the pale brown one of the Eskimo, and the dirty gray one of the European.

—*Hans Zinsser, Rats, Lice and History*

In Chinatown, sixty miles due east of Day Care, Bennett made sure William's second day at school would end differently than the first. After roaming the streets together, admiring the pressed ducks hanging in the windows and giant mangoes displayed on the sidewalks, after going into one store to buy a little jar of balm, its golden lid embossed with a leaping tiger, and another to sample six different kinds of steamed dumplings in order to select a box to take home, after hours of being with people who looked and spoke like his mother, they returned in the evening. Showing me his treasures, William trumpeted, "I'm half Chinese."

"Yes," I said, gratified that the visual impact had done what words could not. And then, out of curiosity, inquired, "Do you know what the other half is?"

No answer. He was stumped.

But not for long. Gradually but inextricably, we both lapsed into English—the language of schoolmates, of teachers, of power, of my ideas but not all my emotions, of his choice but not all his values. Without the words and phrases of my parents, could William under-stand? And without that, could he understand me?

Getting ready for bed that night, he took the picture out of his pocket and returned it, having no use for it now that the real thing was next to him. Noticing it was already showing some wear, we encased it in a plastic holder, and put it on the rocking chair by his bed. For another week or so, pocketing it was the last step in his dress-ing ritual before going down to breakfast and school.

It disappeared from my consciousness until the day I went in to teach the children how to pick up popcorn with chopsticks. Lingering on to watch Miss Glusa instruct a recalcitrant child in the art of bread-making, she beckoned to me once she was sure he had gotten the knack of beating the dough with his fists.

59

"He's having a bad day," she told me.

Referring to the process as well as the product, she added, "It's a good recipe."

Walking with her to the other end of the room, she pointed at the bulletin board and smiled. There, tacked to the lower corner, was the picture. William had been afraid he would lose it during outdoor play and gave it to her for safe-keeping. She asked if he thought the board was that sort of place. He did. And that's where it stayed for the rest of the year. Sometimes weeks would go by and he wouldn't bother with it. But every so often, she would see him saunter over and take a look. And at the end of some of those days, he would proudly present me with a miniature loaf of whole wheat bread. Kneaded by the inevitable frustration of being-in-the-world, it was a nutritious alternative to being stymied. We so enjoyed sharing those tiny loaves for dinner, we asked if he could make bread even on the days when he was feeling good. Very occasionally he could, but not often. Even a Montessori class led by Miss Glusa could sometimes use an extra oven.

Once however, the numbers exceeded all expectations. Entering the room on that afternoon, the aroma of freshly baked bread invited me to breathe more deeply. It had become my habit to sit in the classroom a while before asking William if he was ready to go home. Miss Glusa and I had come to a tacit agreement that my presence was one way for the children to become accustomed to the existence of Chinese in the world, to help make the foreign more familiar. She understood what many of her fellow liberal educators forgot in their commitment to preserving a child's natural creativity: that no human mind can possibly imagine the richness of the world as it is. Throughout William's childhood, I reminded myself of this by thinking of our neighbor, Sandy, someone we had known for years. The first time our good-natured, laid-back son looked up from his crib at her, he screamed bloody murder.

She was his first blond. I would be the kids' first Chinatown.

For similar reasons, I made it a point to stop, with William, at the classroom down the hall, near the exit, whenever its door was open. We would watch the children inside. Sometimes we lingered to comment on a new drawing someone had put up on the wall, or evaluate the shape of the cutouts taped on the window panes. Often our being there would entice the attention of someone inside. If he or she then approached to touch us or just to stare, William learned not to shrink back or avert his eyes or grab my hand. Counter to both my cultures, he learned not to pay attention to his schoolmates' parents complaining about "them." He got to recognize a few of the regulars, to realize that their way of being might require him to move less quickly or speak more slowly, but this was not essentially different from what he did elsewhere. At my parents' house, he modified his pace to their lifestyle; in an antique shop, he must walk with his hands clasped behind his back; and at school, he got to know that being with retarded people was just another aspect of being-himself-with-others. He got to know that "appearing normal" is often no criterion for good value. He got to know because, years before he was born, even while his mother had spurned all four pairs of furry, clunky mukluks, his father was traipsing the woods near Iowa City in something even funnier looking. He got to know because his mother had to hit a homer during fourth grade recess, and because she wore a scarf to the Tenth Grade Dance.

But that afternoon in New Jersey, the patterns weren't just strange, they were wrong. The usually demure had become stilted. They were sidling to their destinations, keeping their backs toward the wall the way I had on the ferry with the Bag Lady. Their eyes on some focal point around which they circled, caution intervened everywhere, obliterating spontaneity, making these children behave too much like "good little boys and girls." The rest, normally raucous were, instead, frenetic—dashing not to get somewhere but to avoid being still. What had once been a blend of legato and staccato was now a movement orchestrated by some invisible conductor gone spastic. The players kept looking to Miss Glusa and her assistant for some other direction but neither could restore the rhythm, only a random halting—a prelude that made the ensuing dissonance all the more unnerving. They emitted uncharacteristic cooing sounds that soothed no one.

Looking around, I saw a new boy at the far end of the room. Larger than the others, I thought he must be at least six. His movements were almost a parody of the children down the hall. Using parts of his body to touch what was ahead of him, he sensed the floor and furniture before moving the rest of himself into the space. Tuning in, I heard him accompany his amoeboid movements with a muffled mewing. Occasionally, it would become a yowling, a high-pitched moan that was intense but never really loud. It reminded me of the time I thought I heard a cat. But my neighbor told me it was a rabbit.

Surprised because I didn't think rabbits had a "sound," she said they do when they've been wounded or are in their death throes.

Around the boy's neck hung a box on a thick string. About the size of a building block, it jerked and swung when he hurried, not always in line with where he was going, sometimes hitting him on a back swing. Intermittently he groped for it, sometimes letting go as soon as he felt it, other times holding it with both hands and shaking it with such vigor I thought it must hurt. And then Miss Glusa would rush over, grabbing something en route. Holding it in front of the boy, she would jiggle it like a tidbit, trying to lure his fingers and attention from the box.

I had done the same sort of thing the first time I saw our dog pounce on a chicken. His own surprise at finally finding it under his paws gave me a moment to distract him. The hen flapped away, almost intact. The boy was more tenacious and, often, Miss Glusa ended up having to pry his fingers from around the box. I had rarely seen her initiate physical contact, and certainly not in a way that smacked of force. Rather, she was available to the children, a person from whom they could seek instruction or to whom they could give a hug. She gave and received either or both with equanimity. Except today. Everything about him told me he was in need of something and everything Miss Glusa did indicated she couldn't provide it. All she seemed able to accomplish was the temporary rescue of the box from his clutches. What I couldn't understand was why she allowed it to stay tethered to his neck. I found out later. It was the boy who was tethered.

After one particularly difficult round, Miss Glusa gave up, daunted by his latest tactic of twisting away from her. I could see that the string had worked itself halfway up his head and he would be injured if the tugging continued. Spotting me, she came toward me. A big woman, her ordinarily firm gait was tentative, as if each step might bring her foot down on a sharp pebble in her shoe. Fitting herself into the little chair next to mine, she muttered, "That stupid box!"

I asked, "What is it? Why don't you just take it away?"

"I can't. It's his hearing aid. Though it's not much use. Most of the time I think he gets nothing but static." She paused, then continued, "That's when he shakes it."

I heard her tears before I saw them. Talking to quell my own, "There's got to be something better than that. It looks primitive."

"I'm sure there is. But his parents don't want to hear about it. Yesterday they dropped him off when we opened at 7:30, and picked him up at 5:30 when we locked up. They briefed me about the box. Later, I tried to tell them that the box was no good. All they wanted to know was why we couldn't feed him supper too, complaining about how stingy the county was. That's how he got here. Some government agency. It's supposed to be temporary."

"Can he talk?" I wondered aloud.

"I don't think so."

"What about Signing?" I pursued.

"I doubt it. His parents just push him, or grab his shirt, or shove him along with a knee in his back."

Apprehending, I again saw his mode of walking, his feeling approach to the objects around him, "Oh my God, that's the only language he knows!"

I shouldn't have said it. Miss Glusa cried.

Her face, rough and "unlovely," had become very precious to me. She was William's first school teacher. And she was a good one. She knew how to nurture a child's individuality within a universe of connections, letting each child be at the hub of a web. She revealed the space, the place, that shouldn't get filled up because, where there is not one thing, there can be everything. She taught how to keep that center open, strong for the possibilities of each person's becoming. Becoming what? Whatever. Miss Glusa knew how to help the children weave their webs and explore their designs. Miss Glusa didn't know how to sign these lessons to the Boy with the Box. Though she tried.

During the weeks that followed, I often heard her tell the other children how to communicate with their faces and hands, how to move slowly into the Boy's arena and touch gently, yet firmly, the body and mind therein. If the Boy resisted the guidance, they learned to resolve the difference without harming the values inherent in the classroom Miss Glusa created. By involving everyone and not just her assistant, they succeeded in restoring much of the old pattern.

Nevertheless, Miss Glusa would express her wish that the "temporary arrangement" come to an end. None of this was of interest to the Boy's parents who continued talking about Day Care as nothing more than the least of what was due them for having spawned a defective child. There is no way of knowing what was on the Boy's mind, or why he chose to retaliate when he did.

It was a Tuesday, the first of three consecutive days that constituted William's school week. When I entered the building, I could see Miss Glusa standing outside her room, neither proceeding in nor going elsewhere. She was waiting for me.

"I'm sorry, Cathy, William was hurt."

"Is he all right? Where is he? What happened?"

"He's fine. There are marks but William is okay. The Boy scratched him." Actually, she didn't call him that. I can't remember his name though, at the time, I thought I'd never forget it.

Her voice low with uncertainty, she expanded, "Yesterday, he struck one of the children with a pencil, close to her eye. It was so sudden. I didn't think he could move that fast. Today we didn't let him have anything sharp. A few times he tried to grab something but the children have been alert and wouldn't let him." She finished with a sigh, "He used his nails on William. I try to keep them clean. But it's hard—they get dirty again right away. We tried to call you, but no one answered."

"I need to see William."

"Yes, of course." Trailing off, she opened the door and, as I went through, touched me, murmuring, "I'm sorry."

Spotting William immediately. I went over to him as quickly as I could without causing any more stir than my anticipated arrival had already made. He looked so forlorn, the red marks contrasting with his demeanor.

"Hello, *MaMa*."

"Hello, William." Bringing him to me, I enveloped him with a calm strength I brought forth from the memory of some other day, some steadier time. "Does it hurt?"

"A little." His fingers gingerly skimmed the dry edges of what had once been baby softness. "It feels stiff."

I laid my cheek by his and let him ease his onto mine. He stayed for a moment then turned silently toward the table where he had been busy, waiting. The drawing lay there, beckoning.

I asked the question he had been thinking, "Would you like to finish? Or would you like to go home now?"

By not sweeping into the room and carrying him away, the first alternative remained a live one. He had created it when he didn't retreat into a corner after the attack; he conveyed its importance when he didn't rush into my arms; he chose it when he responded, "I haven't done the moat. Or the secret room."

William always drew castles that had, imbedded in the individually drawn stones, a treasure room. The first time I noticed it—I who didn't notice for three weeks that Bennett had rearranged the living room— my son conferred a smile upon me equivalent to the Ph.D. I still didn't have. After that, he would give me each drawing to inspect. Whether I found the secret location or confessed my inability to do so, William was equally satisfied.

"All right, William. I'll just go and sit by Miss Glusa. Okay?"

"Okay."

Giving his hand a warming hug, I left him to finish the work he had begun despite and because of the pain. Walking toward Miss Glusa, I passed The Boy with the Box. He was surrounded by empti- ness, like the day I first saw him. His eyes had been following me since I entered. There was a feral quality about the way he watched, making those sounds that Bennett described as coming from an animal who is given human vocal chords, a muted screeching with no content, no reference. For a breath, I wanted to hurt him.

"I'm sorry, Cathy," she again began, "He's liked playing near William. We thought it was because William was closer to his mental age than the others. William didn't seem to mind. Now I think it's because William is the smallest, the most vulnerable."

"Yes, vulnerable." I repeated, thinking less about size than the shape of things to come.

As she talked, I saw one of the girls, a large square bandage taped near her eye, "What about *her* parents?"

"They were upset. But today they said nothing."

"Didn't they report it to the county?"

"I don't think so. You know I've tried everything. They won't lis- ten."

"They will now."

That night I asked William to sit very still while I took pictures of his face. Afterward I made "choo-choos" for dessert (a part of the meal that Bennett was normally in charge of). I had renamed the bite-size balls of sweet bean paste wrapped in glutinous rice flour when, as a teen, I couldn't say it correctly in Chinese. The next morning, after William was kneading the resilient dough for a double loaf of whole wheat bread, I asked Miss Glusa to join me as soon as she could. When all the children were involved in some project, we went to the office. She listened while I placed a call to the agency that had assigned

The Boy. Describing the pencil and scratching incident several times, I was finally put through to the Director. He sounded more sympathetic to his own constraints than to my plea.

I responded, "For starters, he needs a better hearing aid. But even with the best, even if he has somehow figured out what others are saying, he can't say anything himself. He needs to be taught how to sign. He doesn't know how to communicate except by physical contact. And that includes violence."

"Yes, well there's nothing I can do about that."

Sitting taller on my high horse, I spoke with acid, "I'm really sorry you think that way. I had hoped you could be persuaded by the case for this child and the rest of the children. You leave me no choice but to threaten you. I shall do it once so listen carefully. At 5:31 this afternoon, one minute after this school closes, Miss Glusa—the teacher who's been made responsible for that which you are being paid to do—will call me. If she tells me that you haven't yet arranged for this deaf child to be assigned a signing teacher in a situation that can provide the education he needs, then at 9:01 tomorrow morning, I shall deliver the pictures of my son's face to my lawyer, and instruct him to sue your agency and you for endangering his welfare. Furthermore, I shall launch a campaign to convince each and every parent in his class to do the same. DO YOU HEAR ME?!"

He did. And I did. God, it felt good! He got the letter I never mailed to the *Reader's Digest*!!

I don't know if The Boy fared any better as a result. Maybe it was already too late for him—communicating with the rest of the world could never compensate for the shoving and kneeing he got from his parents. Except to confirm that the Director had followed through, in deed, what he promised at 5:14 the previous afternoon, we never saw or heard from them again. Miss Glusa's class resumed, and flourished. When I actually got the roll of film developed, I showed her the pictures of William's face.

"You took these that night? I can hardly see the marks."

"The lighting in the kitchen isn't very good. And my camera isn't very fancy. But the guy at the agency doesn't know that."

Miss Glusa laughed. And I didn't want her to stop. Putting my hand to the side of my mouth, I followed up, "I also don't have a lawyer."

She laughed some more and said, "You don't need one."

And then I laughed. But behind the laughter, I could see the Umbrella Woman smirk, "Did you really think the Chopsticks-Fork routine would work in a world where there is never enough, where selfish parents make violent children? Get involved with strangers and they'll claim your time, give them space and they'll want to take yours. Look at William's face. That's what happens when you let them "swing" and wear red, when you go to Day Care and kiss frogs. Now look at The Boy and tell me you don't feel what I do."

I did. And she was right. I had wanted to hurt him.

Yet acknowledging The Umbrella Woman in me was humbling and, therefore, comforting because the gods wouldn't perceive my seeking "liberty and justice for all" as the arrogance of a know-it-all. When no one is perfect, not even the gods, then noble deeds can more easily arise from ignoble feelings and no one has a monopoly on virtue. When practice can never make perfect, we can openly doubt ourselves and others without losing faith in human effort or resorting to blind faith in the superhuman. But I had gotten to this point between East and West by a map that had been keyed to a legend that no longer existed. How would it be possible for William to arrive in the vicinity when so many of his fellow travelers demanded commitment only to one direction? Whose only good routes had to be straight and narrow?

Miss Glusa got up to help a new child prepare the afternoon snack for his partner. When she returned, what she said was not what I wanted to hear, "Cathy, I'm leaving. I've always wanted my own school and this whole affair was the push out I needed."

"How far?"

"Too far to drive William every day."

I felt her memory immediately. It was a looking back from some moment yet to come, a distilling of her essence into some inviolable part of my brain, a pledging that I would never forget her goodness, or fail to feel my gratitude. It would take her a year to make the move. The prospect of finding another school, another place where our hybrid ways could flourish, was daunting. She had helped me teach the children that proficiency with chopsticks *and* forks was not for the sole purpose of avoiding embarrassment but to provide greater service —not to mention putting popcorn in the lesson plan. What I taught was sometimes a matter of intellectual commitment; what she understood was out of habit.

So William got it both ways, at school and home. What his nuclear family couldn't or wouldn't do was sometimes provided by one anti-dote to individual limitations: the Extended Family. When I was content to place a star on the cactus in the kitchen and tell William it was "the Christmas tree," my sister's husband, Winston, would convince me to lug a full-grown fir to their New York apartment so that he could celebrate according to the principle of "Quantity, not Quality." Annually, William was dazzled: reading "Twas the night before...," leaving cookies by the (permanently blocked-up) fire place, opening presents for six or seven hours, and disposing of an embarrassing waste of wrapping paper. By the time he was five and shedding baby teeth on a regular basis, I got an inkling of how the realities and fantasies were coexisting in his head. It happened one night when Bennett was out of town.

I'd taken William to school with me. While I lectured on what Hobbes meant when he described life in the State of Nature as "...soli-tary, poor, nasty, brutish and short," William drew pictures of castles in the air. Driving home, William was trying out some new technique to extract the latest casualty of growing adult teeth while I, too tired to face cooking dinner, kept an eye out for a restaurant. We both suc-ceeded.

Spotting the bloody incisor on the table, the Chinese waiter asked, "*Will your grandparents buy it from you?*"

Alert to financial transactions of any kind, William was interested but perplexed. He could still understand some of the waiter's words but had become accustomed to conversing in English. (Ever since the week he asked about the malfunctioning car and freedom, I gave up trying to make him bilingual. My ability to explain concepts in the language of my childhood didn't include the workings of carburetors or John Stuart Mill's essay *On Liberty*.)

William looked up at the man, then down at the tooth. I could guess what he was thinking. He knew about The Imaginary Tooth Fairy who gave him real money for actual teeth. He knew my parents, his *PoPo* and *KungKung*, gave him Red Envelopes of money on special occasions. The question before the House was: What did one have to do with the other? Were the three somehow in cahoots?

Quickly, I told the waiter, "*We deal with teeth American style.*"

Enervated by Hobbes in one class, and then the rigors of explaining the logical implications of "If...then" thinking in another, I wasn't up to going into the ontological status of fairies or the limited market value of baby teeth. Also, I wanted to forestall involving my parents. Chinese grandparents of their generation expected children to enter their world, not the other way around. They had done their part in raising future generations. They should now be able to observe their grandchildren, talk to them when convenient, and be proud at the appropriate times. Asking them to remember, let alone participate in, the Tooth Fairy ritual was not reasonable. I flashed back to the time she was renamed "imaginary" and saw it hit the fan.

The waiter left to get our tea and milk, having picked up on my desire to drop the subject. William did not.

"I don't understand. What did he mean? What did *you* mean?"

Overly casual, I let it out as fast as possible, "In China, children get money from their grandparents. In America, they get it from the Imaginary Tooth Fairy."

Then, with much Pomp and Circumstance, I opened the oversized menu and rubbed my hands with gustatory anticipation, "Mmm, now. Let's see. Shall we have your favorite? *Moo Shoo Pork*?"

His neck extended like a turtle so his eyes could see my face clearly. His words were slow and deliberate, "Who is the Imaginary Tooth Fairy?"

Meeting him halfway so he could watch me even more closely, I said, "Who do you think it is?" Then added, "Remember: It's the *Imaginary* Tooth Fairy."

And flashed him a wink and my This-Is-A-Good-Joke-If-You're-Smart-Enough-To-Get-It smile.

Sitting back, he thought. No conclusion came forth. Figuring he needed another clue, I added, "You know, William, 'imaginary' means 'not real'."

No reaction.

"William, *MaMa* is real. *MaMa* always called it the Imaginary Tooth Fairy. *MaMa* tucks you in bed. *MaMa* has access to your pillow. Now, THINK!"

As I started to wonder how, at this rate, the kid would finish kindergarten, he stretched toward me again, stuck out his chin, furrowed what little brow he had, and slowly intoned, as if to the dim-witted, "Maybe the Tooth Fairy is Real, and You're NOT."

A split second later, he gave me a blink and his This-Is-A-Good-Joke-If-You're-Smart-Enough-To-Get-It smile.

By the time the waiter served our dinner, we had gone on to a critical analysis of the drawings he had done in class. Finished eating, while waiting for me, he carefully cleaned the tooth. Holding it toward me, he said slowly, uncertain of his own wish, "Do you want it...now?"

"No, William." Gently, I suggested, "Why don't you put it under your pillow tonight?"

Obviously pleased with my answer, he once again focused on the tooth. Turning it round and round with his little fingers, he said to it, in a voice I could hear, "Santa Claus may not 'exist,' but he's real to me."

Even more gently, I said, "Yes, William, that'll be fine."

During the rest of the drive home, he was quiet. Changed for the night, he tried none of the usual ploys for staying up "just a little longer." In bed, ready for the sleep ritual of song and poem, I asked, "Is your tooth where it should be?"

With a look of gratitude and then, a conspiratorial grin, he clambered down to rummage the treasure out of his coat pocket.

Everything in place, I first sang *You are my Sunshine*, and then recited, "In Xanadu did Kubla Khan A stately pleasure-dome decree...."

As was his custom, William joined in at the end of every line— with the last word.

In the morning, the heft and sheen of the quarter helped resolve his mixed feelings and give reality to his new perspective. That evening, he completed the transition by waiting patiently for his father's return. During the lull between dinner and bedtime, William climbed into Bennett's lap and began, "*BaBa*, let me tell you about the Imaginary Tooth Fairy. Did you know...."

Children can deal with multiple realities and multiple fantasies. However, if, from the time they acquire language, they are asked questions like "What is your *favorite* color?" "Who is your *best* friend?" "Which is the *coolest* game?" they become habituated into thinking, even believing, that there is room for only one at the top and that choosing "the" one is expected, even desirable. And if they are also taught to be singular in terms of being true to one's self and developing self-respect while denigrating the wishy-washy and despising the two-faced, then there is little wonder that, by adulthood, being *multi*cultural is often more problematic than virtuous and being single-minded is more virtuous than problematic.

COMMONWEALTH, COMMON TOUCH

Via e-mail from Taipei, May, 1995:

> Hi Mom, went out with a Taiwanese girl a couple of
> times....not a word of English but a bit aggressive espe-
> cially for a Chinese girl....times are definitely changing
> out here. I don't think this one is a really good idea and I
> know you wouldn't approve...her highlights include blue
> tinted contact lenses and nice legs but didn't go to college
> and aspires to sell cars...well that is putting her in a bad
> light but it doesn't get too much better. This one happens
> to be pretty unintellectual...I'll see.

Biting my internet lip, I wrote:

Dear William, What do you mean "a bit aggressive for a Chinese girl"? Are you being politically incorrect again?

What I wanted to do was rehash the Facts of Life speech I delivered before our twenty-one year old college grad went to live and work in Taipei. Not only had our son arrived in Taiwan when impressionable girls were already transforming every young American male into a knight in denim armor, a.k.a. Keanu Reeves, but William had the added benefit of being photographed in every style of Levi's and being so displayed in department stores and *World Screen* magazines all over Asia.

"Mom, some lady stopped me in the street and asked if I wanted to model blue jeans. What do you think? Should I do it?"

"Sure, William. But just get very *ve-ry* suspicious if they ask you to take off all your clothes."

Happily, he got paid a month's rent and wasn't tempted by the possibility of a new career—"It was boring." On the other hand, tint-ed contacts over nice legs drove me to warn him again about not get-ting carried away by naïve female adoration. It was their fantasy; it shouldn't be his. (Translation: Virgins are off limits and, DON'T GET PREGNANT!!)

He wrote back:

> ...oh by the way, Mom, I don't know whether this was
> clear in the last e-mail but the way these girls operate is
> they get "face" because they have a foreigner for a
> boyfriend. You'll love this—I told her that I didn't want a
> relationship/girlfriend at the moment and she asked
> whether it would be okay if we just "acted" like we were.

"Acted" is the closest translation I can find to *xiang*. But anyway, that's what I mean by "aggressive"...girl does not take no for an answer.

I put my cyberspace foot down.

Dear William, It's been two weeks. Enough is enough. For her sake and yours, get out of this one.

He submitted, maybe.

Hi Mom, Nothing else new except that the girl who worked at the clothing store and has blue contact lenses got hit by a car while on her scooter and has been in the hospital for the last two weeks—fractured skull as far as I can figure out but it could just be some internal damage...her brain is okay though. I went and visited her yesterday. She didn't look too happy. She was getting out of the hospital as I showed up so I guess it is good that I went when I did.

After that, neither of us wrote about her again. Intellectually, my silence was honoring the right to privacy that his silence was developing. Emotionally, my fears wanted to hide him under a very dark blue umbrella. Practically, I asked, "Why ruin a good story?"

CHAPTER 3

MAMA-HUHU

MaMa (HorseHorse)

…The anti-hierarchy movement—a loose assembly, transcending traditional class lines, of people who resist the rush toward global centralization on a variety of political, moral, scientific, or aesthetic grounds.
—*Richard J. Barnet & Ronald E. Müller, Global Reach,
The Power of the Multinational Corporations*

The summer after Rotomac, Bette and I were exported to Camp Winnetaska. So was Marion. It was not co-ed. It was accredited. It was not *MaMa-HuHu*. Taught with more rules than I could memorize in a day, I learned how to swim five regulation strokes and sing songs like *Ninety-nine Bottles of Beer on the Wall* and

> May I ever be most worthy
> Of my native land, America.

Unlike Cook, Lettie and her brother, Mrs. Briggs and her "Girls" never joined in the fun. Always they stayed behind, where they lived, in an area turned so gray with soapsuds and grease that no amount of rain or time ever washed them away.

The Director awarded me several of the much-coveted badges and made Bette the "Best All-Around Camper." He had her name etched onto a plaque alongside previous winners, and hung it in the Dining Hall where we had to sit at assigned tables so somebody could figure out who should get demerits for leaving a mess.

He was the first person whom my family admired but whom I found deficient.

Which is not to say that I didn't enjoy my new skills, or didn't go whole hog for Color War.

> I'm a Greenie born, I'm a Greenie bred.
> And when I die, I'll be a Greenie dead.
> So, Rah-rah for Green Team,
> Rah-rah for Green Team,
> Rah-rah for Green Team,
> Rah-rah-rah!

Teams vied for points in everything: athletics, cabin clean-up, arts & crafts. There was always a winner, and a loser.

Bette and I were both Greenies, so I was doubly proud when she got chosen for the highest award. But I wondered: Would the Director have allowed himself to honor the *whole* Bette? Would his Rules permit him to love her as much as I did if he knew what I did? His standards were so absolute and his demand for meticulous attention so stringent, wouldn't they preclude him from really liking anyone? Wouldn't they have made him scratch out Bette's name if he found out she had once left her little sister in the woods to die? Well, miss lunch.

I tried to imagine how the Director would react if he heard about Bette and her bicycle. It was a good one. Before moving to Teaneck, we lived in Elmwood Park, a city-town that consisted of long blocks with endless rows of two-story apartments and walkways that never cut diagonally across the commons. My sister's bike afforded her freedom from being a mere biped. One day, she rode it to the store. Parking it against the outside wall, she went inside for a loaf of bread. When she emerged, it started to rain just as the local bus pulled up to the curb. Running to catch a ride, she arrived home, delivered the bread to the kitchen, and went about the business of being a twelve-year old.

The next day, Bette went to the line of one-car garages that flanked the driveway behind every sector of the brick neighborhood. Once all the metal doors looked alike. Now people had no trouble finding the one assigned to their apartment—each was marked with an assortment of dents and scratches, individualizing marks left by folks testing out their two, three or four-wheeled vehicles in the driveway before venturing into the streets.

Jerking the scarred door into alignment with the side runners, Bette ducked into the cement niche and immediately turned to the left corner, her grip already set just the right distance to grasp the handlebars. Looking into the gloom, her hands drooped to her sides. The bike is gone. The Bike is Gone. THE BIKE IS GONE. It didn't take long before the whole neighborhood took up the chant. Within the hour, all the garage doors were locked for the first time ever. No one wanted to take a chance if The Thief returned.

About a week later, needing another loaf of bread, Bette got on the bus, got off at the store, went inside to make her purchase, came out, got on her bike, rode home, parked it in the garage, delivered the package to the kitchen, and then went about the business of being a twelve-year old. The next day, it took a friend's query, "Did you get another one just like the first?" for her to realize that the bicycle was where it should be, that The Thief must have returned it during the night. Pleased to have it back, she offered to take her little sister for a ride. Pleased to have the attention, I fitted myself into the front basket. We headed for the woods. After an hour or two of hunting for this and that, swinging from here to there, I wandered from the clearing where Bette had been sitting. Until she got thirsty. Hopping on her bike, she went home for a drink. Later, when asked, "Where's Cathy?" Bette replied, quite honestly, "I don't know, Mommy. Probably with her friends."

Meanwhile, I trudged home, brows knit, head wagging, struggling to comprehend the depth of my sibling's absent-mindedness. In-between, I kept count of how many steps it took to get back and tried to remember if it was the brown or the black bear that was native to New Jersey. Not sure whether a small eight-year old would count as a whole meal or just a snack, or even if bears were carnivorous, I settled on wild dogs. By dinner and the family's story-telling time, I had my hardships down pat.

Could the Director comprehend or enjoy such a story? Or would his Point System demand that Bette get at least Ten Demerits after flag-raising in the morning so that by the time the flag was folded in the evening, she would beg the assembled crowd for the opportunity to confess the error of her ways and prove the sincerity of her penitence by offering to return the Best All-Around Camper certificate. Assuming she could find it.

The next summer, I returned to Winnetaska. My sister didn't, opting, as usual, to get out while still on top. Where was the "Me too, me too" when I needed it? Nobody made me, so I guess it was my decision. Going away was such a luxury; my parents never got to take a vacation. Somehow not to return would seem ungrateful, a verdict against their generosity and judgment.

As a Second-Year Camper, I mostly learned techniques in passive resistance bordering on passive aggression, and the art of talking for three weeks about dancing for two hours at the nearby boys' camp. Had I never gone to Rotomac and known the joy of streaking around the bases marked by clothes too hot to wear in the sun, I might not have become a recalcitrant.

Andee, the Head Counselor, treated my defiance as symptoms of adolescence. Since my parents had never mentioned that being a teenager was an illness, I had no idea to what Andee was referring (though I later realized that mine lasted twice as long and Bette skipped it altogether). What I did know was that putting a warm body into a frigid lake couldn't be healthy.

"Andee, it's freezing out here and I'm not even wet! Can't we do this tomorrow?"

"No, tomorrow we test the Seniors."

"So can I at least put on clothes until it's my turn?"

"No. All Intermediate Swimmers have to be ready at the same time. Think of it as a character-builder."

"What does getting pneumonia (a second time) have to do with building character? Besides, I'm not going to pass Junior Life-Saving anyway so why can't I just put on my clothes and watch?"

"That's not the ol' Winnetaska spirit—quitting without even try- ing."

"It's not a matter of spirit. It's this body. I can't get my arm around Maria. She's gigantic! No way can I do a cross-chest carry on her."

"You know why we teamed her up with you. I thought you under- stood about her shyness."

"I did. I do. And I've been very nice to her. But that's not the point."

"Okay. Maybe we can assign you to Rita for the test. She's about your size."

"So you're going to give me a badge that says I'm only qualified to save flat-chested people?"

"That's enough, Cathy."

In this Measure-and-Mete world, I could neither improvise nor cajole an extra helping of ice cream. Under the Director's influence, I got to believe that a pinch of this was crucial, but a quart of that made no difference. Under his influence, I missed having a birthday.

Camp always ended on my American birthday, the 27th of August. En route, the kids sang to me on the train ride to Penn Station, New York, where our parents picked us up. Since the night before wasn't officially My Day, and because suppers were when The Birthday Girl's table got served a whole cake for dessert, mine never got one, not on my account. I don't remember what the ritual was at Rotomac. There could have been none at all. It wasn't a Big Deal. Or it didn't seem so. Coming from a family that regularly forgot people and birthdays, if all I got was a song, I didn't wonder as I did when leaving Winnetaska, "How much could it hurt to give me the dumb cake a day early?"

It hurt enough that, two years after the second, I went back. I did it to ease the yearning, the still indiscriminate need to measure up to standards, any standards, simply because they existed and were there for the mastering and jurying. Three was the charm. By the time I stepped off the train for the last time, after I got my Birthday Song, and only a song, I was exorcised and could let it go. No longer needing my parents to pick me up from the station, I made my way home. Arriving in Teaneck, I found my mother on the phone. Directing me to wait for her in the kitchen—that was only a few feet from where she sat—she whispered so loudly to the person on the other end of the line, that I knew she wanted to make absolutely sure that I heard every detail of the secret plan they were hatching.

Joining me when done, she asked as if she didn't know, "You listened?"

"Yes, Mommy."

"It was going to be a surprise party."

"Yes, Mommy."

"But now that you know, here, you take the list and call everybody. I can never remember which friend belongs to which mother.

"Okay, Mommy."

"Good. So, how was camp this year?"

The gods may not be omniscient, but for a long time I believed my mother was. When I started to realize she wasn't, I still thought she might be omnipresent. I never thought she was omnipotent, but it took a lot longer to understand the limits of her power. This was what made growing up interesting, even if I didn't know it at the time. In retrospect, it's not simple to sort the "special" from the "ordinary," the "being an immigrant" from being "typical." Take Uncle Jiang. He wasn't a real relative but we automatically addressed non-kin of my parents' generation with an "Uncle" or "Auntie" and their last names. If they were blood relations, we used their first names. Anyway, the Jiangs were the only Chinese with a dog, a genuine pet who lived in the house. His name was Carlos. Spoken with an accent. It could tell who was who, and attacked only people who weren't Asian. Since everyone believed in the Model Chinese stereotype (especially Chinese), this was one smart watch dog. Proud of Carlos' keen eye (or nose), even my mother patted him. When I was a sophomore in high school, Uncle Jiang took me to play golf.

"How was it, Cathy?"

"Daddy, Uncle Jiang picked me up in a *limousine*. With a driver. In a mulberry uniform.

"Yes."

"Who is Uncle Jiang?"

"The Chinese ambassador," he informed me in a "How could you not have known but it makes no difference, I hope you had a good time" kind of voice. So Uncle Jiang went back into the "nonchalant" category, along with a host of other "Generals" and "Honorables." And so when my parents made a fuss before I was to meet the *Agha*, I got nervous. He was royalty. And so was his daughter. Or so close that a dynasty would topple if I spoke out of turn. Later, the dynasty was toppled—but not because I let a "Gee Whiz" or "Cool" slip out.

I asked my mother, "How old is she?"

"About fifteen—not that much younger than you. But she has led a very sheltered life. I think she's been living in Europe, at a finishing school. Her father wants you to take her around New York so she can see the sights—Rockefeller Center, the museum, maybe a Broadway show. He thinks it would be nice if his daughter got to do some ordinary things with people her own age."

"Okay."

"No, no, don't say 'Okay'. No slang. No talk about dates. No rock 'n roll."

My father broke in to expound, "The idea is not to worry him. This is probably the first time she has been allowed to go out unchaperoned. They are very strict. You will have to gain his confidence."

My mother continued, "She knows some English. The proper kind. Probably you'll have to use your French."

At that point, I envisioned sweet Miss Devany rolling on the floor, stricken with paroxysms of laughter, and Madame K, last year's language teacher, standing by, bigoted arms crossed, red pencil in hand, fully ready to add a second E to the first. I was tempted to say aloud that even Madame K's bias was not totally responsible for the C average I'd received for the subject itself. But I didn't. Officially I was studying French therefore, officially, my mother could summon it forth from the primordial syllabic goo of my vocal cords.

Dressing for the occasion was a family affair. I had to look old enough to be a credible chaperone. Lipstick. Innocent enough to waylay doubts about my character. Not red. Sufficiently sophisticated to inspire respect. No pony tail. Practically functional to reflect my familiarity with the streets of New York. Medium heels. And since I was the hostess, enough money in my purse to cover the tab no matter how much she would insist on paying the bill. By the time I donned my coat, I was so intimidated by the prospect of my stint as a tour guide, I couldn't enjoy another "first"—brunch at The Plaza.

The pace of the meal was very leisurely. That gave me time to calculate. Theoretically, I already knew what to do with the dozen or so forks, knives and spoons flanking both sides of my main plate. It was the stemware and ancillary dishes that I had no rule for. So I watched, not drinking or buttering until someone else had done so and I could go around the table, mentally assigning what belonged to whom. I was pretty sure neither our host nor his daughter would have jumped up and pointed a mocking finger at me if I reached for the wrong one, but I wouldn't have put it past the waiter standing behind me. Each of us had a minion, at the ready to light a cigarette, replace a soiled plate, provide an extra radish. I had the feeling that if I had been too tired to chew, they would have done the honors for me. I wasn't certain if they were programmed to stop my hand in midair lest I touch the wrong glass and cause The Plaza God to swoon at such gaucherie. Powerful as our host might be, I doubted even he could protect his guests from the wrath of such a powerful deity.

Thankfully, the two fathers dominated the conversation so I didn't have to get overloaded with that complication. And the daughter was so demure she barely existed. With not one "okay" escaping my lips, I passed muster and we were sent off to "Have a good time" when the coffee was served.

As I rose from my chair, I caught one of those looks from my mother—the kind that's calibrated to stop a speeding train on a dime in less than two seconds. I nodded to her, conveying my reassurance, "Don't worry, I won't lose her. She'll be safe with me."

Out in the brisk wind, a taxi was opened to us immediately. Before I had a chance to say we could walk to Rockefeller Center, my companion was seated and directing the driver, "To Times Square."

Not knowing how to say, in French, "As long as we're in a cab, let's go to the Metropolitan first," I got in too, figuring we could walk back to the east, check out a few theaters, get a cup of hot chocolate while watching the ice skaters and then go north to the museum, unless she preferred to see one of the musicals. As the cab wended its way through the traffic, I tried to anticipate the fare and the tip while inquiring about her school. She responded by asking if I had a boy friend.

I thought, "This is some kind of test, right? If I say 'yes,' she's going to tell the driver to turn around and report to her father that I'm a bad influence. The driver's probably in on it. He's a member of the Palace Guard and has been told that if anything goes wrong, the N.Y.P.D. will find him lashed to the hotel flagpole in the morning, dripping blood on the people passing below."

I obfuscated—easily done considering it took five minutes to get out three simple sentences. "*Mon, uh, Ma école est public. C'est, uh, c'est coed. Mes amis sont féminin et masculin.*"

I lost her attention. Vowing that I would henceforth give more of my own to Miss Devany, I resorted to single syllables and pointing: at Central Park, "Parc" and at the horse-drawn buggies, "cheval." Arriving at Times Square, I couldn't blame her for getting out as fast as she could. She headed west instead of east.

By the time I caught up to her, she was entering one of the porno-graphic movie houses. Running so I could block her way, I desperately accompanied my "*Non, non. Mal place!*" with stuttery waves of refusal. Shrugging, she proceeded down the street. I should've worn sneakers. Walking side by side, exchanging pleasantries was not part of this young woman's repertoire. A few more end runs and I wondered if "finishing school" in Switzerland meant the ribbon at the end of a one-minute mile track. Finally, she hit a cinema where I recognized the actors listed on the marquee. It still looked pretty sleazy, but I had to buy tickets quickly so the cashier wouldn't send the cops in after her for trying to get in without paying. Finding her in the darkened the-ater, I sagged with relief. Even if she didn't want to stay for both fea-tures, I had some time to get my breath and to try and explain enough of the facts of life in the Big City to get us both through the day with-out mishap. Given the choice, I believed the trade-off a good one: a bit of her innocence in exchange for my hide.

My respite was short-lived. Two sailors, confronted with an empty theater took one look at my ward's beaming smile, sat square in front of us and turned around to make our acquaintance. I tried to give them one of those freight train looks but they didn't seem to recognize it. Or maybe it too was so short-lived that its devastating effect had no time to take hold. My companion—the proper, sheltered, innocent Demure One—was chattering away with just enough "Pardon my English," and "How do you say ___?" thrown in to make her French accent irresistible. Not that the sailors had any intention of resisting. They recognized a "pick-up" when they heard one.

Grabbing her arm and our coats, I hauled her out. No amenities.

No "*Excusez-moi.*"

Although I never got a chance to use the French I had prepared ahead of time—"*S'il vous plait, permettez-moi. Vous etes mon invitée*"—I did get to rib my parents about their presumptions. For about 35 years. Over and over I could tell the story. It was a good one for, embedded in its composition, were layers: reassurance about my virtue and, with it, recognition of their success in preparing me for a world that could be risqué. Yet gaps were insinuating themselves—between their respect and my lack thereof. I started to think that they liked, too much, people like The Director, to hear tiny hints that, really, it would be better of I weren't so *mama-huhu* about his rules. Over and over the Plaza story was used because the punch line delivered no lethal blows to what they wanted me to value.

Yet these stories became harder to come by because I couldn't help but detect that, really, it would be more to their credit if I did more resemble The Ideal Tourist whom they initially pictured to be the Agha's daughter. The more *comme çi, comme ça* I became about measuring up to these standards, the less "neither here not there" they were about setting them up. Rather than confront myself or them with our difference, I became more timid about taking chances with their reactions. My individuation was "so typical" of growing up in America, but also so "special" because I had no Chinese friends to talk to whose English was also becoming less Chinese. My mother was not yet confrontational—instead, the less I revealed to her, the more she insisted she knew me inside and out.

...*HuHu* (TigerTiger)

At the personal level, racial identity is decisive, but even more important is one's perception of one's own gen (roots)....The Chinese notion of roots is what gives rise to the varied, often conflicting understandings of Chinese identities; it contributes to the shaping of destinies of Chinese in foreign countries.

—L. Ling-chi Wang, "Roots and Changing Identity
of the Chinese in the United States"

Maybe my parents did know me and the gap had more to do with my inability to express the more painful facts so they could become stories that would get their attention and interest. Whichever, my parents were still adept at doing things like finding Marion's Mom to transplant us both from the no-rule-of-thumb Rotomac to the rule-for-every-occasion Winnetaska, or planning a party to resolve my love-hate relationship with birthday cakes. Whether I withheld some facts or repeated only the old stories, or they withheld some judgments or ignored the inappropriate subjects, at school, I was taught the facts but was never asked to do the more fascinating exercise: wonder about their truth. So I believed there was such a thing as Truth.

As I fell into the habit of always skirting the issues that my parents ignored and were silent about, I went through a serious stage. A very serious stage. So serious, I bought a diary. I wanted to write and remember, tell all and never forget, commit to paper and, thereby, pledge a troth between the child I was and the child I would one day have. I would express my innermost thoughts and make these truths available to the future. At the very least, the child's child would be eternally grateful for my effort.

After each entry, I locked it. Since all the diaries at the store came with a tiny key, I rationalized that my particular purchase was not in outright defiance of our communal household where interior doors were rarely closed and no one ever knocked or locked. Nevertheless, I felt better about using it once I realized my mother had no trouble picking it open. What I didn't realize as I inscribed the plans of a would-be parent to the child-that-would-be was that when one writes with indelible ink in a solitary diary, the words have staying power but the "library" changes. We say things like, "It takes all kinds, " and "You are what you eat," to our young children and then wonder "Where did I go wrong?" when, as teenagers, they show up with green hair and nose rings or, as adults, expect three-course meals every day.

Take Mr. Gunner, my high school biology teacher. Could he have predicted that his lecture on Hybrid Vigor would one day lead William to write, "I was raised by a Chinese Confucian mother who teaches Western philosophy and aerobics; and a Caucasian Jeffersonian father who makes art and practices Tibetan Buddhism"? Could Mr. Gunnar have imagined that the information he gave us about ovaries would produce my philosophy of cooking? Or for that matter, anything else I would just as soon not do—like shopping or digging ditches (some call it "gardening"). There I was, back from our honeymoon, my cup of steaming coffee in hand, ready to luxuriate in the tranquility of reading the paper. Without looking up, I heard Bennett sit down. After a few minutes, I realized he was too quiet. Putting down the paper, I saw him sitting there, bolt upright, a hand on either side of an imaginary plate, holding a nonexistent fork and knife.

"What're you doing?"

"I'm waiting."

"For what?"

"For breakfast."

It must have been the shock, because I actually got up and made the "American breakfast" my father was so fond of—bacon, eggs, toast, juice and coffee. At lunch, Bennett appeared out of nowhere and sat again, waiting. Same at dinner. Day in, day out, it was the same. He could be creating the most important piece of artwork to hit the scene since Picasso yet, like clockwork, he'd show up at that kitchen table and wait. Worse, he kept muttering things like, "meat" and "potatoes." I didn't know they were addictive, but I guess when your mother has fed you that sort of thing on a regular basis, it can be. Anyway, I started to bastardize the Chinese dishes with extra slivers of beef. As to potatoes? "No way. Eat rice."

This went on for a while. Then one day as he sat and waited, he announced, "I decided to be a vegetarian."

They say that a quick blow to the head can be the cause as well as the cure for amnesia. It worked for me. Remembering Mr. Gunnar and those ovaries, I informed Bennett of my new Philosophy of Cooking: I was born with just so many—so many eggs, so many dinners, so many trips, so many ditches. When they're gone, they're gone...and there's no use wishing for more. Ovaries, not women, run out.

Cultures who have respected the crone, the post-menopausal, know this. The dynamics is natural, mathematical—not personal, and certainly not moral. If everyone knows that they're going to run out (and that, probably, the later ones aren't nearly as energetic or enthusiastic as the earlier), then everyone can look at *this* one as, possibly, the *last* one. So: Appreciate the appearance of each, but Be Prepared for their total disappearance. Eggs, dinners, trips, ditches—when they're gone, they're gone. That's how it goes and there's no one to blame.

Surely, if all the Mr. Gunners knew that "facts," like "words," don't occur in isolation and that embedded in each subject are lesson plans for other topics, then students could learn how to *shuai* (or, in English, be "interdisciplinary"). Surely, if we taught that feelings are facts too,[5] and that words are a form of action that can hurt worse than sticks and stones, children—William—would be that much ahead.

"William, do you realize you're being awful to your father?"

"Yes, *MaMa.*"

"According to Dr. Spock, you're probably going through the Oedipal stage."

"What's that?"

"That's when little boys become jealous of their fathers and want their mothers all to themselves."

With lots of nods, he concurred, "Okay."

(It didn't seem to bother William that he didn't know the meaning of the word "jealous.")

"On the other hand, Chinese don't believe in these stages."

"Oh?" William's head, now at a standstill, indicated some realization that this piece of information might alter the scheme of things, though he remained noncommittal whether he would accept the proviso.

"In any case, William, *BaBa* can accept the idea that you may not like him very much right now. But what is totally unacceptable is your being rude to him."

With a nod, he seemed to close the subject with another "Okay." Then, as an afterthought, "*MaMa?*"

"Yes, William?"

"What's a 'stage'?"

"In this context it refers to different ways of being. Do you remem-

[5] A phrase I first heard from a friend and colleague, Carlos Antonio Torre.

85

ber the woolly bear caterpillar we found last fall?"

"Yes."

"Do you remember why we kept it in a jar all winter?"

"Yes. We were waiting for it to turn into a butterfly."

"That's right. Insects go through different stages during their lifetimes. Each change is called a metamorphosis. Had the Woolly Bear been more cooperative and not dried up, you would have seen it happen. In any case, people go through stages too. You've seen pictures of *BaBa* when he was a small boy, before he changed into a man and then into a *BaBa*. Now some changes are more noticeable than others—you can see the difference between *BaBa* now and when he was your size in the pictures. However, other changes or stages are only noticeable if you observe the difference in the way someone acts—like when *BaBa* became a parent and started doing things like bathing you and loving you, or when you became Oedipal and started treating your father like garbage. Now some experts say there are stages that everybody must change into or go through. But I think that, even if they're right, it's still possible to choose how you go about it. I think that when you understand what's happening, you can control it more. That's why I tell you these things."

Not getting an "Okay, *MaMa*," I acknowledged to myself that William was more involved with his Tinker Toys than my lecture, and, realizing it was past his bedtime, I ended the one-sided conversation with, "William, it's late—time to go upstairs and change."

Without protest, he went to his room, giving me the feeling that, once again, I had talked a subject to death. I should have stopped somewhere around the Woolly Bear part. Five minutes later, instead of calling me to let me know it was time to buzz Bennett in from the studio for the bedtime story, William came back down, dressed in the "Kissed Carson" vest I had made for Western Night—a tan suede dotted with red felt lips. Ill at ease with the traditional theme of his school's annual gathering, I had convinced people to come as Wired Earp and Annie Oakleaf, Sockajaweara and General Custard, and make an event of celebrating puns rather than guns.

I started to reprimand him for not being in his pajamas when he forestalled me by saying, "You just said to 'change'—you didn't say into what."

For that, he got another fifteen minutes play time, Bennett got more civil treatment, and I had the pleasure of deciding that the combination of his triumph and my lecture was irresistible.

But once William left the controlled environment of our relatively isolated house and entered the world of school, simple combinations became harder to come by. This realization came in the form of Eric. Before Eric, William chased chickens or was chased by dogs. Eric, on the other hand, was a human. This made a huge difference—to William and to me. To William because he could now chase and be chased by the same entity. To me because Eric turned five and persuaded his mother to have something called a Birthday Party.

We had always marked William's birthdays with presents and, sometimes, a special dinner. But certainly, I hadn't been so foolish as to invite pre-adults *en masse* into the house. My inclination was to keep the house so that it was always ready for guests. Yet my Teaneck memories—of building forts at Jan's—also made me want it to be comfortable for William and welcoming to his cohorts as long as no more than one or two showed up at a time. We hadn't spent all those years renovating the place only to have it destroyed in two hours.

So William knew about celebrating his birthday. He just didn't know that most of the American population regarded having the celebrant's friends—as in children—to be a necessary component of such occasions.

Walking into Eric's house, careening with hyperglycemic little people, festooned with balloons and presents and streamers, I could tell right away that William thought this was a Good Thing. One look at Frankie, Eric's mother, and I knew otherwise. I found her in the bedroom, trying to become one with the corner wall. Had she been a cartoon, her eyes would have been drawn as spirals and there would have been lots of "parentheses" around her head.

"Oh Cath, I should've listened to them about The Rule of Thumb. They knew what they were talking about. I should've followed The Rule of Thumb."

"Frankie, you're babbling. What're you talking about?"

"The Rule of Thumb, Cathy. *The Rule of Thumb.*"

"Frankie, sit down. Now, what's this Rule of Thumb business?"

"Eric's five. I should've had six. You're only supposed to invite one more than the kid is old. That's the Rule of Thumb. And now, I've got even more than too many. Keith's...Kent's...whazzisname's mother. She drops him off and his kid brother and their toddler sister. Can you believe it? She comes to the door with all three and a bottle of Kool-

Aid or something. And leaves. I swear the two are still in diapers! Cathy, whaddami gonna do? Have you seen what it's like out there?"

"It is impressive."

She paused and I thought she was quieting down. Then, "Omigod. I don't have enough prizes. Everybody should get a prize. I don't believe only a few should get prizes. Some people do. But I don't. Cath, I can't go out there without enough prizes. It just won't be right. I just can't...."

"Frankie. We'll do this together. It's okay. You do food. I'll do children."

"The prizes...."

"Don't worry. In their state, I could give out carrots and they'd think it was special."

We did it. It happened in some kind of time warp when a minute equaled a day. But we did it. I formed a circle with those hundreds of legs and arms and mouths and we played games I hadn't thought of since Rotomac. William among them, alternated between galloping joy and immobilizing fascination at seeing his mother putting her right foot in, then putting her right foot out, then putting her right foot in again, and then shaking it all about.

After the last one left, Frankie and I would have smiled to each other had we had the strength. Standing by the door to see us out, Eric, momentarily still, politely thanked us for attending his party. I wished him a wonderful year.

"Thank you, Mrs. Bean. Isn't it great? Now that I'm five, I don't have to take a nap anymore."

I didn't know William could do a double-take. He did. "What did you say, Eric?"

Covering up his ears, I pulled his head out the door just as Eric repeated himself. I was too late. In the car, William asked, "*MaMa?* What did Eric mean about five-year olds not having to take naps?"

"William, some people think that, as children grow older they don't need naps."

"*MaMa*, I'm five. Can I stop taking naps? Like Eric?"

"No, William. We're Chinese. Because you're five, you can stop taking *two* naps."

A sigh. And then a deep breath, "MaMa? When I'm six...."

I knew what was coming. "Yes, William?"

"When I'm six, can I have a Birthday Party—with children?"

"William, we're Chinese. We don't start getting personal Birthday Parties until we're sixty—when we begin a whole new cycle. Until then, we all grow one year older together at the Chinese New Year.

"When will I be sixty?"

"In the year 2034."

"Oh."

"All right, William. Since we're also Americans, how about a com-promise?"

"What kind? How?"

"Do you know why *PoPo* calls you *Little Tiger?*"

"Yes. Because I was born in the Year of the Tiger. Like her and DaAyi."

"That's right. You and *PoPo* are both Wood Tigers. This means you are exactly sixty years apart in age—the time it takes to go through the full cycle of twelve animals combined with the five elements so that all the different kinds of years have had a turn. Your *DaAyi*—my older sister—is an Earth Tiger and only 36 years older than you. I'm a Water Horse. My father—your *KungKung*—was born in 1911, so he's a Metal Boar. Chinese like to refer to the Animal Year they're born in. It's special because it only happens every twelve years. Not as special as the sixtieth. But pretty special. So maybe we can do something special in 1986, when you're twelve years old. It'll be a Fire Tiger year but I'm willing to compromise if you are."

Trying to figure how long that would take, William got lost between the right thumb and the left index finger.

Holding up seven of my own, I said, "*Then* you can have a Birthday Party at home. With children. Okay?"

Although there still seemed to be entirely too many, it was still less than two full hands' worth. And a lot less than sixty. "Okay, *MaMa.*"

"Good. Because I think it'll take me between now and then to work up to the idea."

He looked worried, wondering if this was a caveat, a way out for me at the last minute. He knew that I taught Logic. He didn't know exactly what that meant—except to listen ve-rry very carefully to my choice of words.

I continued, "In the meantime, William, I'm sure you could discuss this with *BaBa.* Maybe the two of you can think up something that would be as satisfactory to you. And less traumatic for me."

"Oh yes!"

William was delighted. He knew his father was a pushover. He also sensed that being male, or simply Bennett, if there was a pre-determined number of eggs, dinners, etc. in him as in me, his father would metamorphose or mutate or, in this case, take the concept of a Birthday Party and make it reappear, intensified, in some unexpected guise. Whether it was art or dumplings, that was the way he made things happen.

"Cath, try this."

"What is it?"

"Don't ask. Just taste."

Biting down, I encountered a lump. A very pleasant lump. It had the kind of texture I love—still chewy and somewhat glutinous despite the soaking it got while cooking in a broth that had both clarity and complexity. "It's very good. What is it?"

"Look around."

I did.

"Notice anything missing?"

Playing the game, I replied in the negative after checking to see if the kitchen sink was still where it should be.

"The counter. Look at the counter."

Able to see more of its surface than had been the case for about three days, I cautiously affirmed, "It's gone."

"That's right. It's in here," indicating the bowl in his hand.

Unbelieving, I opened the garbage bin. Finding the telltale box crushed into a space with too few dimensions to hold it, I searched for the leftovers that he invariably wanted to throw out and that I, forever remembering the toiling rice farmers, insisted were good for another serving. Still skeptical, I asked for a second taste. Gleefully, he spooned it into my open mouth. Knowing what to look for, I was able to detect the prime ingredient, "Pizza. You made Pizza Soup."

"Pretty good, eh? I simmered it long enough to reconstitute the dough, but not so much it would lose the resilience of your petrifying process."

Appropriating the bowl, I agreed, once more enjoying our difference.

It had been why I had married him. But being male, or Bennett, every so often vestiges of some earlier incarnation would appear, and he would make some pretty confounding requests like having Sunday Dinners on Sundays, in the late afternoon, with objects like hams and roasts to carve. While we thoroughly enjoyed such meals at his parents' house in Iowa, there was nothing in my genetic makeup from which such atavistic hankerings could arise. In this, William was a bit of a throwback to his father's side. Reinforced by the society at large, some hankerings persisted well into his teens.

"Mom?"

"What is it, William?"

"Will you bake me a birthday cake?"

"You've got to be kidding. You know I don't do cakes. You've never been particularly fond of cake. What's wrong with *BaBa* making another Birthday Pie?"

"This year I want a cake."

"Okay, I'll order one from the bakery."

"No, Mom. I'd really like you to bake a cake for me."

"Isn't it enough I've invited the Gallaghers and Schumans over for dinner tomorrow?"

"Just this once, Mom. It won't hurt."

"Yes it will. I'm allergic to flour."

"No you're not."

"I'm sure I could be if I work at it. Besides, Chinese don't bake. We steam. It takes less fuel."

"We've got an oven."

"We do?"

"Come on, Mom. Please?"

"You know, you're getting as weird as your father."

"Please?"

"Very well."

"Thanks, Mom. Could you make it a Chocolate one?"

"I suppose. I hear Pillsbury makes a great mix."

"No, Mom. From scratch. I want you to make the cake. From scratch."

Figuring I couldn't fight nature, but mentally calculating that this would use up every one of those "eggs" I owed William for omitting baby cereal from his diet as long as I did, I consulted *The Joy of Cooking*, made a list, bought the ingredients, and started the impossible process around 7:00 on the eve of his impending birthday. Every hour or so, Bennett and William would check in on my progress. Around 11:00, William gave me one last pat on the back before retiring. At midnight, Bennett did the same. By one in the morning, I had managed four layers of chocolate cake, stacked so that the 1/2" sides were balanced by the 2" ones. Sure that everybody was sound asleep, I went into the laundry room where I had hidden the can of ready-made icing. Lured by the ad on television, I bought the kind that's so easy, the woman spreads it with a knife she cuts out of paper.

"What's that, Cath?"

"What's what?"

"You weren't really going to put that store-bought dreck on William's Cake, were you?"

"I thought you were asleep."

"I thought you needed some encouragement." Handing me his Craig Claiborne's *The New York Times Cookbook*, "Here, try this."

"You're kidding. Remember his recipe for zucchini bread? He tells me to 'Grate the zucchini and set aside,' and then never mentions the ingredient again."

"No, this time it's complete."

1. Melt the chocolate in the top of a double boiler over hot, not boiling water.
2. Sift the sugar. Add the sugar and butter to the chocolate, stirring until smooth. Remove the saucepan from the heat and add the water, one tablespoon at a time. This cools the mixture a bit.
3. The mixture must be lukewarm when it is used or it will not spread or ooze from a tube properly.
4. Spread the icing on a cake or use it for decoration.

Everything went well until somewhere between the fourth sentence of Instruction Number 2 and Number 3. Number 4 was Mr. Claiborne's idea of a joke.

Less than a quarter way around the first lopsided layer, the stuff coagulated. I tried doing the double boiler routine again. The mixture did not do "lukewarm." It went from hot to cold almost instantaneously. Finally, softening it with the heat from my hands I spread it with my palms so as not to destroy the tenuous relationship between the 1/2" and 2" parts. The result was that three-quarters of the "icing" took up permanent residence on only one-third of the cake. The rest looked like the savanna when what was once mud is cracked with thirst for the rainy season. Giving up, I covered the mess with confectioners' sugar and went to bed. It was 3:00 AM.

To this day, William insists it was a "great cake." Never mind the sugar went all over the dining room when he blew out the candles.

Never mind he had to pop the whole thing into the microwave to nuke it so the steel knife could get through the icing. Never mind that, the following year, Mr. Gallagher preemptively offered to bake the cake. Liking us too much to chance our ingesting another one of Mr. Claiborne's, the Gallaghers took turns, amongst themselves, to produce a safer alternative.

"Cath, I don't know anyone who loves birthday parties more than you do."

"Kate Gallagher, how can you possibly think that? We've known each other since the kids were in kindergarten."

"You can't fool me. I know."

For years thereafter, like clockwork, on our birthdays, a cake appeared on our doorstep so that the Beans would not miss out on a great American tradition just because there happened to be a Bao in the batch. By the time the kids were ready to graduate high school, we had consumed many home-baked Gallagher Cakes, each uniformly iced and susceptible to cutting. Until Devin's last contribution. This one came out of the oven with a large fissure running through the top almost dividing the layer in half. Sticking a miniature signpost on top, instead of a candle, he wrote, "*Beware!* Earthquake Zone" next to a cut-out man falling into chocolate oblivion. When his mother saw it, she insisted on stopping en route to our house, to get a store-bought one. The second cake was brought in first for proper effect, but we ate the other for taste. In an earlier time, she would have shamed Devin into baking another. But now, you see, she was older. Chinese-American, Irish-American, we're born with just so many eggs, dinners, trips, ditches…and cakes.

In this way, William had multicultural birthdays—dinners in our dining room with Gallagher cakes, Hay Rides on Interstate 80 with store-bought cookies. This latter was Bennett's alternative to Eric's No-Rule-of-Thumb type of party. He didn't disappoint. They would pile bales of hay in the back of the van, gather up the three who are still William's friends—Devin and his older brother Sean, Eric, and whoever else was part of their group at the time—and drive into New York. They would browse through William's favorite places: The Forbidden Planet with its shelves full of comic book exotica, five stories of Pearl Paint art supplies from which each could pick out two dollars worth of party favors, the Harley Davidson store with its mean machines, studs and spikes, and leather accouterments for all manner of sport, even biking. They ate *dim sum* lunches at packed hole-in-the-wall Chinatown luncheonettes, impressed that the agile waiter knew how much to charge though he never wasted time writing any of their orders on paper, and then really impressed when Bennett explained he did it by counting the numbers and *shapes* of the serving dishes which had been accumulating on the table. The next year, the kids helped the beleaguered waiter by systematically piling the crockery.

They eagerly took turns holding Bennett's hand because no one wanted to miss his running commentary on the urban wonders. They felt like city-slickers, "in" where the action was. They swaggered, looked at the folks in the West Village, and debated whether green hair was better than orange. One time, Bennett stood before a UniSex Hair Salon, and said, "Let's do it."

Horrified that their dreaming might become a reality, one tugged at the big hand, pulling it back toward the street, "No, Mr. Bean, I don't think we should. I think my mother wouldn't like it."

"Are you sure? This is your chance."

"Yes. I mean No. Mr. Bean. I'm sure."

"But look! Everybody's doing it."

"*Please*, Mr. Bean, let's go to that nice museum you were telling us about."

They walked backwards down the Bowery, trying to spot "wino's," not realizing they had tripped over several in doing so. And on the way home, while eating cupcakes and drinking pop, they whispered about what a shame it was that the bus had stopped and blocked their view just when they noticed the pictures of nude dancers displayed in the theater across the street. The next year Bennett took them to his friend's photography studio. The walls were covered with people unemcumbered by clothes. On these tours of New York, the first-timers mostly expected what their parents did. They were never disappointed when, instead, William's *BaBa* had other ideas.

So while William looked forward to the Year of the Tiger, he didn't wait around for it. By the time 1986 rolled around, I had thought Going-To-New York For William's Birthday had become such an attractive tradition that he wouldn't remember what I had said about his 12th year. No one forgot. Not William. Not Bennett.

When it was time for the invitations to go out, I was torn between wanting as many and as few as possible. Writing to the children on William's list during one of the coldest winters in years, I kept wondering if spring might come early, in time for his birthday—like February first—for otherwise how many parents could I realistically expect to drive over half an hour each way through such terrible conditions for a two-hour party? (Shorter if I could manage a squeezed-down version of the requisite components of this intimidating ritual.)

On the other hand, the more who came, the more furniture, pottery, sculpture, I could kiss good-bye. There was only one solution: I decided to have two parties—an indoor one for the parents and an outdoor skating-sledding affair for the children. I would be in charge of the former, and you-know-who would get the latter. The prospect of all those children *with* their parents was less frightening than just a horde of mini-people all on their own. If choreographed well, I could arrange it so no one not eligible to vote would get beyond the greenhouse doors to the inner sanctum.

It was William's job to do the public relations. His friends were at an age when the main attraction to party-going was the going: the being out of sight of parents and they being out of mind. The *mise en scène* of spinning the bottle or delivering kisses to the post office could not be set before adult eyes for where was the risk, the fun, if, at any moment, they could look in and see what you thought you were doing? The New York Gang knew Bennett was no threat to their preadolescent fantasies, he not only exposed them to nude paintings, he pointed at them and discussed their virtues. But normal parents? No way.

What I couldn't assign was the weather. It had to be sunny enough to warm the greenhouse for the refreshments routine, but cold enough to sustain the ice and snow. I got the sun, but not the cold. The deities must have been one wish behind and gave me the spring I had hoped for. By mid-morning, the snow was mostly in clumps, and though the pond was still covered with a foot-thick layer of ice, the ice itself was totally covered with over an inch of water. By noon, the pond looked like the fish might surface momentarily and I had no choice but to prepare some makeshift games for the children to play indoors. Ready for the onslaught, I started to take a last tour of farewell through the house-as-I-knew-it, when Bennett came in, grinning. "Don't worry. They won't come inside."

"Why? What've you done?"

"You'll see."

There is a special kind of advantage in being married to someone with the ecstatic brain waves of an eight-year old and who can take a two-dimensional image, spin it in his head like a holograph, and make it reappear, intensified.

That afternoon, I had a wonderful time, indoors, with most of the parents. The rest had joined Bennett outside with thermoses full of hot chocolate, a bonfire to roast hot dogs, and still enough snow for snowballs. As to cold drinks: all the soda was half immersed in the middle of the pond too far for any casual reaching from the shore or the bridge. Only a fastidious few could spare the time to come in for the bakery cake or make use of the modern plumbing. They were too busy trying to figure out how to get the soda—that elixir of life so sparingly doled out by their health-conscious parents.

When they first arrived, Bennett had told the kids he had put the soda out there that morning so they'd have a ready supply while skating. Unfortunately, he told them, the sun had melted the ice and, alas, now he feared it might be too thin to tread on. That was the bad news. The good news was that he had a lot of equipment at their disposal—fishing poles, ropes, snowshoes, material for a very small raft, planks, ladders—for getting out there safely or retrieving them. And because he was the adult who tried to dye their hair green, they entered the world he concocted and looked at the pond for what he proposed: ice that was possibly too thin to walk on without life-preserving caution.

One and a half hours later, while some of the children were having the mother of all snowball fights and the rest were still trying to hook and rope the soda, Eric was skinnying out on the ladder they had laid down in the water while Sean held one end, presumably to stabilize it from a foothold nearer the shallow shore. It isn't clear exactly how or when one or both figured it out. Maybe it was when Eric slipped and didn't, as expected, sink into oblivion, or when Sean realized he was in fact standing on solid ice despite the surface water. Whatever, they reached the pile of aluminum treasure. It wasn't long before the pond was a scramble of children sliding, sloshing and splashing their way to quench their youthful thirst.

Half a day of warm weather was not enough to undo a whole winter's worth of freezing, or the fondest wish of a Young Tiger.

"*MaMa...BaBa*...thank you."

Responding in kind—with words that American etiquette says must start with family but which I was still self-conscious about if in my Chinese mode—"You're welcome, William." Heaving an exaggerated sigh, I added, "William?"

Shifting from "*MaMa*," he went into the American mode of address, "Yes, Mom?"

"Maybe we can do this again in 1998, when you're twenty-four?"

"That's cool."

"But only if I like the friends you have then as much as I like this batch."

"It's a deal, Mom."

What I didn't say to my pre-adolescent was how much I already missed hearing the *MaMa* of old. Oddly, Bennett never became a "Dad" but remained a *BaBa*. I also didn't ask William the question I hoped would never arise as an issue, "Will you and your friends find pleasure in being with us then?" After we have driven you to so many places and possibilities, and encouraged you to examine closely the enduring and the ephemeral? What and how will you choose when we are no longer steering, when we're around mostly for the ride? Will you be there as a tour guide, highlighting only the showplaces, or will you feel comfortable and confident about showing us the eyesores as well? Will we? For as much fun as we had, I detected a yearning that suggested he was a throwback to his grandparents in more ways than an occasional Sunday Dinner or once-in-a-lifetime chocolate cake could satisfy.

MaMa-HuHu (HorseHorse-TigerTiger)

When I asked William what he might ~~like~~ need for a present, he asked for some bedroom furniture that would accommodate his height, stipulating, "I don't want any more antiques. I want some real fake stuff."

CHAPTER 4

HOW DO YOU SAY "I LOVE YOU" IN ENGLISH?

IN CHINESE?

IN AMERICA?

HOW DO YOU SAY "I LOVE YOU" IN ENGLISH?....

A man who sees the world only through human relations is inclined to be conservative, because in human relations the end is always mutual adjustment.

—Hsiao-Tung Fei, China's Gentry

Between my first and second stint at Winnetaska, my mother said, "You're living in America, you should know about American religion. Why don't you go to church with your friend across the street?"

At the time, it seemed a perfectly reasonable suggestion given the letter I had written from camp.

> Dear Mommy and Daddy,
>
> The Director said I should be in the choir. Most of the kids are Jewish, so I guess they have to settle for me (ha ha). Anyway, we sing at churches on Sundays. I didn't do so well at the first one. I clapped when the soloist finished—she was really good. Nobody else clapped and I started to feel sorry for her. Well it turns out nobody's supposed to clap in church. And then they passed this basket around. I didn't know we had to pay to go to church. So I took the pennies out of my loafers. But it was hard, the leather's still stiff. Anyway, one of them went flying. I guess I really goofed. Dr. H. said I should take some of my canteen money next time.
>
> Love from Butterfingers (ha ha)
>
> p.s. Can you send the leftover name tags? Mrs. Briggs said some got ripped off in the wash. She's from North Carolina. She looks just like Aunt Jemima on the pancake box.

Imagining her daughter disrupting a solemn service out of ignorance would naturally lead my mother to conclude that I needed some education in this field. Exporting me to church would teach me how to pray properly, sing traditional hymns, and make offerings according to the rules. I was going to be a Regular Christian.

Needing clarification only about which "friend across the street," I asked, "Claire?"

She said, "No, Janet."

Next port of call: Trinity Lutheran Church. My mother picked Jan instead of Claire because, somehow, she knew the Gunthers were

Catholic and Catholicism was "too much"—all those saints clamoring for the same kind of attention demanded by Chinese ancestors, living and dead. Or maybe because we didn't know any Episcopals yet.

Jan's church was full of "sons"—Olsons, Swensons, Carlsons, Johanssons, Tonnessons. They were all so nice. I could tell the same joke over and over with great results—my Swedish accent got them every time. And I didn't even have to try out for a part in the Christmas pageant—who else could be a "Madonna of the Bamboo" without a lot of make-up and a wig? On the other hand, no one seemed to wish they could have the part instead of me. They were all so giving. They cradled me in their generosity and I wanted to be with them, to correspond with them.

In the spirit of Rotomac, I went to the services as well as attended classes, choir practice, Luther League meetings and socials. Going to church and coming home became routine. I would get in the car after Sunday School in Tenafly, humming,

> I will make you Fishers of Men,
> Fishers of Men, Fishers of Men.
> I will make you Fishers of Men,
> If you follow Me.

and head for home, a Disciple of Jesus, ready to reel 'em in. Arriving in Teaneck, I'd emerge from the car, a Follower of Confucius, no relation to Adam and Eve. The transition that occurred en route was natural, part of having *shuai*, of needing to "swing" into a different mode—like an athlete who cross-trains or a prison guard who's also a lenient mother.

At school I found out about dinosaurs, at church I studied *Genesis*. In both cases, I did well on the exams and, therefore, in neither case did it occur to me that my parents had to be involved. (When algebraic functions made me wonder if I would make it to the tenth grade, I tried to take ten minutes of my father's time and expertise. I got three hours. He would have given me more but I preferred *I Love Lucy*, and settled for a "B.") In the Chinese scheme, learning flowed from the elder to the younger. When it had to go the other way, the shift in direction was made with very good reason and *a lot* of diplomacy. My teachers at school never asked that it be otherwise. Bert, the church secretary, however, urged that, having allowed Christianity to be done unto me, I had to do it unto others.

"Cathy, is that your mother in the car?"

"Yes. The Olsons are going somewhere after the service."

"Why don't you invite her in?"

"She doesn't mind."

"Still, she could come in and look around."

"I think she'd rather wait outside."

"Well, I just thought she might like to see how well you're doing here. Maybe meet Pastor Frieberg."

"My father's waiting to be picked up—we usually go to Chinatown on Sundays to shop and have dinner."

"That sounds wonderful. You know, some of our ladies would love to learn how to cook Chinese style. Do you think your mother would like to teach a class? It'd be so nice to have all the Bao's here on Sundays. Think about it, Cathy. Remember, part of being a good Christian is to share Christ's love with those we love."

In a quandary, I knew enough to know this was not what my mother had in mind. Involving my parents in church would be like asking them to be a Greenie during Team Week. What I wasn't sure about was the extent to which she expected me to "do well" in a case when the doing involved believing, and believing meant *every*body. I loved the universal brotherhood stuff, but putting non-"sons" in with Swedes was not a natural next step for me.

"I don't think so. I mean, about the cooking. It wouldn't work out—she doesn't speak English very well."

She didn't if we compared her to Winston Churchill or Queen Elizabeth. So it wasn't really a lie. And my mother wouldn't have minded—she often deterred an unwanted exchange by pretending she didn't speak English. She got rid of a lot of door-to-door salesmen that way. Their bullish intent and bearish ways were no match for my dainty mother. Cowed by her small hands fluttering "No, no...." to whatever they were selling, they withdrew down the steps, their own arms up to quiet her seeming agitation, or defend what was left of their own composure. Often they would convey apologies for not understanding her language, for intruding into her world—one in which they were too big, too clumsy, too hairy. The ones who were sent away never knew that their entry had been blocked by a woman with a backbone of steel. The few who made a sale knew. By the time they managed to pocket the price of one item for every three my mother retained, they were grateful for the one. Yet they always left smiling. Somewhat bewildered, but smiling.

I tried fluttering "No, no…" hoping that Pastor and Bert wouldn't force me into an outright refusal. I was caught at a point where no variation of the Chopsticks-Fork Principle applied. Whatever I did would be a breach of etiquette. If I helped the church try to seat my parents at the Communion Table, I would be placing them in the position of having to say "No" for themselves and admit that their daughter didn't know well enough to avoid such an embarrassing situation. If I continued to shield my parents from unwanted and unwarranted interference, I would be intimating that the Christian menu could only appeal to those with less universal tastes or, more horrifying, that my parents were the ones with the less refined palate and couldn't appreciate what was being served.

I tried to plead ignorance, to pretend that Pastor was extending one of those pro forma invitations that no one acts on. When that didn't work, I tried to compare the situation to writing letters from camp: as long as I did it, Bette didn't have to. Likewise, my parents did what I couldn't by driving their share of the carpool. Surely no god could be so unreasonable, so inefficient, as to demand that everybody be or do the same as everybody else?

Yet the minister kept insisting that I had "The Way, The Truth, and The Light," and I must take it home. He put such zeal into it. How could I bear to disappoint him? Or the person I was when I heard him? I prided myself in being one who followed instructions well, who pledged allegiance with fervor. Was I benighted by some Dark Force into believing that *shuai* was good when it wasn't? But if I wasn't a dupe of Darkness, was I then a hypocrite? I'd never experienced having something like that believed of me. Not by friends, people who still liked me. The thought put me off balance—it was so final, eternal, and, worst of all, *personal.*

Pastor's insistence seemed to force a choice. I succumbed. But how to do it? What did I know about being a missionary? It's not as if I had much to go by, having only been on the receiving end of preaching. I knew Pearl Buck had tried this sort of thing, but the vision I got from that piece of information was Paul Muni made up to look Asian, plowing *The Good Earth*, and Louise Rainer being so wretched as a peasant that they gave her an Oscar at the Academy Awards. Nowhere could I picture myself in this scenario. Historically, Chinese had amalgamated many religious traditions, both foreign and domestic, so I knew about being accommodating. *Proselytizing* and Loving Everyone

(or No One in Particular) was something else altogether. My inexperience notwithstanding, one Sunday, the calling survived the twists and
turns of the ride from church, and my mouth got home and said
words like "Believe" and "Christ" to my mother.

I didn't just blurt it out, the words had to be transfigured, then
painstakingly arranged before they could be imported for domestic
consumption. Into the late afternoon, they were still too blatant. What
was appropriate before a large congregation was too gross for a family
of four. As I joined my mother to prepare the five dishes she planned
for dinner, half my mind reformed the stubbornly absolute phrases
into sentences with greater subtlety, while the other half followed her
instructions on how to deal with the ingredients. Some were slivered
or shredded. Others were diced, sliced, mashed, chunked, molded,
corrugated, minced—whatever it took to produce the requisite shape
and condition for a result that would be wonderful in its consistency,
coherence and taste, by itself, and in relationship to whatever else was
served.

As I was sorting through the possibilities for translating "sin," "salvation," "confession," and "resurrection" into effective persuasion, the
counter, table top, refrigerator, sink, dish rack—all available spaces—
filled up with little plates, bowls, cups and jars of ginger, eight-star
anise, wood ears and day lilies. I didn't want to leave anything out, the
way my mother did. For however many times she prepared banquets
for family friends, inevitably, two or three days later, she would find
something that had been temporarily stored and then forgotten.
Window ledges, doorsteps, hooks in the garage, the basement clothes-
line, even the bathtub, held the overflow that our little kitchen couldn't
accommodate. On the other hand, since the feasts were always so abun-
dant and the potential combinations so numerous, the overlooked was
never missed. If she had written a menu, we could have been sent out
on a scavenger hunt, list in hand. But the profusion was never recorded
except in her mind, disciplined by her confidence that, this time, she
would remember it all. Instead we discovered them, one by one, quite
by happenstance like the salamanders at Rotomac. Presenting whatever
we found for my mother to identify, she would hold the cup and shake
the shriveled contents like a tea-leaf reader, divining backwards its original source and for which dish it had been destined. Depending upon its
value in cost, preparation time, and power to enhance taste, she would
cluck her tongue or exclaim "*Aiiya.*" It was always a shame, but never a

regret. My mother rarely wasted her energy on might-have-beens, however delicious.

By the time everything was ready for the actual cooking, I was still mulling the strategy of my crusade. During dinner, the words kept getting stuck in my throat and were then swallowed along with the soup or rice. Finally, everybody rising to clear the table, the pressure to say something became more powerful than the need to be thorough, and I spewed forth bits and pieces of sermons I had heard. Although utterly incoherent, the emotional force of my delivery was, nevertheless, sufficient to stop everybody in midair. As they sat back down so I wouldn't be stranded, I finished with, "...you should go to church for the sake of your eternal soul."

Thankfully, I was saved from further isolation as everyone picked up their chopsticks and intently sorted through the dishes for another morsel. A few minutes later, rising again, my mother noisily stacked bowls. Looking at one with too little left over to be of use tomorrow evening, she said, in Chinese, without conviction, *"Can anybody eat this? What an inconvenience, a waste...."*

Hearing myself speak, I felt so righteous. Hearing her silence and her words, I felt so stupid. I was thirteen and didn't know there are some imports that must be retooled, or best left at the dock, or even sent back to their point of origin.

Though I stopped saying, "Believe" and "Christ" to my parents, they never seemed surprised or disappointed that I remained an intensely dutiful Christian. When I told them that I had passed my Junior Confirmation test with an A+, they accepted it without comment. When I told them that I could not be Confirmed without first being baptized and that I needed Christian sponsors for the ritual, M. Gardner Tewksbury and his wife appeared for dinner.

All my church friends already had godparents. I prayed for a couple of my own. What I got was an eminent scholar and renowned China missionary who handled chopsticks and chattered in Chinese better than I could. Forgetting that my parents could find anything they wanted, I thought the Tewksburys came into my life by divine intervention. Their credentials were so impressive, no one in the congregation cared that they were Presbyterian. At a time and in a town when lives were marked and "tracked" from birth, I already knew "just by looking," who would wear white, as opposed to blue, collars, but I hadn't quite gotten the nuances of "Christian" beyond my Jewish friends' distinction of "Gentile" and awareness that not being carried down the aisle to be baptized, weighing in around eighty, instead of eight, pounds, was unusual.

It was all too much. When I stood between my parents and god-parents to be cleansed of my original sin, I joined the two babies and cried uncontrollably. I was absolved. Even though only two of the four who flanked me knew the Lord's Prayer, their presence kept me from having to stand alone in front of the Pastor or speak for myself to the congregation. I belonged.

After the benediction, my mother walked beside me and said, "Enough." So much crying was unseemly at a baptism. Tears were for funerals. And that made them flow more copiously. I didn't yet know how to regard an option tentatively, only how to choose or reject it irrevocably; I thought that I had to belong and believe forever when I only needed to consider it seriously for the time being.

Baptized, I went through the Junior Confirmation ceremony the following week. The visual contrast between me and the overwhelm-ingly blond Nordic assembly with which I could now identify was no longer significant in the eyes of God. I was "saved."

And so were my parents. Like the photographers at the Easter Parade, parishioners who met them up close refrained from crowding or shepherding them. One soul per family would suffice. But just in case I wasn't as smart, my mother reflected my enthusiasm back to me by answering the doorbell one day.

"Hello. How are you today?"

"Fine, thank you."

"We're Jehovah's Witnesses and we would like to talk to you about Our Lord Jesus."

"Please, come in."

I couldn't believe my mother said that. All the other times, she pulled the "Sorry, I don't speak English" routine.

Sprawled on the rug surrounded by books, I watched them give my mother their evangelical spiel. It was, would be, a hard sell. I grinned with relish, looking forward to some version of the "salesman sce-nario." The Fisher of Men part of me was somewhere in Tenafly as I mischievously wondered what the odds were on the Witnesses leaving with their product line in tact. When they finally paused to await her response to their query, "Are you a Christian?" I heard my mother say, "No, I'm a Buddhist."

I thought, "Really? This is news to me." I had always been under the impression she wasn't "religious," that we were "Confucian." As my mind wandered to all those statues with the big bellies in Chinese restaurants—my only association with the word "Buddhist"—I heard, "Believe," and "Christ." And then "...go to Hell."

My mother? In Hell?! The image was ludicrous. The Devil himself would kowtow before her self-assurance and then jump to quench the fire and brimstone lest she tire of fanning herself cooler. The Witnesses weren't the jumping sort, but they did bend a little, having some difficulty imagining their God sending a fifth of the world's population to perdition. More if we counted the non-Chinese heathens. And this out of love.

"I don't think so," was all she said to them as she graciously invited them to leave, and "Have you finished your homework?" was all she asked of me as she tried to straighten the rug underneath me.

That's what she asked, not what she said. My mother could have been a law professor. All her questions were leading, loaded, or both. She could talk about one topic and cover six that were never mentioned. I didn't always have the insight, foresight, and hindsight to get it all or put it together but, when I did, I felt the power surge of being Cassandra and Sherlock Holmes simultaneously and, on occasions like this one, their horror and melancholy.

Thus, my mother let it be known I would proceed into the Promised Land on my own. Although family members are in the same boat, each is not required to get off at the same ports of call. While she was left in peace to wait in the car, I entered my final year of preparation, passed the Senior test, and was then re-confirmed. My parents attended that ceremony too. As they faithfully appeared for Parents' Night at school, piano recitals, ballet performances, they were in the audience when I received my First Communion and a personalized copy of The Holy Bible. On the cover, "Cathy Kwei-yee Bao" was inscribed in gold. On the presentation page was written, "No one who believes in Him will be put to shame, Romans 10:11." It didn't seem right. I asked the printer to scrape off the original, and put the shorter "Cathy Bao."

Not long after that, it didn't matter what was written.

"Pastor?"

"Yes, Cathy?"

"That pamphlet we got—about how to argue with Catholics—I'm

a little fuzzy on the 'By Faith Alone' part."

"Well, Cathy, the Catholics believe that, in order for people to get into heaven, they must have faith *and* do good works. Of course, you know from Confirmation classes, what that led to."

"Indulgences. That was like trying to bribe St. Peter into letting you in."

"That's right. So what isn't clear?"

"I guess the problem is how we get the faith to be saved."

"By the Grace of God."

"Isn't that a little unfair?"

"Not at all."

"But why does He give it to some people and not others?"

"Because we are so weak that, without the help of God, no one would be good enough."

"So why not give it to everyone?"

"Because God knows that some people will not receive His gifts."

"But if God knows that ahead of time, then they really can't help it and it'd be wrong to punish them. I mean, what kind of choice did Judas have what with Jesus looking right at him and saying, 'Truly I say to you, one of you will betray me, one who is eating with me.'?"

"Cathy, it's like God is in an airplane and He sees you driving over a bridge. Now God knows what you don't—that the bridge is broken up ahead. So God knows what's going to happen. But you can't see the future, so you decide to keep on driving."

"But Pastor, if I knew about the bridge being busted, I wouldn't keep driving, not if I could help it."

"Well, in a way, you do know that there'll be trouble ahead if you ignore The Lord's Commandments. So you should know not to head in the wrong direction."

"So I should do good works instead of bad? But that's what the Catholics say."

"Yes, you should do good works. But you are saved by faith alone."

"No matter what I do? Or don't do?"

"Yes. With the courage of Christ on the Cross, the strength of your faith will lead you to do the Lord's will. As Jesus said at Gethsemane, 'Not my will, but thine be done'."

"I don't mean to be disrespectful but, being God, Jesus kinda had a leg up on being courageous. Besides, it's not like we can't not do His will. I mean, if God wills it, that makes it as good as done."

"Cathy, I know it may seem confusing, but that's when we need to have faith."

"Does it mean mine isn't strong enough because I have all these questions?"

"No. Your questions are a sign of your faith. But at some point, you must put them aside. Remember what Christ said to Doubting Thomas, 'Blessed are those who have not seen and yet believe.'"

"Pastor?"

"Yes, Cathy?"

"I'm not asking for proof. I just need it to make sense."

Whether it was because Pastor's image of God reminded me of The Director at Winnetaska, or "Singing the praises of the Lord for all eternity" just didn't strike me as much of an incentive for the here and now, my questions and his answers ceased to be important. What gained in significance were cultural losses he never considered, risks he didn't know were worth taking, exchanges that were not relevant to him. He had talked about God's mansion having "many rooms" but, increasingly, it sounded like they were pretty exclusive spaces with no doubles or triples for people whose relatives drove carpools to church, called long distance from a camp phone, and kept watch over family traditions from ancestral heights. They, like Jewish friends and Catholic neighbors seemed to be forever locked out for lack of the letter but not the spirit of God's law. In Pastor's universe, where only the divine could truly make a really real difference, mortals weren't left with much to get excited about.

And getting excited is what I do best.

When I stopped going to church during my first year in college, my mother never asked why. I figured her silence meant she now had confidence in my ability, Chopsticks-Fork style, to pray, sing hymns, and make offerings according to the rules—that is, be ritually competent like a good Confucian. I, on the other hand, got more vocal. After getting a B+ in a Philosophy of Religion course, I took A. J. Ayer's stance and argued with everybody, without regard to race, gender or national origin that statements with "God" in it were, literally, nonsensical, i.e., incapable of apprehension by the five senses—which is all we've got. Only a few thought this was fun.

Then, twenty-six years after I became a Regular Christian, I realized how little I saw of what had gone on at Trinity Lutheran. The refocusing happened when I attended the Epiphany service at St.

Thomas Church in New York to hear a colleague's son sing. Filled with the sounds of the boys' choir and the lingering clarity of young Rob Streetman's voice, I gave no ear to the sermon that followed. I was confident the visiting bishop, though resplendent in the robes of his high Episcopal office, had nothing to say that I hadn't heard before. Mentally dozing, I was startled by a clapping. As more hands joined in to thank the guest cleric, mine automatically rose to do the same as everybody else. But I couldn't complete the action. Chopsticks-Fork notwithstanding, I was too shocked by the impropriety to care that I was the only one in the congregation not making noise. With a grimace I thought, "Clapping, indeed. In church, of all places."

I was beside myself—the Winnetaska camper who didn't know how to behave in a simple New Hampshire church next to the Philosophy teacher who could run logical circles around the likes of Pastor next to Martin Luther incarnate. The next time I saw my mother, I did what I had never done before or since, I asked how she *felt*, emotionally, "Did it bother you that I took religion so seriously?"

Her response was slow in coming, and brief. "No. You were young. A teenager. In America."

Amazing. She hadn't sent me to church to understand Western Civilization; she'd figured that if I was delivering sermons to her, then she didn't have to preach at me. The carpooling back and forth had been her installment payments on a dark blue umbrella policy for insuring against the moral risks of growing up with unfamiliar customs like co-ed camps and adolescence. Or was it the other way—that the American in her had become too "familiar"? She already believed that, every day after school, I had milk and cookies. Cookies? Maybe. Milk? No way.

Her new pseudo-memories created the kind of world where kids have after-school snacks because their parents did what they were supposed to. So if the kid didn't turn out the way she was supposed to, it was because the younger, not the elder, had failed to fulfill her role. In this way, my mother hinted that my need to be or remain a Christian had only been a preliminary to the more fundamental failing of my adulthood—the one that she could not be silent about or change. Having provided me with every opportunity to be a "Regular" in both cultures, I was to do my part by striving for a life achievement award as a contributor not only to the Chinese family identity but also to the national American one. Then and now, I couldn't agree more, or be any less grateful. But her thorough and wondrous preparation of this Chinese-American ingredient happened when there was so much to get excited about in the *irregular* places where I could venture because, ironically, she had gotten on and off the boat into a Chevy, beguiled salesmen, staved off cooking classes, shamed Witnesses, knew people like the Tewksburys, and gave me a room of my own.

At the time I chose not to acknowledge what she didn't say aloud. Instead, I began to adjust my biography with her actual or retrospective distrust by taking Pastor out of the niche I had put him into. Thinking about him for the first time in decades—not as an intellect, but as a person—I couldn't help but recall a comment Bennett had made about my approach to teaching. "Cathy is a missionary."

With humble apologies, this B+ student whispered a belated prayer. "Thank you, Pastor, for having given me your attention *and* your interest."

Unbeknownst to me at the time, Pastor had conversed with me and, thereby, conveyed a new norm for relating to people who were otherwise unrelated, a way of being with others that could not be described by degrees of Confucian obedience, authority, trust, labor, modesty and, sometimes, affection.

What else had I left unsaid? Like my mother, I have counted on others to keep alive some of the choices I haven't made. But unlike my mother, I wanted to remain curious about the paths not taken, to wonder if there should be a regret or whether energy spent on might-have-beens could still be delicious. As, in a moment of Zen clapping, I could see/hear the issue of God alive again—not as a "truth" but because, in a world where people, even parents, don't *have* to love you, where we have to *learn* to say, "I'm Okay, You're Okay," and where silence is considered golden, isn't it wonderful to hear children sing, "Jesus loves me this I know, for the Bible tells me so"? When it's both so hard and so easy not to be perfect, what is said is telling and what is not can keep open wonderful and dreadful possibilities—like trying to create a culture that will provide the words and opportunities to express as much about what we love as how we despise, about what we hate as how we cherish. And about loving and despising, hating and cherishing one and the same.

HOW DO YOU SAY "I LOVE YOU"...IN CHINESE?

Culture hides much more than it reveals, and strangely enough what it hides, it hides most effectively from its own participants.
—Edward T. Hall, The Silent Language

Had William been old enough, he would have remembered the first week of 1975, when we gathered on my mother's 60th birthday and I got the idea of how we could celebrate his non-Tiger dinners. But at the time, William was not yet two and I had to remember for him so he would know, in retrospect, the source of the joy he was storing.

With friends of the family, we shared a *Huo Guo* or "Fire Cauldron." In the center of the table was a large charcoal brazier, filled with simmering chicken broth flavored with ginger slices, chopped scallions, and sprigs of cilantro. Surrounding them were plates, each displaying thinly sliced beef, chicken, and flounder, or bite-size scallops, shrimp, oysters, and clams. All raw. Bowls held uncooked spinach, Chinese cabbage, water cress, snow peas, varieties of mushrooms, and tofu. All was placed so that each person could reach as many different ingredients as possible. Starting with a fresh egg, each diner first created a dip, adding as much or as little of the soy sauce, sesame oil, peanut butter, hoisin or bean paste, chili, and oyster extract as his or her taste dictated. Then, with chopsticks or wire scoops, each picked up whatever they wished to eat, held it in the broth until the desired degree of doneness. If it hadn't escaped, the morsel was dipped and eaten. Or traded. Or tossed. Or set aside until someone was old or wise enough to appreciate its culinary virtues. Throughout, we compared consumption rates, took breaks, replenished drinks, exchanged seats, told stories, toasted ourselves, and rearranged plates to supply less carnivorous or more herbivorous diets. Toward the end of the meal, noodles, symbolizing long life, were put into the broth that was now rich with flavor from all the cooking, trading, tossing and losing. No one stayed in the kitchen to work while others enjoyed, each individualized the menu, and everyone shared in the making and eating of the soup that resulted. All in all, it was a delicious experience and a better metaphor for *E Pluribus Unum* than "melting pot" or "smorgasbord."

Had William been old enough, he would have also remembered the day after the big party when we continued the festivities and I got an idea of what it would take to be an extended family in America.

Going to a restaurant, we were three Chinese daughters with our parents, Caucasian husbands, and Hybrid children. Two languages crisscrossed the table along with the dishes. The words and food, translated and transported, were such a hodgepodge that the originators of either would have been boggled. Intermittently, one who didn't speak any Chinese asked of those who did to be enlightened about the conversation. My mother and Bette, too engrossed to be interrupted, got into the habit of turning to Bennett with a "You do it," before rushing ahead with their follow-up. Often Bennett obliged with a best guess based on his ten vocabulary words and eight years of observation and repetition. Twice the children told a joke in English that led to a convoluted discussion as to why it was or was not funny in one, both or neither language—a device I later used in the classroom.

Finally, out of the clamor came full stomachs and a game plan: the women, more uncomfortable in high heels than hungry for dessert, would take the children home and change before going directly to the theater while the men would finish their meal and arrive at the box office in time to get tickets for the movies. After double-checking the address, all the women leaned to one side or the other to locate where their discarded shoes had wandered during the meal. The searching seemed to take longer than usual and was accompanied by a lot of hushed whispers that led everyone to look up at the same time. That's when we realized that all four wives had been passing money under the table to their respective husbands, instructing them to pay for the dinner and tickets before one of the others beat them to it. The hush turned into a sheepish silence, and then everybody laughed.

Only the children didn't join in. To them, this was typical. They didn't wonder how it could be that people with roots in traditional and Communist China, in the midwest Plains and a Fisher's Island beach, in Brooklyn, New York, and Teaneck, New Jersey, came to sit at a round table and not feel compelled to rationalize or quibble about precisely who conspired what for which reason.

Not that we couldn't have debated, as we have since, who loses or gains face by being treated or treater. On top of that, at least one of us thought it appropriate that men shouldn't be disturbed by such trivialities as handling money, while another believed it was about time that women learned how to do it. Some of the money was in a purse because it belonged more to its earner than the spouse, while some was carried in a handbag because the spouse was subject to fits of dyslexia.

I felt all those reasons. A Chinese traditionalist, I need to facilitate so others can maintain their chosen roles. An American feminist, I act on the principle that money is power so people will pay serious attention. A philosophical pragmatist, I pay the check so the waiter gets 15% instead of 51%.

That night, no one insisted on being understood by those who might have disagreed. Our differences had been subdued by our laughter and getting to the theater on time—*The Godfather, Part II* was not going to wait for us to sort out who had been repressed, suppressed or impressed.

It was an oversimplified and fleeting moment when the love that Americans believe makes the world go around joined forces with the balance of influences that Chinese consider cyclical. It was a clear moment, between past and future, when Asians were not too much bound by the mutual dependence of their roles, and Westerners were not too easily separated by the happenstance of their individuality. It was one that allowed me to look at the same circumstance and see two situations, not simultaneously, but tangentially. One occurred in a web-like world of interconnections, where the strength of the whole requires some filaments to be longer, with a few more centrifugally than centrally placed, where the triumphs, failures, points of attachment, sensitivities and tears exist yet belong to no one in particular, where singularity is not easily assessed or justified, where the delight and success of the moment was because all the couples could afford to be the "winner" or "loser" so there was no competition, and each person was able to cede or accept the honor and cost.

My other perspective revealed a world of atomic persons contained within a pyramid shaped by republican, corporate, or metaphysical laws, each creating a structure where there is room at the pinnacle for only one president, C.E.O., or God, where being "lower" always means being amongst the increasingly numerous masses, where individuals can move free and equal within the constraints of the system to form a variety of elements, where being at the top or the bottom can be both rewarding and lonely, where being understood is personal and differentiation an obligation, where the delight and success of the moment is recognition of how each individual arrived at the table and chose to be aligned with the others.

As William got old enough to remember more, to be propelled by the momentum of his memories as well as mine, I drew on everything

I knew about these many ways of loving and living and kept silent about none of it except, possibly, the most crucial.

Daily, as we commuted to and from his new school, we talked. American talk, Chinese talk. Travelling further northeast than where Miss Glusa had taught, we had plenty of time. He could have stayed at Day Care another year but there was no point without her. I looked elsewhere: for a school that went beyond kindergarten, for one that didn't require there to be losers. Hoping that some of what Miss Glusa had conveyed to William could be attributed to the Montessori principles and not just her personality, I was reassured soon after William started classes.

Going into the new school one day, I saw a boy wandering through the halls, looking down at something in his hand, then up, down and up, all the while counting to himself. He'd walk a few steps and then turn abruptly, go for another two or three, and then do an about-face. Worried, I asked him where he was going.

He replied, "I don't know yet."

Holding out his hand, I saw a compass and a piece of paper with directions: two paces north, one pace east, etc. He explained further, "But when I get there, I'll know where it is."

The same openness pervaded the Quiet Corner—a little area partitioned off with low bookcases and a few pillows on the floor. Children could go there just about any time they chose, to sit and read, or lie down and think. I used to tell my students about that corner. I would urge them to "Go home and think" about the source of all meaning, or the difference, if any, between emotions and feelings, between knowing *how* and knowing *that*. Regardless, most would quickly raise their hands with the "answer," even as I alerted them, "It takes time to think."

And talk. Bao talk, Bean talk. The former more concerned with conclusions than reasons: "William, see that building in front of the hospital?"

"Yes, *MaMa*."

"That's a nursing home. Now you're my Little Insurance Policy against old age, so you'll never put me in one of those, will you?"

"No, *MaMa*."

The Bean Talk more focused on reasons: "William, I changed my mind, you can put me in a nursing home if I'm in the latter part of the second stage of Alzheimer's disease because, at that point, you will appreciate the difference and I won't."

"William, see that statue in the park?"

"Yes, *MaMa*."

"It commemorates the American soldiers from this area who fought in the wars. But you should know that just because countries become enemies, that doesn't mean the people living in the countries should hate each other...."

Often William initiated the lessons, "*MaMa* why do the cows have to be fenced in? Why can't they be free?"

"Well, William, being free isn't just a matter of going where you want, or doing what you feel like...."

"Pictures too?"

"What do you mean 'pictures'?"

"Why must they be framed? Why can't they be free?"

"I don't think the issue of freedom applies to cows and pictures in quite the same way as it does to humans...."

"*MaMa*, why do you smoke?"

"Because when I was young, I thought it was part of being a grown-up. Now I'm addicted and that means...."

"*MaMa*, why did the children laugh when Melissa forgot to pull up her *duankuzi* after going to the bathroom?"

"William, it could be because they appreciated her eagerness to get back to her project. Or it could be that their parents taught them that clothing is a moral necessity because the human body is...."

"*MaMa*, is *fanguan* a Chinese word or an English one?"

"It's Chinese. The English is restaurant. *Fan* means cooked rice and we use the term for 'food' in general. *Guan* means...well, I don't know what *guan* means but when you put it together, it means 'restaurant'."

Sometimes as we drove, I just wanted to know what was on his mind.

"William, if you could change something about me, what would it be?"

After an agonizingly long time, "Nothing, *MaMa*."

Relieved, then suspicious he was being too diplomatic, I asked, "Honest? What about my yelling? I've been doing that lately. Wouldn't you rather I didn't yell at you?"

Without a pause, he responded, "It doesn't mean anything." And in so saying, he told me how much he cared for me.

"Really? I spend all that time and energy yelling at you and you tell

me it doesn't mean anything? *Aiiya!*" And in so responding, I affirmed
that the feeling was mutual.

Not once during his early years did William hear his mother say, "I
love you."

Until I was twenty-three, I didn't even know how to say it in
Chinese, only "I like you." When I finally did ask my mother, she
looked at me as if I had just asked for details about the northwest sector of Mars. Then, without looking at me, she quickly said, "*Wo ai
ni.*" Her eyes still averted, she followed up with an admonition that
this is the not the sort of thing one *says*. Except, ahem, in private. And
only to a husband.

Although I had made up Chinese phrases for body parts that I
couldn't bring myself to ask my mother about, *ai* wasn't added to my
vocabulary, and I drove to and from his school unabashed that this
word remained unspoken. There was so much to say about other matters, so much Old Talk and New Talk.

"William, did you make your bed this morning?"

"Yes, *MaMa*."

"William, have you ever noticed that I hardly ever make my bed?"

"Yes, *MaMa*."

"Why is that, do you suppose?"

"Because it's in your room."

From this I knew that he knew that if I had to spend time making
my bed, I wouldn't have enough for a career or to plan a Tiger Year
party, with children. Whereas William, when he was still making his
bed on a daily basis, was not yet responsible for his laundry, sewing,
and ironing in addition to his homework. Throughout, he was learning that neither rooms nor people are "equal" as in "the same," though
access could be equalized. No Bean was permitted to play in the same
way or with all the toys in every room—not if we also wanted to
entertain a guest (whose parent might come in and see the mess), or
eat regularly (since cooking and cleaning were scheduled on an Either-
Or basis). Yet Bennett and I did seem to have more space under our
control than he had under his. Remembering how our dog would
compulsively mark his territory, especially after a rain, we assigned at
least one drawer or cupboard shelf in each room to William. When he
decided his dining room drawer was perfect for storing chicken feed
and the desiccated woolly bear, that was his business, provided it didn't
endanger house or home. That was The Deal.

Concurring by word and deed on A Deal was often our *modus operandi*. If his father absolutely had to paint the lawn at a time when outdoor art referred only to objects put on the grass, not made of it, and sprayer cans cost more than our clothing allowance, then his mother would make do with hand-me-downs. If his mother yearned for fresh soy beans but kept forgetting where the garden was, his father made them appear where she could find them, near her car. What William heard and saw in the negotiating wasn't "A United Front" (we weren't at war) but how very different his two parents were, and how the difference could create a home, and how doing so was the way they loved each other.

It takes time to recognize and develop Deals. We didn't talk much about Bad Deals, and never about Raw Deals. In the process, *shuai* got higher billing than absolute rules, and William learned how to transform Ordinary Deals—like the contents of his lunchbox—into Good Deals. Basically, if he wanted to go to a Montessori school that put 200 miles on the odometer every week, then eating store-bought cookies and hundreds of defrosted sandwiches was part of The Deal. Since I was again teaching full time, and since Henry Ford had been so ingenious as to revolutionize the auto industry with the assembly line mode of production, I saw no reason why we couldn't adopt his method to increase efficiency in the lunch box business. Thus, periodically, we covered the entire kitchen counter with slices of bread, applied the peanut butter, then the jelly, laid on the covering slice, cut the result in half, wrapped each in plastic and stacked the batch in the freezer—enough to last a month or more. The bonus was that the frozen packet acted as a refrigerant for whatever else he put in the box. By lunch time, the sandwich was thawed and everything else was kept nice and cool. The only people who had trouble with the arrangement were other parents.

"I've never heard of freezing peanut butter and jelly sandwiches."

"On whole wheat bread," I added.

"They must get soggy."

"I wouldn't know. I've never eaten one."

Their kids had no such problem.

"Hey, William, what will you take for those cookies?"

"That."

"What?"

Pointing inside his schoolmate's box, "That."

"You mean this?"

"Yup."

"You mean you're gonna give me two cookies if I give you carrot sticks?"

"Yup."

"You've got a deal. Uh, William, tomorrow (chuckle, chuckle), tomorrow we should sit together again for lunch. Whaddya say?"

"Sure."

Probably William and Eric would have become friends without the exchange but the process may have taken longer for not being as subtle. This kind of learning—what others consider a Good Deal—went forward when William had his first bad dream and started talking about leaving the lights on at night and sleeping in our room. Bennett suggested that a Guardian might be a better way to ward off any uninvited callers. He had just finished carving a wooden bird head. It was dark green and had a large red beak with round white eyes encircled by dark brown. His inspiration had been one from a Pacific Northwest tribe he had seen at the antique store. Failing to talk the price down, he made his own. William had been admiring it.

They both agreed that if it stood under the bed, beak pointing up, it would be a formidable Guardian. Not only did William get to keep The Bird and himself in his room, he learned that noting the artistic merits of an object was one way to acquire it from his father.

Before I could decide whether I liked this mix of metaphysics and aesthetics, William took the matter out of my hands with another Deal. His friend, Devin Gallagher, was preparing for his First Communion. This meant they had less after-school time to think things over together. One day, lying between the house and barn, each sucking on the end of a long piece of grass, they were discussing the arguments for and against the possibility of God's existence, and the pros and cons of going to catechism classes. By the end of the afternoon, Devin was still Catholic while William seemed quite content to suspend judgment until testing on the Shroud of Turin was completed. That weekend, however, he spotted an ornate silver crucifix at one flea market table. Watching him circle and handle it, the woman allowed him to haggle the price down to the half dollar he had in his pocket, figuring that the difference was her contribution to the Lord's work. William hung the cross above his bed, another Guardian, "In the meantime, just in case..." and a better deal than going to catechism classes.

Sometimes a Good Deal and the Chopsticks-Fork Principle work in tandem as when my willingness to adopt the table manners of the host brings in more invitations. Given my aversion to washing vegetables, juggling tableware in exchange for eating a meal cooked by somebody else is definitely a Good Deal.

The tricky part of negotiating is to convey that not everything is negotiable. Once William knew better and worse, I had to forestall cynical manipulation by being up front about intentions and motives.

"William, what I'm about to offer you is a Bribe. I do so because, right now, I don't have the patience to do it some other way."

He got to relish those bribes. That was an open secret.

"William, if you don't take the Bribe then I shall interpret your refusal to come from a lack of consideration, and that leads to unfortunate consequences. In other words, this is also a Threat."

I made it sound so serious that it could be a joke...yes? Another open secret. Another way for him to learn not to be hypersensitive about his own worth or overly suspicious about other's motives, about how to live in a pyramidal world populated with webs of good relationships. Small talk. Big talk. Attention and Interest. Love and Respect. All cueing him and me to the possibilities, each nuance prompting us to this, rather than that. Our way of conversing was so obviously intelligent, it took most of the first Parent-Teacher Conference for me to comprehend that it might not be intelligible.

"Mrs. Bean, we need your help. There are some things we just don't understand about William's behavior."

"Like what?"

"Well, you know that in the morning, the children are downstairs for all the sensory learning like drawing, cooking, etc. And then they go upstairs in the afternoon for the language and math skills. Now William is usually cooperative, except when it comes to the blocks. We continually have to remind him not to spread out so much. He isn't quite impolite but, clearly, he finds this very annoying. The other day, when I told him it was time to put them away and go upstairs to work, he said, "You mean *play*" and proceeded to ignore me. He always seems to get those two words confused and the other children laugh at him. I've tried to explain how it is for kids who are bilingual, but it's hard for them to understand. Anyway, could you help us out with the blocks?"

Smiling, I explained, "My husband makes art for a living. Before

William could walk, Bennett—Mr. Bean—would take him to the studio and prop him up inside one of the big Chinese urns and let him watch. Later, when William's feet were more reliable, he was allowed to roam in the studio provided he touch or use nothing without permission. Bennett has made some pretty bizarre objects out of some pretty inexplicable stuff. Often there's just no telling, by looking alone, what's a work-in-progress and what's not. Anyway, as far as William is concerned, building things is 'work,' and the way to do it right requires integrity and respect for the process. This means that no one messes with someone else's work. Maybe your best bet is to say that constructing *and* taking down blocks is how that kind of 'work' is done."

"I see."

"About the word mix-up: we read or take out the Scrabble game and score sheets in the evenings, so he associates letters and numbers with playing. I'd leave that alone. If you think about it, it's a nice kind of confusion. Maybe the other kids will pick up on it."

"Yes, I can see that. Now, there's one other thing. It's hard to pinpoint, but William seems to get inexplicably upset on occasion."

"Like when?"

"For example, the other day, he drew a particularly nice castle. I told him so. Not only did he ignore me, he seemed almost unhappy about it."

Relieved that I could offer another cool, rational explanation, I responded, "I don't mean it the way it sounds but he ignored you because your opinion is irrelevant."

"Irrelevant? I'm his teacher."

"Yes, of course you are and he knows that. But we've got two things going here. One is that I've tried to counter the traditional Chinese attitude that the Teacher automatically has authority and must be held in high esteem—so much so that it suppresses student initiative, the willingness to question, even to chance embarrassing the teacher by asking one 'the superior' can't answer. Secondly, we've tried to teach William to guard against flattery, especially when it comes from people who have not otherwise earned our respect. He doesn't know about your degrees or experience. You may be 'the teacher', and that status gives you some prerogatives, but you still have to prove to him that you're in a position to render opinions about his art work."

She responded, "What do you suggest? I mean, I think it's important he pays some attention to what others think."

"So do I. Why don't you do this: ask if he would do a castle draw-ing for you to keep. When he's finished, look at it and find the secret room he always puts in there somewhere. Then, as an aside, mention how well it's placed, or suggest a better one."

"Okay. But that still doesn't explain why he was upset."

I did the best I could, considering my own distress at her insis-tence, my mind racing to find the words, the story, that would explain to her, to me. "Maybe you can understand if I tell you about the time I was in college, when I contracted *residual pneumonitis* and didn't get to campus until four weeks after classes started."

On cue, she murmured, "Oh, that must have been hard on you."

Without elaborating on how it—my second bout with pneumo-nia—was kind of inevitable, I went on, "Going into midterms that semester, I knew that, no matter how well I did, my grade average would be closer to a D than the A I thought my parents expected. Calling home, I prepared my mother for the dean's report. Her response, "Well, you did the best you could under the circumstances," put me into a depression that lasted several weeks."

"I don't understand. It sounds like your mother said the right thing, supporting you during a bad time. Why in the world would this depress you?"

"Because, for the first time in my life, I chose to put her in a posi-tion of having to excuse or explain my behavior. Of course I had done my best. She knew that. And I knew she knew. But I made her *say* it. I didn't let her be silent."

"Silent?"

I couldn't stop. She was William's teacher and he needed her to know who he was and that meant "family business." So I pushed on, "All my life I was expected to do my best; to do so was not in itself praiseworthy. To have to say the obvious ends up meaning that I need-ed to hear it, as if, somehow, I really hadn't done my best. And if that were the case, it's best left unsaid, letting time and better effort be the proof of one's remorse or good resolution. It's like I was always work-ing for a "No Comment" report card. For even though the American part of me wanted to hear the soothing words, they didn't mean the same in translation and the Chinese in me should have known better. So I tried to make the situation 'normal' again by sending a hand-drawn birthday card to my father, a token of me, by me, to him—like the ones I used to make in grammar school."

By the time I got to this point, my narrative was already too personal in either culture but I hoped she was sufficiently polite to bear with me. She did, "Yes, I much prefer the homemade to the store-bought."

"But it only made it worse because, a few days later, I received a check in the mail."

"I don't get it."

"Well, there I was, trying to turn the clock back. Instead, they concluded I hadn't planned well and must have spent all my money."

"What a misunderstanding!"

"Which brings me to William. I've tried to do it both ways: to let him know that excellence is the tacit criterion, and to let him know when he has done well."

"Yes. So what's the problem? Why was he upset when I praised him?"

"Well, the trouble is: it's a lot easier for me to talk about criteria than to say the simple words of praise. So he's not used to hearing them. So maybe he thinks the opposite when he does."

I didn't need to add, but I did, "And maybe the only affirmation he gets is my silence because...well...because I've never mentioned loving him."

I said it to get it out there, in the world, to make me look at what I had done.

Her face white with horror, her teacherly manners couldn't gloss over the revulsion she felt at suddenly finding some alien species sitting across from her. For in America, not saying "I love you" questions, even demeans, the loving. Here, actions rarely speak louder than these words.

With the next parent already waiting her turn, there was no time to explain so I quickly concluded the conference by reiterating the part about the castle. Thanking her, I left for the relative tranquillity of rush hour in the hallway.

How could she comprehend? Did William? Did I? In Teaneck, despite the customs exchanges that took place, my world was still a bifurcated one. I had tried to ameliorate the separation for William with talk, attention, and interest. Had I gone too far? Or not far enough? In a world of Guardians but no God, Bennett and I were "it." There was no Creator to guarantee self-worth; no eternal salvation when new effort was no longer required, no loving "forever ever after," no omniscient Perceiver who sees into hearts regardless of others' misperceptions. The family was as close as William would ever get to unconditional love. Now I was unsure whether my parsimonious praise had reduced him to a state of eternal hungering, of stunting self-deprecation. When home is in a culture that honors and expects the unspoken, but school is where people "say what's on their minds," isn't it inevitable that the American will ache to hear words that the Chinese will not say? In any culture, is it more grueling for people to think they're speaking the same language when they're not, or to speak up and risk misunderstanding?

In a pyramidal world, saying "Thank you" and "I love you" is how we establish appreciation and confirm relationships. In a web world, they indicate lack of faith in the strength of the ties that bind. Most all of us experience both. When defined by a role—"homemaker," "breadwinner," "Daddy's little girl"—we know the pain of being taken for granted and not hearing the words that would transform the script into a way of loving, of being lovely, of being needed and wanted as individuals and not merely as part of a tangle too complicated to unravel. Yet as individuals, endowed with inalienable rights to be independent, we also know the terror of being unable to utter the word "we," the self-loathing when "I" is not enough, the desperation that comes with realizing how tenuously the casting of our lives depends on others saying "I do."

Further, had my silence created more than just a void? Our households so often seem to include an extra member, one born of our minds with the power to steal our hearts. The phantom member can be a sibling, parent or child—the one that never is, but is always wished for. Whether we have created these idealized selves out of "fondest hopes" or "worst nightmares," out of fantastically invincible heroes or villains, they can become the too-real rival for real affections, making this "extended family" the most frequently cited object of unrequited love.

Driving home that day, I told William about the conference, all except the part about the secret room, and asked him to think about it. By the end of the week, I started to leave him notes around the house. Notes signed with a ♥ and a ⌣ .

Immediately, William reciprocated with ones ending in a ♥ and a bow-tie ⌣ .

><

Soon Bennett joined in with a bearded version, ♥ ⌣

Leaving each other notes on the fridge, under the pillow, in a shoe, got to serve many purposes because of how much we wanted to be present to each other and how little we were all three in the house at the same time.

Beat the dog and feed William. Or the other way around. ♥ ⌣

In this way, the father got instructions and the son knew his conduct was on a par with Rug, the Dalmatian that was supposed to lie still and be my alarm system. Instead, it was faster than a speeding bullet, leaped high enough to catch a chicken on the fly, and barked only when people left.

Thanks for the oatmeal. ♥ ⌒

In this way, Bennett acknowledged my thoughtfulness in preparing his dinner before heading out but also hinted that what I left on the counter could be improved upon by using up one of those shopping trips.

Dear Mom & BaBa (this is mostly in reference to Mom) ♥ ⋈

In this way, Bennett didn't feel left out though he sometimes wished he were. Once when I didn't know he was bringing an art collector from New York, I left a note in the middle of the kitchen table. Next to it was a giant rat trap, a very large box of poison, and a huge shotgun.

ONE WAY OR ANOTHER—KILL IT!!!! ♥ ⌣

He didn't even try to explain. Some "family business" is like that. But whatever the subject, amongst ourselves, we did our best to elicit a smile and not just give information.

At the same time the notes appeared in our lives, I swallowed hard and verbalized the ♥ with a "Love you" (in English). William then got used to saying, "Love you too."

In this way, we now end all our conversations. Just in case holding hands and Good Deals are not enough, and saying the word "love" isn't redundant. Just in case being in America means we are freed from traditional frameworks and discover the need to love and be loved in more ways than our ancestors thought were necessary or appropriate.

HOW DO YOU SAY "I LOVE YOU" IN ENGLISH? IN CHINESE" IN AMERICA?

When William's Chinese had degenerated to Bennett's level, and he was enrolled in Weekend School for kids who needed help with their "native" language, I heard the teacher instruct, "*Ai* means 'love.' As in *Wo ai ni*, or *Wo ai* America, or *Wo ai* Hot Dogs." Afterward in the car, I warned William about using "*Ai*" in the presence of anyone from PoPo's generation...especially when talking about hot dogs.

Later, on the phone with my mother, William was doing his best to capture her interest without straining her attention. Winding up the short conversation, he said, in English, "Well, bye, *PoPo*," and, for the first time, added, "Love you."

Several seconds passed while he listened. Then, finally, he hung up with another "Bye."

"William, What did she say?"

"Nothing."

"Nothing at all?"

"She sort of cleared her throat, then started to say something. Then stopped. Then said, 'Okay, Bye,' and hung up."

Since then, I have heard my sister's son on the phone with his *PoPo*, ending the call with, "Love you."

I have also seen bumper stickers—**Have you hugged your child today?**—on the cars of Chinese parents who speak English with an accent.

My mother is gone now. I left her without confessing any regret for the patterns I wove into the family fabric. She left me without saying, "I love you." In English or Chinese. I'm sure her silence was not perceived by the gods or ancestors as remarkable. What they might have heard was a voice saying, in English, "I hate you and everything you stand for." But since I never mentioned the lapse, in English or Chinese, I expressed my gratitude to her, Chinese style, so the heavens couldn't be sure which dictionary was operative until she was ready to explain in person. Or I can translate. Meanwhile, I accept that, however much we may yearn that it be otherwise, it can take more than one lifetime for a lifetime of changes to unfold and the wrinkles to relax—though some may never be ironed out to everyone's cultural satisfaction.

After her final departure, my father chose to learn how to journey without his companion of 65 years. Sitting on the couch together, we revisited many scenes, perceiving them from the present, even project-ing them into a future. Though he walked more slowly, willing his right leg nearer the left, our conversations lasted much longer than the time it used to take to go from Teaneck Road up Cranford Place for I had his attention *and* his interest. If I had not hoped for both, I may not have known I must always give both to William. In English *and* Chinese. Because we're in America.

William managed to put a lot of this in a card. Pictured on the front is a cat, looking concerned because she's hanging by her paws to a telephone wire. William's handwritten note surrounds the imprinted message:

> Dear Mom,
> Another Happy Mother's Day
> CHEER UP!
> Because you finished another chapter and the tax season is
> over and...

Opening the bottom half of the card, there is an elephant hanging off one of the cat's leg, looking involved but not particularly con-cerned.

> it COULD BE WORSE
> Because the IRS might have audited us and I might have
> decided to stay at home for a few more years!
> Happy Graduation and thanks for not screwing me up!
> Love, William

CHAPTER 5

JUDGE AND JURY

JUDGE...

One day Yingtai got word that the Hangzhou Academy was admitting new students. She pleaded with her father to let her go and study there. The old man objected strongly, for in those days the daughters of rich families were not even allowed to show themselves outside the gate, let alone attend a school away from home. However, his daughter's persistent entreaties disarmed him and he finally consented on condition that she go there disguised as a boy. So one fine day, in the guise of a scholar and accompanied by her maidservant, Yinxin dressed up like a page, Yingtai took leave of her father and set off for Hangzhou, happy as a bird freed from its cage.

—*Hua Jiqing, "The Story of Tragic Love,"*
Women In Chinese Folklore

When it comes to crimes of the heart, not loving one's children tops the list in America; amongst Confucians, the worst is for a child to exhibit a lack of devotion to parental needs, whether as an infrequent visitor or a permanent resident. An American parent can "get a life" only if the child's physical and emotional requirements are secured; a Confucian child has no respectable life if the parent has no greater dignity as a result. The Western ideal is for every child to happily develop his or her full potential; the Asian goal is to burden parents with nothing more onerous than lots of bragging rights. For Americans, to confess that one doesn't love the child is to make matters worse whereas for the Confucian to confess having less than total filial devotion is to constitute most of the remedy.

As the crimes escalate in gravity, terms like "inhumane" and "unnatural" become more applicable in both cultures but, in America, intentions almost always aggravate or mitigate the felony, while Confucians assume that public actions rarely belie private motives because appearances are presumed to coincide with reality. If the offense is perceived as a threat to a popular institution or person, then both cultures are equally capable of rationalizing severe punishment, claiming that the whole is being dangerously undermined by a part, or that the unconscionable condition of a part is the result of some flawed interpretation of the whole. Similarly, when things still don't work out the way they're supposed to, both have been known to depart from their respective norms by appealing to methods and virtues usually associated with the other approach. Yet when it comes to appearing in the courtrooms of life where we judge ourselves, our families and our peers, Americans generally cling to the principle that, even if one has confessed, one is officially innocent of the crime (that is defined by all those mitigating circumstances) until proven guilty by the accuser according to due process, while Chinese tend to believe one is already guilty of a crime (for having been accused at all) but admission of it can restore innocence. According to Mark Elvin,

> Conviction required confession,...The objective of the system was not "justice"—a term for which there is no satisfactory Chinese translation—but rather social discipline and the maintenance of the social structure, as with the rules governing a Western army, school, or church.

"How do you plead?"

"Guilty."

"No, you don't," the judge whispered as he leaned toward me.

"Excuse me, sir?"

"I said, 'Your plea is 'Not Guilty.'"

"Can you do that?"

"Yes."

"But I was on the other side of the road—so I wouldn't hit the parked cars."

"I know that."

"It was my fault entirely."

"Mmm, yes. Well, there's a difference between driving in the country and driving in the city...."

Still thinking of him as my friends described him—"the hanging judge"—I tried to match the dreadful preconception with this kindly, even folksy, man. Like a good priest with an inexperienced penitent, he reinforced the value of confession even as he hinted that so much remorse was commensurate with far greater sins than I had committed or, presumably, was capable of contemplating. Had we been alone, I would have been soothed. But we weren't, and I wasn't. Although I couldn't see my mother sitting in the back row, I could feel through my back her profound disapproval of the spectacle: her daughter, Vice President of the Student Council, in public court charged with a crime. That I was to receive Teaneck's Junior Citizen-of-the-Month award the next day would not balance the ledger. The contrast of the two ceremonies could only intensify the shame that this one occurred at all.

The presence of a dozen or so schoolmates didn't help. All they were lacking was the popcorn. They came to the hearing reminiscent of townspeople gathering around the scaffold. Their curiosity and conversation turned the fearsome into the festive. These were the same friends who had been so serious when I, recently licensed, drove my parents' car into a tank, cleverly disguised as a full-sized Buick. After inspecting the accordion damage to the front-end of an already compact vehicle, they were convinced that it would be months before I could again sit behind the wheel. The trauma would be too great.

Had it not been for my parents' concerned, but matter-of-fact, response to my telephone call amidst the flashing lights of police cars and ambulance, I too might have indulged in some long-term hysteria. Instead, they ascertained my escape from bodily damage, borrowed a car, picked me up, dropped me off at home, and proceeded to their "Double Ten" party. As soon as our car was repaired, they asked me to drive to the store on an errand. It never seemed to occur to them that driving so soon after the accident might be difficult. I had no choice but to be aggressive and adopt their attitude. To do otherwise would have been a bit silly, especially considering how much they enjoyed the irony of their daughter scheduling a head-on collision on the tenth day of the tenth month: Chinese Independence Day.

Being in court was another matter. I had been made meek by compliance with my mother's stern instructions to remove all traces of my red nail polish, to comb my hair into a prim bun, to don my most sedate clothing and, once seated before the bench, to refrain from greeting my friends. Lady Justice may be blindfolded but the deities would be watching for any sign of defiance or disrespect.

Yes, I could feel the severity emanating from my mother's upright body; there was no need to look at her now. I had seen her grimly watching other defendants approach the judge, be fined, and then proceed to the clerk's desk, woefully taking out of their wallets the requisite amount. I had been feeling the gravity of pulling her into this inhospitable place where no one knew or cared who she was, where her rectitude and poise were no guarantee of consideration or outcome. When I saw her looking at the other violators, seeing their submission, anticipating my own, it was irrelevant that we both knew it was an accident that had brought us here. It had been *my* accident. And being the mother, she was as vulnerable to the proceedings as the daughter. When I watched her watching the accused, I couldn't see them as citizens, protected, even empowered, by a system of laws and

rights. If she perceived defendants as a group, undifferentiated by individuality, uniformly diminished, then I did too. If she was now,
through no fault of her own, a member of this group, then it was my
responsibility to mitigate the effect and act as honorably as the situation allowed.

"...So be sure you pass closer to those parked cars. That way, you'll
stay on your side of the road. Will you promise to do that?"

"Yes, sir."

"Well, good night, then."

"Uh, good night, sir. Uh, thank you for the advice."

"You're welcome. Next case!"

Walking back down the aisle, my friends' faces alternated between
disappointment and admiration. They had come to see me writhe as a
system of rules drew the line, leaving me for the first time on the
wrong side. Instead, they saw the judge mandate a wiggle in the
straight and narrow that placed me back on the right. It would be
weeks before his reputation would be restored, before his image could
once again scare summoned dragsters out of jeans and into slacks. I,
on the other hand, was assured of presidential prominence.

By the time I reached my mother's row, I was calm with vindica-
tion. She, however, was frantic, "Up there. You pay up there. Hurry!
They'll come after you."

"Mommy, I don't have to. The judge let me off."

"Don't be stupid. Go back and pay. Quick."

"It's okay."

"It's not 'okay'. Everybody's looking."

I couldn't explain that they were looking because our hands and
mouths, chattering in Chinese, were more intriguing than the hushed
proceedings going on in front. People who can exchange words that no
one else understands have the luxury of holding private conversations
in the open. We get so used to relying on the language barrier, we
sometimes forget it's not soundproofed as well.

Already responsible for my mother being in court, I had no credit
left to spend on an outright dispute of what was or was not true. So I
kept silent until our audience lost interest.

"See. No one's coming."

Assessing the situation for herself, she firmly escorted me out of
this unpredictable official world, and drove me back to our house—
where nothing was ambiguous.

Four years later, a friend and I were reminiscing while on a sort-of date. Once voted the "Most Popular," he was now an existentialist. About to march in the South alongside other civil rights activists, he was feeling the obligation to disavow some of what he had once been. Chronicling the thoughts that took him from the mainstream to the fringes, he ascribed one of the early and more portentous, to something I had said when, as he put it, "I finally got up the nerve to talk to you, even though I never did get the guts to ask you out." There were only two of us at this "reunion," and it was not that long since we had graduated. But the experience was the same. Whether it's the twentieth or thirtieth year, whether there are hundreds or a few left, we can gather together and start where we left off—in the unresolved, unrequited relationships of our youth when we scribbled our dreams in the margins of our notebooks even as we drew the lines around us. We may add and cross out new designs, but that high school configuration seems indelibly stamped into our psyches with the ink of teenage hormones and the fixative of Commencement Day. At reunions, the old blueprint emerges and we jostle ourselves back into or out of positions that no longer exist but still matter, if only for the time it takes to make an entry.

Looking at my handsome friend, hearing him give me stature I never thought I had, I wanted to embrace him for the might-have-been. And then throttle him for being too late. Through his eyes, I revised myself into someone who had enough presence that a fellow of his good looks had to think twice before approaching me. I saw myself, for the first time as what my father envisioned for his daughters—a woman who can turn both heads and minds. Gratified, I nevertheless had to deflect the compliment my friend paid me. I didn't want the deities to think that I lacked one of the other crucial elements of the truly authoritative: humility.

"It wasn't as if I was any free thinker. I didn't choose to view some things differently. It kind of comes with the territory of being the only Chinese in town."

"We never thought of you as 'Chinese.'"

"I know. Mostly, I wanted it that way. Whether I should have is another question."

"Whatever, you still scared me. I was on the edge. Ready to ask what you thought of me, not ready to hear it."

Meandering from there, he did concede that I couldn't have been too far "out there," since I got the Citizenship award around the same time he got one. With that, I told him my "hanging judge" tale. He looked puzzled.

"You knew they fixed it."

"Fixed what?" I asked.

"The ticket."

"Who did?"

"The Junior Citizen Committee."

Paul then told me what he and a few other classmates knew all the time: that I had been "not guilty" because the committee had persuaded the judge to rule in my favor. Its members were afraid that if the local paper featured an award recipient in the same issue that it reported her conviction, the readers might question the committee's judgment.

How many people knew the story ? How many of them knew what I didn't, but thought I did? It was my worst nightmare—being misunderstood. Silenced by the passage of time, I couldn't go back and explain that I had been an unwitting beneficiary, that I disapproved of judge and committee rigging the outcome. With righteous indignation, I would have preferred being "guilty" of the actual charge, to being "innocent" by collusion. Unforgiving, I condemned them all for the injury done to me.

"That's not how it's supposed to be!" I blurted.

On an emotional roll, I ignored the irony of a Chinese "minority" protesting treatment that put her *above* the law. Entering the era that was to become "the '60s," some of my college friends and I were propelled by skepticism and hope. It was a mix that made us admire the effect of Malcolm X's words on an audience—people who sat taller for having heard them even when they rejected the message. We hadn't given up on "the system." We still expected the Halls of Justice to be a forum where ideal minds think objective thoughts about colorless people. At the time—before the Warren Commission and the Watergate Hearings—we didn't really expect the other option of cynicism and helplessness could be a way of life. Sometimes we talked that way, but we didn't really *feel* it.

Then I remembered my mother. I recalled how she had endured the uncertainty with me. Picturing my supplicating hands, holding her "face," exposed for judicial review, I remembered how frightened I was to share the responsibility of something so precious. And for what?

Certainly not the ideal that I had abstracted from my life in America, and to which I had pledged my allegiance. If the citizenship committee had gone so far as to influence the judge's verdict and make the hearing a sham, why hadn't it gone a little further and told me?

In the kitchen the next day, preparing dinner, I reminded my mother of the incident. The indignation squeezing my voice as I told her about the rumor. I waited to receive her commiseration.

"What judge?"

"Don't you remember? After the accident."

"What accident?"

"When I got my license—on Double Ten."

She showed no sign of recognition. Cleaning the scallions, my resentment gave way to a new problem—how to jog her memory without disturbing her mood? As I stumbled through other key words—"The Junior Citizen Award," "Teaneck High"—I avoided the ones that might trigger a recalling of the vulnerability, the shame.

My mother surveyed the myriad of dishes that kept separate the ingredients we had prepared and readied herself for the flurry of combining it all. Once the oil in the wok was searing hot, there was no time between a handful of this and that to be timid. Assured that everything she needed was at hand, she looked up with eyes that asked, "Why are you bringing this up now?"

What was the point? She had no reason to recollect what was of no use anymore. I was now a good driver. The memory was like the measuring cups. Stored in some inconvenient shelf, they were there for us, if the need arose. Otherwise, learning how to produce the right balance of tastes for however many were eating was best done in terms of one's own handful. My self-righteous flustering over some impersonal standard of measure didn't make any sense in that kitchen. Moreover, watching her poised before a stove that would soon be shooting flames and spitting oil, I knew she could just as well direct its fire if it suddenly became a dragon. How could I have presumed that her standing could be effaced by a traffic ticket?

Having broached the subject, however, I felt committed to continue. So I repeated the rumor. She was pleased to hear it.

From her viewpoint, I had confessed my fault and been duly processed by the rules. It had been an accident caused by too extreme care, not negligence. The other driver, herself unharmed, had been reimbursed for the little damage her Buick sustained. The fine charged if I had been proclaimed "guilty" was worth less than if the committee lost face. After all, the honor it regularly bestowed was part of the township's way of inspiring civic effort and pride amongst the citizenry. And though she would have much preferred that I had never been summoned to court, it was a ritual to establish authority. Despite his lenience toward me, the judge quickly restored his reputation to its former fearsome stature and, thereby, its capacity to deter anyone from thinking that either he or his court had gone soft. Satisfied that my pristine and meritorious behavior had solicited intervention on my behalf without any instigation on my part, she shared the credit I received. Order had been restored—not by law, but by quiet mediation, not by going to the extremes of one side or the other but by taking the Middle Way—Confucius' way. And probably Aristotle's. This was the stuff of Chinese-American Dreams. Unfortunately, when fairness is in the eye of the beholder and what's self-evident to one group is not obvious to another, this can also be the stuff of Chopsticks-Fork Nightmares, a kind of cultural double jeopardy with judge and jury operating from different ideas so that what's Doing Good to one is Doing Violence to the other. Or worse, when the judge can never be juried and the jury is unjudged.

The nightmare happened on our Senior Class Trip when I became an escapee from a Chinese concentration camp. A psychiatrist might explain my teenage prank as a symbolic expression of being "barred" from my own childhood, or a subconscious effort to trivialize Iron and Bamboo Curtains to counter a lingering fear of being left behind like *SanSan*. I, however, tended to go along with my parents on this: assigning a maximum of one consciousness per person and categorizing all behavior as subject to will power. (Freud never made it big in China. Thus, when my younger sister once said she was depressed, my mother's advice, "Stop it," made sense to me. Though an aspirin would have been a nice gesture.)

In any case, I doubt there was any subliminal meaning to my choice of fiction. I became a prison survivor because a school radiator had sneaked up on me and seared its serial number on my leg. I may actively control my will but I'm often quite passive about—even oblivious to—the physical world around me. The branding took place a week before our pre-graduation trip to Washington, DC. The classroom windows were open and the air was warm. Too warm. Someone had neglected to tell the custodian that spring had come early, and so the heating system was still on. In need of some fresh air, I stood at a window. Nearby, were the heavy iron coils that exuded the hot breath of the monstrous boiler steaming in the subterranean depths of our educational fortress. By the time the pain reached my brain and I pulled away, my calf was red from the burn. A day or so later, I noticed the redness had become a mirror image of the marking on the radiator valve—6031.

When my mother saw it, she shrugged, figuring, I guess, that few would ever get close enough to her daughter's calf to notice it was numbered. No one blamed, let alone sued, the custodian, or the Principal, or the School Board, for deformation of a lower limb. The incident was, at most, a reminder that we live in a world of "things" outside our control. That she didn't even bother to extract from it some moral lesson about taking greater care was an indication of its negligible status in the scheme of events. I took my cue from her and blamed no one. But I did have this number on my leg. And it would be such a shame to waste it.

My mother was right that no one would notice; she was wrong that no one would see it. A lot of people saw it—every gullible one I could find. Some believed because the news was too titillating for them to be concerned about veracity. Others believed because they had watched movies in which Alfred Hitchcock regularly transformed the familiar into the frightening. And still others believed because we lived in a town that housed many Holocaust survivors whose real memories substantiated my claims.

All were primed because, in the '50s, few knew much about China. Between its Bamboo Curtain and Eisenhower's Containment Policy, most Americans connected the "Far" East to the near-at-hand through the bifurcated menus of Chinese-American restaurants, or the "two-faced" familiarity of Caucasian actors made up as Charlie Chan. Similarly, two Bao sisters in a town of 35,000, in a school with no other Chinese, aroused no xenophobia—we spoke English without accents, were officers of the Student Council and members of the popular Sigma Tau sorority. Yet we were not "familiar." Thus, when I said that I'd once been "6031," they all believed me. No one asked why such marvelous information had not been revealed before. No one checked the chronology to find out how I knew so much about the Brooklyn Dodgers '47 line-up two years before I was supposed to have been incarcerated by the Communists on the Mainland. The ease with which 6031 came into existence made it mandatory that someone else appreciate the ingenuity of my new persona. Keeping one's own cleverness a secret required an independence I didn't possess. Enter Karen. Together, we were able to expand operations. We even fooled the Russian spies.

My mother had dubbed her "The One with the Big Eyes." Yet they were slightly almond in shape, and dark. Her hair was half black, and half prematurely white. Her coloring made her appear older, an exotic blend, quite different from the usual bobby-soxer. I, of course, always looked different in a country with fewer than 240 thousand Chinese among the 180 million. So when we toured our nation's capital and put a little distance between ourselves and our classmates, it wasn't difficult to mislead strangers into perceiving us as distinct from them.

Sightseers smiled as they overheard Karen "translating" the Gettysberg Address into "Chinese" for me, an obvious foreigner learning about the great President "Rin-Con." Some patted my bobbing head, and gave my friend a "thumbs up" sign to encourage her good work. Karen's gibberish—made-up words from popular songs with a little Pig Latin and a few "Ah so's" thrown in—sounded just about right to the untrained ear. It was good enough to convince the Soviets when they approached us in the hotel lobby.

"*AAAIYA!! Solja, solja!!!*" I cried out as I grabbed Karen's sleeve.

"Cathy, *oo ee oo ah ah ting tang walla walla bing bang. Ellbay oysbay.*" Now within earshot, they heard Karen comfort me as she intermittently translated, to no one in particular, that the "bell boys" were not enemy soldiers in dress uniform.

"Excuse. Please. Is she from China?" They asked, pointing to me.

"Yes. But we try not to talk about that. The memories are too terrible." My attractive interpreter whispered as I stood by suspiciously eyeing every bellboy who passed.

"Oh? How is that?"

Realizing their interrogation might seem equally suspicious, they added, "We are here from Moscow. But for the convention. We make maps."

Looking as if she understood exactly what they meant, Karen put her arm around my shoulder and said, "She escaped."

"From China?"

"Worse. From a Chinese Camp."

Hearing this, they nodded as if to say, "We understand."

To make sure they did, Karen gently instructed me, "*Owshlay eglay*," and pointed down as I demurely consented to "show leg" to them, heaving a sigh of despair as the brand came into view.

"This is incredible" they chorused. Or something like that. After exchanging a few words in Russian, they continued, "Please. We would like to talk some more, have you meet my wife and the rest of our delegation. Maybe tonight, after the speech? Around 10:30? We are in Room...."

We never heard their room number. Our attention had gone toward the chaperones who were now herding the Teaneck contingent away. Afraid they might see us strays and interrupt with the unwelcome truth, we mumbled our gratitude for their kind invitation and moved close enough to the school group so that the teachers didn't notice anything wrong. Fortunately, the Russians were called to a meeting, and we managed a nonchalant and seemingly coincidental saunter into the restaurant after the "American school children" with whom we had nothing whatsoever in common.

Hidden behind our menus, we guffawed the best moments to each other as we bent over dinner plates. Later, we chortled the glorious details to our roommates as we hunched on our beds and hugged our pillows for support. By the time we were supposed to do what every red-blooded American student had done before us—prowl hallways in search of illicit fraternity parties—Karen and I were exhausted. After a thousand historical sites and a million giggles, we were content to wash our hair and forego getting soaked in anything more heady than self-congratulation. Having already perpetrated so much mischief, we were too tired to violate the Principal's injunction to stay in our assigned rooms after curfew and drink nothing more potent than soda, juice, milk, or water. Our triumph, and our sore feet, kept us exactly where we were supposed to be that night—until thirst overwhelmed us, and we went searching for a coke machine.

In wet hair and bathrobes, Karen and I took off in the opposite direction of where we thought our teachers were patrolling. And inadvertently toward the KGB. Peering around corners, and then scurrying to the next safe haven, we found no refreshment center. Just as we started to retrace our route, a deep voice said, "*Katya, Karin.*" Turning, we saw one of the Russians. Conscious of our inappropriate attire, "Karin" sputtered an explanation while I babbled in Chinese. Ignoring our discomfort, he insisted that we quench our thirst. His wife and fellow delegates, who just happened to be in the nearby suite, would be so honored. Thumbing our noses at the Principal's rules was no temptation, but another chance to masquerade before Cold War adversaries was irresistible. Exchanging shrugs and "What the heck" looks, we followed him into their headquarters, scared and delighted by the prospect of intrigue.

We may have fooled the men that afternoon, but Mother Russia was another matter. It's possible that half a head of white hair could divert the woman's eyes from the youthful sheen of Karen's freshly scrubbed face, but nothing short of a nuclear explosion could have distracted her from the visual effect of my feet. One glance at the gigantic Mickey Mouse slippers and she knew that we were refugees from nothing more sinister than a classroom.

With a smile that's universal to all tolerant parents, she graciously served tea and polite chitchat about the vicissitudes of life in a prison camp. Sensitive to our plight, she didn't detain us longer than our mortification could stand. Her husband, now aware of his wife's deductions, gave us a hearty "Good-bye," as we backed into the hall, not sorry to let their door close on a skit that had run one scene too long.

Anxious to get offstage lest our too-obliging audience decide we might want to do an encore, we didn't move one step before the curtain immediately rose again with the sound of another deep voice calling, "Karen, Cathy." The Teacher Patrol. Caught in a different act, we instantly dreaded the review. Here were critics who had been forced to watch out for wayward students when they would much rather be doing exactly what we were forbidden to do.

"What're you doing out of your room?"

Once again Karen was the first to explain, "We were looking for a coke machine."

With a dismissive glance at the girl whose "C" report cards did not warrant their attention or surprise, they focused on me.

"At this hour? In your bathrobes?"

"We were going to bed. But then got thirsty," I truthfully pleaded as I tried to edge down the hall and away from the just closed door and the convivial sounds coming through it.

My movement failed to draw them toward me. However, my words did elicit dismay and disbelief. "Surely," their slowly shaking heads conveyed, "someone with my grade average would not compound a simple—even expected—transgression by insulting veteran teachers with such a feeble excuse?" The script was now in their hands, and we had no choice but to remain a silent, as well as captive, audience.

Still unmoved, the one then looked down at her clipboard, and with exaggerated haste flipped through her lists to find names and record misdemeanors. The other, eyes glazing over, droned the lecture that he must have already given a dozen times that night. Karen and I stood between them and the door, listening to both parties.

"...Especially you, Cathy, you ought to know better than to..."

His colleague interrupted, "Wait a minute. This room isn't on here." Upset that the roll might be incomplete and that they would actually have to crash a whole party instead of just citing the hosts assigned to the room, she looked up and asked, "Who's in there?"

"Some of those map-makers here for the convention. One of them said he wanted..."

And that's as far as I ever got. They heard "CONVENTION," then "HE," and their minds were off and running. Looking through our bathrobes and slippers to what must have been underneath, our crime was now of the flesh, not of the spirits, alcoholic or otherwise.

Unlike the "boys who would be boys," we weren't just reprimanded and sent back to our room for the night. Our sentence implied that girls who would be boys were inherently flawed. For the rest of the trip, if not touring or eating, we were confined to our rooms. With foreboding hints of further punishment, we had plenty of time to agonize about what was going to happen when we got back home, when options besides mere containment were available: summons to the Principal's Office, letters to our parents, or—the worst—not graduating. But nothing more was done, at least officially.

Karen's immense relief at finding herself still part of Commencement cleared her mind, and left it free to concentrate on plans for our sorority's trip to the Jersey shore (that my parents couldn't object to without mentioning the unmentionable). My distress was not so easily resolved. Yes, I was a member of the graduating class and that was a relief, but I was "relieved" in another way. I was relieved of my past, my reputation. No longer a "good" girl, I could do no good.

If they believed in community, it was to protect it from the likes of me rather than in its power to inspire reform among those who might threaten its well-being. If they thought I could be rehabilitated, it was only if my desire to be made moral survived the punishment. If they decided it was justice to isolate me, then it was my business, not theirs, what effect this might have on those who had invested themselves and their caring in me. Having withdrawn all diplomatic recognition of the "little ambassador," they saw as little of me as they thought of me.

They had taken the years of my, my family's, effort and achievement, and used them to make my guilt weigh more heavily against me. They made me wonder, "What was it all for?" so that what I remembered in English became more inaccessible than what I forgot in Chinese. They recalled nothing that would prompt them to ask, "What really happened, Cathy?" Instead, they envisioned what the Patrol had pictured, and rewrote my biography in their minds.

Except for one: Mr. Lurie, my chemistry teacher. When he did ask, I nearly cried, grateful that someone connected my past to the present with the benefit of the doubt.

Showing him the now faded number, I told him how I got branded: first as 6031, and then as a "bad girl."

"And that's the 'sex scandal' I've been hearing about?! What a bunch of gossips!"

He was the first one who came right out and said the word "sex." I didn't hear my mother use the word until I was about to get married. We happened to be driving by a barber shop that had just opened up.

"Humph. 'Unisex.' Why do they have to talk like that?"

They don't. But they do. I speak the Chinese of an eight-year old, but I think in the English of a very liberal Democrat. When sex, gender, and adolescence don't occur in the one but are pervasive in the other, maintaining identity, let alone innocence, can be a tongue-tying experience.

...JURY

There is an ambiguity, then, as to which is just or unjust, the institution as realized or the institution as an abstract object.

—John Rawls, A Theory of Justice

When I went to court, I had my mother. When William went to the principal's office, he had an advocate behind him.

In 1985, William and I had the great pleasure of deleting peanut butter and jelly from the shopping list. Although I had some reservations about sending him to a parochial school, we both thought its cafeteria and school bus would go a long way toward making up for its deficiencies. Bennett tried to concur, hoping the difference between himself and his father would cushion William's first experience with regimentation. Thirty years before, when shipped out of Iowa to attend the prestigious prep school of his forebears, Bennett did miserably. Chided by his father, "Son, if your grades don't improve, we'll have to take you out of here," Bennett proceeded to flunk every course available. Except Religion—no one was allowed to flunk Religion. Rather than stay at a place where students hazed each other into conformity and obedience, he preferred disgrace. I was sure history would not repeat itself. I was overly optimistic.

The moment I saw William step down from the school bus I knew his world had been rearranged for the worse. The portion he had occupied that morning had been expansive, now it was too small even for an eleven-year old. So intent was I on his shriveled condition, I didn't notice that there were more children than usual looking at me through the film of dust that coated the bus windows as I stood by my car in the Town Hall parking lot. Later, I felt their stares when they reappeared in William's nightmares.

Once in the car, I asked, as quietly as I could so as not to pain him more, "What happened, William?"

"I think...I guess...I've been expelled. A few soft breaths later, he added, "I'm sorry, *MaMa*."

"Why, William?"

"I don't know. I mean, I do. But I don't. Anyway, there's nothing you can do about it."

"Why do you say that?" I asked. Not because I had become one of those parents whose presumption is that the child is always innocent, but because William was now a seventh grader. One and a half months earlier, he had been a sixth grader at the school's elementary division. The idea of skipping a grade first occurred when I saw his homework assignments. It became a necessity when I went to the Open House a month later and met his teacher, Sister F.

"I was hoping, since William has already read all the books on your reading list, it would be possible for him to write reports on books from the Upper Division list."

"I should say *not*. He's flunking math." She whipped out a folder with his name on the front and then dramatically opened it up. Gnashing the grade on top with the corner of the copper strip running along the edge of the wooden ruler that seemed a part of her hand, she snarled, "Look at this!"

Turning it over and slapping it down before I had a chance to see anything but the 58% at the top, she pointed at the second sheet, "And this."

Craning my neck to look at what was below the 62%, I started to ask why she had given no credit at all for answers that were faulty only because they weren't aligned on the page in the same direction as her corrections. Raising my eyes to meet hers, I saw such malice in her face, I backed off. Triumphant, her eyes locked on mine, voracious. Feeding on my dismay, she didn't want to miss a second of it and used her hand to feel its way back to the folder. Peeling away Exhibit #2 to uncover the next piece of damaging evidence, she sneered, "And *this*!"

Blinking myself from her stunning fury, I looked down. And smiled. Obviously, William had finally figured out that the key to math was writing the numbers in perfectly aligned columns. Facing her, I let some of the smile remain as I angled my head toward the folder, half quizzical, half invitational. Her curiosity overcame her voracity, and she looked down. When she saw the 98% at the top of Exhibit #3, she went ballistic. Dropping the pile on the desk, she curled each of the remaining sheets into her fist in a mad search for something more damaging. Finding nothing below a B, she took up her ruler again. She slapped the palm of her other hand to underscore every word of her decision. With each sharp rap, she implied that it was my flesh that deserved—would benefit by—the corporal rebuke. "Well he can't. He'll read what everybody else reads. He's in sixth grade, he's in *my* class."

Not for long, Sister. Aloud, I said, "Thank you for your kind consideration."

Two and a half weeks later, William was in the high school building where students had a different instructor for each subject and no one's day could be dominated by any single person. At the very least, this guaranteed variety. Of the options available, it seemed the best. I had ruled out the public school when the local principal, not much of an educator to begin with, had been indicted for child molestation, and his successor followed up with a scandal of a different sort. None of this would have been an issue had his old school—that went through to the eighth grade—not decided to commit a slow form of suicide. Where once Montessori principles were encouraged in all people, now it was tolerated only in the very young. When the Board of Trustees didn't like what some of us were saying about the situation, it asserted its right of ownership and banned parents from meeting in the building or talking in the parking lot. With its suspension of the First Amendment, I told William that it would be more sad to witness the death of a good school than not to see his friends on a daily basis. Also, I couldn't help but remember my mother's wisdom, and added that this was as good a time as any for him to learn something about what Christians believed. (William had all along been getting the Judaic view from his Uncle Kogan who gave him *Bible Stories For Jewish Children*, as well as books about the War of Southern Independence, "Because we cannot have this po' chil' growin' up to be another Heathen Refugee from Godless Communism like his mother. Or worse, a *Yankee*.")

I believed that if we talked him through this exposure, it could all be interesting. When Sister F. said, "The reason children get good grades is because they pray to their guardian angel," I laughed that, based on her assumptions, William must either be in league with the devil or have cheated. When another nun announced "Good boys are silent boys," I told him that his *KungKung* had been China's national debating champion in Chinese and English. When a third justified segregating the girls during recess with, "We don't want them to grow up as tomboys," and then reprimanded William for replying, "You've got to be kidding," I showed him the scar I got from playing football with the Cathie twins. On the other hand, when a fourth suggested, "Pray—it won't kill you," William conceded that bowing one's head rather than looking around was worth her peace of mind. Basically, he accepted The Deal that I had negotiated with the principal—the school would overlook his unbaptized status if he took seriously the value of studying its religion. He also accepted my waiting in one of the school's classrooms, grading papers, in exchange for attending his first dance. Pressured by deadlines, I didn't want to waste the hour driving back and forth twice. When almost finished, I found William and told him where to meet me in half an hour. Thirty minutes later, I heard,

"Hey, Will. You aren't going, are you? It's early."

"Yeah, well, my Mom's been waiting and she's got to work in the morning."

"You mean, like, she's been here the whole time? I mean, you know, like watching? What a drag!"

"It's the price of getting an education."

The following month I did the double round trips and picked him up at the official end of the next dance, pleased to give his friends the slack he and I already gave each other. Because our family life didn't revolve around him, didn't burden him with being the center of our attention, he had the luxury and obligation of expanding into others' worlds to witness a wide range of triumphs. He went to the State Department for his uncle's swearing-in as the ambassador to China even though, early in his career, Winston had been told that marrying Bette would destroy any chances for an Asian assignment. When I took him to where Jacob Javits sat amidst medical tubing, William said nothing while he placed his little hand on that giant's and gently squeezed. He knew how difficult it would be for the Senator to speak because we had taken him to visit Mike. Having seen his father's former student use the same courage to paint with a mouth-held brush as it once took to train circus bears, William understood there was history in wheelchairs. When he went to Boston for his Aunt Margaret's wedding, he wasn't skeptical to hear one of the guests, Corazon Aquino, thanking friends for their support in helping a Filipina housewife become president of her nation. And he could feel the exuberance of our friends being "out" when attending a costume party in Colorado where some of the flappers turned out to be men. Thus the transition from one kind of schooling to another went smoothly until that day he stepped off the bus.

Driving home from the Town Hall, I heard how Mr. H., his English teacher, had stood before the class to announce that William had plagiarized his book report; how the man had marked down additional demerits when William denied the accusation, and then a bunch

147

more when William claimed he never heard of Cliff Notes; how he closed the subject by saying, "And don't think you can send your mother in here to change my mind. I won't talk to her—parents will do and say anything to get their kids out of trouble."

Doing all I could to remain calm and get the whole story, "Did he talk to you in private before doing this?"

"No."

"What happened next?"

"Nothing." A moment later, "*MaMa?*"

"Yes, William?"

"Everybody believed him."

I could barely hear him, but I got the message, the question. His English class met in the morning. Marinated in their false belief for most of the day, he was thinking no one, including me, could doubt the man's words. What a change in so short a time. This had been a child who would go to all sorts of extremes to find a synonym for any word that I suggested. If I argued that mine was more appropriate, he insisted on his. Knowing our son, the idea of taking a whole essay from someone else was absurd. His ego wouldn't let him.

"William, of course I don't believe him. It's all some terrible misunderstanding."

Immediately, his shoulders resumed their normal position and the anguish started to seep from his face. To speed his recovery, I extended a bit of my ego to bolster his, "He had no right to do what he did in front of everybody. But you know, William, maybe he's not as picky as I am. Maybe he was so impressed with what you wrote, he thought it came from a book."

In the house, I went to the rolodex by the phone.

"*MaMa*, he won't talk to you. He said that would make it worse."

"William, he lost his chance to talk to me when he didn't first confer with you."

The next morning I had an appointment with the principal. I tried to convey normality. William would take the bus as usual, while I followed in the car. Waiting in the lot, I saw one child go over to him when she didn't see me leave and overheard her ask, "Is your mother coming to help you clean out your locker?"

"No," William said in his most casual tone, "She's coming to get Mr. H's liver."

His exaggeration would help him get through at least one more day of enduring what has always been my worst nightmare: being wrongly accused. I hadn't told William all that could still go wrong. Throughout the night, I wrote scenarios: Mr. H. hit by a car and dead before he can testify; Mr. H's office ablaze, burning the exonerating evidence; Mr. H. and Sister M conspiring to rid the school of the boy who didn't pray for good grades. Yet the worst was not from the cinema, but my own past: Mr. H. as the off-spring of Madame K., the French teacher who failed me in effort, the one who would never change her opinion of what I was worth. When my mother was to meet her on Back-To-School night, all I could say to prepare her was, "She doesn't like me." I wasn't sure she understood what I was trying to say until the moment she saw the grade and didn't say, "Why an E?" Not then, not ever, did we use the word "racist" at home. It was as if the word, the concept, was beneath our dignity. And why it could always take me by surprise.

Following the yellow school bus toward the Delaware Water Gap, I tried to pick William out from the tops of heads that I saw in silhouette. I couldn't and started to panic. Speeding to close the distance, I had to prove it wasn't like those dreams when you run harder but get further and further behind. Almost tailgating, I saw myself dead on the road, William unprotected. Dropping back, I approached the toll booth marking the New Jersey-Pennsylvania border. The bus was already across the river. Resisting the urge to push the accelerator, I concentrated on compressing my anxiety and fear into hard, rational resolve. The time would have been better spent reviewing techniques in shadowboxing.

"Yes, Mrs. Bean, I did have an opportunity to speak with Mr. H. and have informed him that you *may* be in today. He is in his office now."

"Yes, Mrs. Bean, I can understand why you *may* not wish to see Mr. H."

"Yes, Mrs. Bean, I can see how this *may* have upset William."

"Yes, Mrs. Bean, of course, you *may* confer with me afterward if you think it may help."

In the presence of so many "mays" and crucifixes, my righteous indignation was too gross, too much, uncalled for. "Mrs. Bean" was no match for Sister M. Deferring, I walked down the hall to Mr. H.'s office, knocked on the door, and sat by his desk in the chair indicated. Immediately, he rose to stand over me. I listened with half a mind, still astonished that I had been so deftly maneuvered by Sister M.

"...William's report on *The Red Pony* was so obviously...."

Puzzled, I interrupted him, "What are you talking about?"

"Steinbeck, Mrs. Bean. You do know *Steinbeck*, don't you? The great *American* writer—*John* Steinbeck?

"Yes. It's *The Red Pony* that I don't...."

"Well, that story just so happens to be one of Steinbeck's...."

"Excuse me, that's not what I meant." Feeling my resolve return from its time-out in the corner, "What I want to know is why you're talking about it at all. William's report was on *Of Mice And Men.* Remember? You approved the substitution because he had read *The Red Pony* last year at his old school."

Flustered by the unexpected rebuttal, he lowered his body and voice into the chair, "That can't be. I have it right here...." Picking up a sheet of ruled paper, one edge ragged with the scraps from having been torn out of a wire-bound notebook, I knew immediately it wasn't William's. A second later, he did too. Groaning, "Oh my God. It was the one lying on top, with the name covered. It looked like William's...." For a few more seconds, he looked from one to the other. Giving up, he looked up, eyes pleading.

There was no charity in me, "You didn't even bother to check did you?"

Now decidedly impolite, I informed Sister M. of the error and walked out. Within days, Mr. H. did too.

Awake, William was vindicated. Indeed, he enjoyed a surge in popularity as "the kid who got Mr. H. fired" as opposed to "the kid who skipped a grade." Asleep, though, he spent many nights running from the memory. Holding him then, his eyes wide open, his dream mind terrified, his throat choking out screams about the Big Man chasing him and the Jelly Beans surrounding him, I wanted Mr. H.'s liver and Sister M.'s heart. In the dark, I could still hear her say, "Yes, Mrs. Bean, there *may* have been other 'incidences'. Yes, Mrs. Bean, your visit the other day did convince me we cannot continue to hope he *may* change his ways." Her favorite word intensified my dislike for the "Mother May I" game.

During one of those nights, I noticed the silver crucifix was gone. Sometimes Guardians can give us their perspective. From above or below the bed, they can divert us long enough to take a breath in order to sort the mental from the real monsters.

The next year, Sister M. was transferred to another school, one that the bishop thought could use her firm administrative hand. I don't know what happened to Mr. H. Maybe he learned something and is now an exemplary educator. As far as I know, Sister F. is still in a classroom somewhere, job-secure in her black habit.

Meanwhile, unbeknownst to me, William was executing his own revenge. I found it out early that summer. Bringing in the mail, reading his report card, I called him from his room. Looking grim, I handed it over. Although I had chosen the Montessori system to protect us both from the legacy of my mother looking at a long line of "A's," but only saying, "Why a "B" in ___?" and the anguish of standardized tests perpetrated by the lurking behemoths, SAT and ACT. However, as soon as William became subject to a grading system, I had succumbed to its embrace, one arm from the East, the other from the West. As much as I didn't want him to, he quickly learned to dread those quarterly assessments.

Holding out his hand for it, his body flinching under my gaze, he scanned the report. Looking up, he grinned. I grinned. Big, broad, shit-eating grins. For there, amongst the B's and C's, was the only "A"—in Religion.

JUDGE AND JURY

That was one of the last moments I could read William's mind clearly. By the time he was a sophomore at Blair Academy and wrote the following allegory, I knew for sure only that he had Hybrid Vigor and had been seriously processing the stuff of our lives. I recognized his patience and his kind of quiet finality in the parable, but exactly what he meant always eludes me. Each time I read it, I decide differently who is who and what is what. I've never asked him for his interpretation. Not knowing reminds me that we must continually update our respective dictionaries and that it does make a difference that he isn't an ear of corn.

The Tree and the Man

At some time, in a world, at a certain place was an ancient tree. The tree was beautiful in every aspect, in color, in shape, and detail. Under this tree was a man who was as ancient as the tree. The man was beautiful in the way of the tree, in color, in shape, and in detail. The man sat under the tree among the roots which had grown around him. The man talked with the tree, sharing deep thoughts about the universe.

The man and the tree talked and argued for many years while the outside world was growing, learning, and discovering new ways of thought. The day came when the man and the tree had agreed to all the solutions of the problems of life. The man went outside, away from the tree, to tell the outside world of the revelation that he and the tree had discovered. When the man stepped outside into the world, he encountered something totally strange to him.

The world that the man found was much different from the world he had left many, many years ago. The outside world had grown, had learned, and had discovered new ways of thought. The man traveled the concrete lanes—once dirt roads—to talk of his revelation to groups of learners. The man stated his revelation and was ridiculed. The man defended his revelation with arguments he had used with the tree, but was mocked. The students tore apart his revelation, citing happenings that the man had never known of. The man was rebuked and laughed at and he walked away downcast.

When the man at last returned to the tree, his manner was normal as if nothing of consequence had happened outside. The tree, being very curious about what happened, asked the man about the outside world.

The man answered, "We have saved their world and all is well because of us." When the tree heard this, he was overjoyed and congratulated the man. The man, smiling faintly, asked, "What is the answer to the question of life?"

Even now you may stumble upon a man in a chair of roots talking animatedly with a tree on life, the universe and everything, but the subject of the outside world never comes up.

CHAPTER 6

BETWEEN PAST AND FUTURE**

**A title by Hannah Arendt

155

BETWEEN PAST AND...

...What are the experiences of girls coming of age in a culture that contains the need for Women's Studies?....Adolescence poses problems of connection...in Western culture, and girls are tempted or encouraged to solve these problems by excluding themselves or excluding others—that is, by being a good woman, or by being selfish....Yet the problem girls face in adolescence is also a problem in the world at this time: the need to find ways of making connection in the face of difference.

—*Carol Gilligan, Making Connections*

Five months before my fifteenth birthday, I asked, "Mommy?"

"*What is it?*" she responded in Chinese.

"Gene Conway is on the phone," I informed her in English.

"*Jean? Which girlfriend is that?*" She asked in Chinese.

"Not 'Jean,' Eugene. He's a boy I met at Jan's party last night."

Mentioning Jan's name in a sentence, English or Chinese, was always helpful. I needed to do something reassuring, to counter the effect of saying the word "boy" without any other qualifiers like "Uncle So-and-So's son," or "Little" (as in minuscule).

"*Oh*," she replied. In any language, her tone expressed a fervent hope for a different end to the conversation than the one anticipated. And the dread of imminent disappointment.

"He wants to know if I can go to the movies next Saturday."

"*Jan too?*"

"Not really. But maybe Jan will be there."

"*Do you want me to drive you?*"

"Not really. We can walk."

"*So you'll be back before dinner.*"

"Not really. He asked me to go to the evening show."

"*You're going to walk in the dark?*"

"Don't worry, Mommy, we'll go the short route."

"*From Cedar Lane?*"

She knew, short or long, it would take half an hour.

"I've done it a hundred times, we won't get lost. It's okay then? He's still on the phone, waiting."

This too was helpful. Making people wait unnecessarily was rude. Making them wait so we could discuss the matter would indicate a lack of unanimous agreement—not the family image we're supposed to project.

"*Hao*." Since this means "good" or "fine," the exaggeration served as a directive as well as permission.

"*Wo chu gaosu ta.*" Using Chinese to tell her that I would go and tell him, I signaled my understanding of her conditional consent, and then underscored it by going back up the stairs to the phone in her room at an unusually dignified pace despite my fear that Gene might have grown weary, waiting for us to build a canal between cultural and generational oceans.

Because I *speak* Chinese but *think* in English, my bilingual experience doesn't afford me as much leeway in which to navigate as those who can speak and think in both languages. Sometimes I can make up for the lack by being mindful of the terrain beneath the surface of people's words but, other times, just saying it is the problem. I remember going to bed the night I realized that, one day, I'd have blond hair and blue eyes. If I was good. Assuming the position of all those angelic (fair-haired and fair-skinned) little girls I'd seen on Christmas cards, I kneeled, hands folded, head bowed, and prayed.

Now I lay me down to sleep.

I pray the Lord my soul to keep.

Then, afraid my mother might come in and find me in such a compromising position, I got into bed and figured it couldn't make that much difference if I finished up prone as long as I signaled my intention with folded hands.

If I should die before I wake,

I pray the Lord my soul to take.

As soon as I spoke the words I got really nervous. There I was, on my back, arms across my chest, like Bela Lugosi in his Dracula coffin. God may know it all and stick to His plan no matter what, but deities can get ideas they hadn't thought of. This could be another "Me too, me too!" situation. So I took back the first part right away, adding enough of an addendum to clarify any remaining confusion, but not so much that they might think about it too much, and finished up on my stomach,

And bless Mommy, Daddy, Bette and SanSan. And Miss

Diamondis (she's my teacher)

Not sure if an incantation worked if only half of it was said out loud, I did know that, in any system, "being good" meant I was the sort of person who didn't just think of herself too directly.

Being aware of these nuances can lead to hypersensitivity but it has also helped me steer through some pretty tricky waters. It may be that my parents would have allowed me to go on a date without all that verbal maneuvering. On the other hand, I do think the back-and-forth did help a little in reassuring my mother. It certainly made me feel better about subjecting them to what sends most parents, Chinese or American, directly through the roof: dating. Nine years later, I know it made a difference with my future mother-in law. At the prospect of her son and me driving from their house in Iowa City to mine in New Jersey, she, despite her Stiff Upper Lip tradition, asked/told me, "You *are* going to drive straight through, aren't you?"

Without the slightest upward movement of my lips, I replied, "Oh no. It's a thousand miles. My mother made me promise we'd only drive in daylight. Otherwise she'd be worrying the whole time about us being out in the dark."

"Oh."

I would have liked to have given her more, to explain that my mother was not totally daft in demanding that we stop at a motel. But I had to balance her need against what was expected of me as a representative of the Bao family. My mother's seeming naïveté came from her reluctance to give any outward indication that the unacceptable would occur to her and therefore to me or the deities. (Chinese gods don't read minds either.) Since the operating premise was that a member of her family was incapable of ever considering actions associated with people of lesser moral fiber, whatever she and I said had to jibe with that premise. To explain all of this to the folks in Iowa would have undermined her logic and the reason why she always acted as if I could be trusted. It's also why, when we arrived at my house, I made no mention that the trip had indeed gone as both mothers hoped. But I did happen to leave the two receipts for the two rooms sticking halfway out of my purse—that just happened to be lying on the kitchen table (as she had once left the diary that came with a little key lying open in my dresser drawer).

This may have been blatant, even unnecessary, but the leeway I gain in being bilingual also puts me in deeper waters because I only sort of speak Chinese. And I only started to think in English when I was about nine. The gap between what I've done and what I remember doing, between what I say and understand, and what my audience hears and intends, means that, no matter how often I've navigated the route, there's a likelihood of finding myself in a fjord created by the linguistic separation, an opportunity to lose and find myself, as well as those who travel with me.

Waiters get the brunt of it. When my tongue wanders off to the wrong Chinese place, "soup ladle" becomes "toilet paper." Making just the right tone in Mandarin is equally important and difficult—trying to get "rabbit," my unreliable voice box produces "vomit" or "map." Ordering "duck," I ask the waiter for "teeth;" intending to "buy," I "sell." And the most difficult: if I want "ten" anything, I get "shit." I get away with a lot because people look at my face and hear what they expect.

If a conversation ranges beyond the limits of the vocabulary I carried from my childhood, I go into my Treasure Hunter Mode. Like a pilot trying to locate a sunken ship using only historical records and unreliable instruments, I take the words that I recognize and use them as markers to align my position with the original. Once in the vicinity, I activate my sonar for the yet unknown. As the conversation proceeds, I quickly assess each sounding. Does it indicate proximity to the meaning I've given the markers? Sometimes I can confirm my guess by diving in with what I think is an appropriate comment.

I recall one family discussion about some poor man in China who was incarcerated because his left hand was defective. People from all nations can be cruel to those who are physically different. But prison?! Outraged, I interjected my condemnation. With a collective sigh and the tolerance they would give any Martian who took a wrong turn and steered for the Norwegian Sea instead of Andromeda, they explained that the man's crime was *political.* He had been punished by the Maoists for being insufficiently "leftist."

Oh well. The mental gymnastics I performed during all those talks around the kitchen table was good training for other situations:
- I can put together jigsaw puzzles without bothering to look at the picture;
- I can read "God is the greatest most high on a pedestal" and urge my student to reconsider her philosophical interpretation of St. Anselm as well as take no offense when 25% of one class, opting to write about "mercy killing," entitled their papers "Youth in Asia"; and
- I can make do with no early childhood of my own.

For the memories I gathered when I thought in Chinese are inaccessible to me. They're in Mandarin. But I remember in English. Although

I speak my childhood Chinese "directly" without having to translate from the English as I do with my school-learned French, it's been more than fifty years since I thought or remembered or dreamt in my native tongue. Without vivid experiences to recall, what there was of me before my diary of thoughts commences is less clear than what I could deduce about the not-too-dexterous man in prison. The few details I have are the biographical bits mentioned by my parents and the snapshots from their sparse collection of photographs. Coming from a culture that didn't presume its children to be interesting *per se*, I considered it self-centered to be too curious about events that could have no relevance in the family history. As children, we were more important as worthy receptacles for our elders' wisdom than we were as movers and shakers in our young and, therefore, un-noteworthy world. With my younger sister still in China and my older one summing up those years with only one word, "crybaby, " my link to my past is only through a few childhood friends who knew me when I was still forming memories in Chinese. Recently talking with one from fourth grade, Bonnie puts me in the peculiar position of hearing someone tell me what I once told her about being in China so I can know third-hand what she knows second-hand about my first-hand experience.

Sometimes I felt justified to turn attention to myself if I needed a missing link to satisfy some bureaucratic inquiry like "Is my birthday figured by the American or Chinese calendar?" If my parent answered with an anecdote, I might have a chance to ask for more before their focus shifted away or they stopped simply because they thought I already knew by virtue of some inborn knowledge. I never wanted to admit that my genetic memory was not as specific as I would have liked. On the other hand, appearing in my consciousness, almost full-grown, has not been a matter of deprivation so much as curiosity. Beginning with the earliest available, my 1946 passport picture, I can only "remember" what someone else once saw through a camera lens. These secondhand views into my past sporadically chronicle my transplantation from China until, around nine, the first-hand images start to outnumber the ones in the family album.

These gaps may have kept me from a complete map of my past, but the treasures and traumas were never "lost." They just weren't available for personal examination. Connected to the distant past through family and common sense, I could still claim them as mine.

Many who arrived in this country when they were very young, are unable to fully share in the reminiscences of the "old country." Feeling left out of the family circle, they sometimes compensate for their lack of memory by believing and acting as if there's nothing worth remembering. I wasn't always a full participant—hearing more bare "facts" than family stories—but I never felt the need to reject in self-defense. It's usually been sufficient that *someone* in the family remembered my early youth. It didn't *have* to be me in particular. Besides, reasoning as Aristotle did in his proof of the Unmoved Mover, I've been assured that, since I'm an adult, I must have had a childhood.

Between the past I partially had and the future I wanted fully was that first summer after my high school graduation. Kids seemed to disappear behind veils, uniforms, dressing room doors, and bandages, then reappear with a wedding band or military haircut, a more sophisticated wardrobe or a simpler nose. If they then met up with an old classmate, the difference in their appearance or status didn't generate the kind of excitement or gossip that the change would have once caused between Phys Ed and Biology classes. Yet, like that moment just before we step in front of the mirror, there is expectation and dread.

"Well, what do you think?"

"I'm not sure. The color's a little weird. Maybe it's the pattern—too busy. It sure is sleek. You almost have a waist."

"Forget the material, this is just the prototype—the one the tailor makes from my measurements. It's not meant to be worn so they use cheap cotton. I try this on and then send it back to Hong Kong with instructions for adjustments. Then they make the real one out of silk."

"What a lot of trouble for a dress."

"It's not just 'a dress.' It's my first. After they make my pattern, they file it. Then, any time I want another one, we send a color sample and tell them if we want it plain or fancy, with trimming or frogs. Look at this."

"They made that, too?"

"Yeah. The slip has to be perfect so the slits line up with the dress."

"Your mother is doing this? I mean, she thinks it's okay for you to go out with your legs showing like that?"

"She wears them. Grandmothers wear them. Legs are ok. Breasts aren't except if you're nursing."

Holding out a patch of red that I had snipped out of a magazine,

"What do you think about this shade?"

"Fine. I guess. You'll look...well, you'll look...so *Chinese*."

She was right. I was going to college and somehow I needed, wanted, to be more myself—though what kind of "Chinese" was not at all clear. Then and since then, I could look at myself in the mirror and, half the times, see what Karen or others saw. Other times, I could look and see only the readiness but none of the details.

We were all trying to see ourselves through different eyes, by different standards. And the expectation, relief, confusion, and resignation at what we thought would be reflected back was momentous. We were no longer children and we wondered if The Real World of college, labor, boot camp, whatever, would notice. And if they did, could we live with it?

Most evenings that summer I sewed after work; one Chinese dress wouldn't be enough for college life. I had set up operations in the basement. My father had renovated it and that allowed me to make a mess without disrupting my parents' need for orderliness, and to stay up long after they went to sleep. It wasn't large, but it did have a partitioned area that contained a toilet, sink and small mirror. Before that second bathroom had been installed, I couldn't function too independently of their schedule because the first and then only one was right next to their bedroom. Putting in the light fixture downstairs had almost cost my father his sight in one eye. Holding the screwdriver above his head, it had slipped, and just missed the cornea. But telling visitors about the near tragedy allowed him to call attention to his handiwork without coming right out and boasting it was a one-person job. (Chinese gods can get jealous so, if you've got to call attention to yourself, it's safer to do it on a "good news, bad news" basis like "knocking on wood." That way, they'll think twice about taking what you've got because their fortunes can take a turn for the worse too. And if you also give them the credit for the situation not turning out worse, that's even better because they're not above flattery either.)

After dinner and the dishes, I would sit at the card table, turn on the TV for company, and create fashions that I thought would be appropriate for every eventuality that a college could offer. Between steps I would eat, sometimes ingesting pounds of fruit. I never tried anything on until it was done. Mainly because I didn't need to—I had been making my own clothes ever since I put my doll away forever. Besides being cheaper, it was more direct, since anything off a store rack had to be shortened anyway.

The night before I was to leave for Boston, I was frantically finishing a project. The day before had been my last commute so I spent the time packing the car with everything but the last-minute items, including the matching skirt and vest, still in pieces. By 3:00 a.m., the basket was full of scraps and peach pits. The television flickered black-and-white scenes of supernatural gore. I had already seen most of the week-long series of horror movies and didn't need to look up to know what was going on. I was too exhausted and excited to miss getting the "good night's sleep" that my mother had recommended before retiring herself. She knew I was working on adrenaline but felt compelled to give me the good advice even though there wasn't a chance in hell I would stop until everything on my list had been checked off.

When I bit off the last piece of thread to try it all on, I almost decided to wait until the morning, when it would be cooler and the wool less stifling. But the need to see what I had done—if only in that small mirror over the sink—overcame my reluctance to aggravate the humidity of a hot summer night. Undressing and dressing, I went into the bathroom and tried to stand away from the material as I turned on the light. In the background, I could hear a wounded werewolf howl the pain of his final transformation. Then, in front of me, I saw what was going on behind me. My face was bright red, distorted with swellings. My lips were gorged with blood. The scream began from the surprise, and then ended with the realization that this is what they would see on my first day at the University.

I tried to wash away the effect of eating too many peaches, too much residual spray. When that didn't work, I went quietly to my room, afraid my parents would suddenly step out of their room and be startled by the grotesque results of an allergic reaction. I crawled into bed and waited for any telltale noise. Hearing something, I whispered , hopeful, "Mommy? Daddy? Are you up?" They weren't. Too old to do something about my fears, I closed my eyes, resigned to being alone with the image that crept up from the basement. I lay in the dark, unable to stop a parade of strangers, each one finding me more horrifying, with no intention of getting past first impressions. And just when my mind would start to fog over with sleep, the cuckoo clock would detonate the silence with the fact that another hour had passed. Then, again alert, I distracted myself with plots to murder the always cheerful, brightly colored wooden souvenir which my father had brought home from Germany. But my cartoon-like vision of the persistent bird, hanging from the end of its broken spring, with "stars" for eyes, would eventually give way to more nightmare visions—me in my beautiful red silk Chinese dress with a face even my mother couldn't love.

I must have slept because it was suddenly light. It took a few seconds to remember that I had a problem. I tried to tell, by touch alone, if I still had one. Finally, closing in on the mirror above the dresser, I focused on the mild remnants of the night before. By the time we crossed the Massachusetts border, my face was normal. At least to me.

Several weeks later, I tried to reproduce that blood-curdling scream at the first try-out of the campus season. It was the most difficult part of the script. After several calls to return and read, my confidence was intensifying along with my screams. Much shorter than my only remaining rival, I emphasized the difference by wearing the flattest of shoes. Not usually pleased to be only five feet tall, I deliberately paraded my diminutive stature near those who had already been chosen for the adult parts. And when, after the final call-back, the Director asked if I would feel comfortable playing the role, I started to preen myself to be the first, maybe second, frosh ever to win a leading role at my college's famous Arena Theater. Trying not to sound too excited, I responded with a "Yes," buttressed by all the reasons why I could identify with the feelings of the young heroine.

And then the Director asked, in a voice so gentle that it belied the force of his revelation, "But do you think that a Chinese can play the role of a Jew from Amsterdam?"

Or maybe he said, "...*should* play...."

Until that moment, it never occurred to me that my Asian features were factors on the stage, the one form of make-believe I knew how to get involved in. Yes, my parents would constantly remind me that I was the local representative of all the Chinese who ever existed, but this responsibility didn't mean I couldn't do everything else that any upstanding American could do. A member of the Playcrafters in high school, I had been cast as an Austrian princess as well as a pre-teen from Dixie. That stage, and the town and time which created it, somehow made it possible for me to believe, without aforethought, that I should try out for *The Diary of Anne Frank*. After all, if Loretta Young could be Chinese on the silver screen, why couldn't I be Anna? I doubt if even knowing then what I know now—that Hollywood had "rules" about such matters, that a white man could only kiss a "Chinese" woman in the movies if she wasn't really Chinese—would have changed my attitude.

While I was preparing for college and the '60s, the precursors of events to come occurred against such friendly backdrops that their revolutionary character was not starkly apparent. When in 1959, we voted in a female to head the Student Council, President Ginny holding the gavel wasn't so alarming because she also twirled the Head Majorette's baton. When Jon made a big deal about unilateral disarmament and refused to sit under his desk while the rest of us scrambled under ours, never wondering how a piece of wood would protect us against a nuclear attack, he, on weekends, wore a football helmet across goal lines while Wesley, the first Negro to be a class officer, cheered. When my friend and I gained admission to the "shop" class after little more than a "Why?" and a "Why not?", anyone who cringed at the unprecedented sight of girls using machinery were comforted by the sound of our giggling over the screech of the jig saw. People had known me for years. I was not "exceptional," let alone a challenge to assumptions. There was only me so, quite naturally, I had been a typical "banana": yellow on the outside, white on the inside. It was only when I left town that my inside realized it had a lot to learn about being Chinese on the outside to people who didn't know me and who rarely saw the other 279,999 Asians living in America at that time.

Once in college, the pace of my learning increased, but the lessons were rarely anticipated, either on-stage or off. Even before I arrived on campus, I was certain that the college had made a mistake when I saw that my room was to be shared with a Chinese from Teaneck's neighboring town. I wrote to the admissions office that, indeed, I wished to benefit from the policy described in the handbook, that stated something like:

> Dormitory assignments are made with the view that people of different backgrounds, from diverse places, can live with, and learn from, each other.

The school's response that there had been no error didn't keep me from bubbling to Adee, the first Black I knew from south of the Mason-Dixon (and my future roommate), "Gee, you're so lucky to have a single. How did you manage it?!" And when she looked at me as if I were a rare but probably harmless specimen that somehow survived extinction despite segregation and lynching, my embarrassment didn't make me think any less of myself for being so dense.

Although The Diary's director did teach me that the face of terror had to be disguised in something less universal than a scream, and the Admissions Office was the catalyst for my feeling a new kind of camaraderie when "we" later discovered that the one person of color who got white roommates had neglected to send a picture with her application, my racial naïveté immunized me against the effects of too much bile. So resistant was my capacity to be surprised—and pleased, and hurt—that these doses of reality were not potent enough to change my basic chemistry, my legacy of being from a secure and caring family, my belief in the American Dream. The moments when what I saw happening didn't align with what I expected ought to happen, I blamed no one in general. In those days, I, like most Chinese immigrants, was still a Republican.

While being "in the know" made me feel sophisticated, it didn't make me an addict, craving the aloof high of cynicism. What these shots from the "real world" did do was help me build up a tolerance for repeat performances so that, by the time I outgrew the protection of my childhood innocence, I had developed another antidote to getting "my fill." For no matter how often one has "seen it all before," one can learn to see the old moves as new plays, with no act that can't be differently reviewed, with no scene that can't be altered. Like the one that took place just before Thanksgiving during that first year away from home.

Dragging into the dormitory, I had been exhausted by fear of my own teammates. Their pre-feminist approach to sports had transformed field hockey into a jousting match without benefit of armor. Or insulation. Or rules. In outfits more suited for a beauty pageant, they had charged and hacked without regard to goal or sides. Bruised and sweaty but cutely attired, I was informed by the receptionist that I had callers. Looking toward the sitting area, I saw five young Chinese men, slouched in lounging poses. As I approached, they made no move except with their eyes.

"Hi."

"Hello. I'm Cathy Bao."

"Fine, let's go."

"Go? Where?"

"Out."

"Out?"

"With us."

"Do I know you?"

"No, but we know you." And they waved a booklet at me. Flipping through, I saw a listing, some elaborated with pictures. All female, all Chinese, all attending schools in the greater Boston area.

Finally comprehending, I quietly explained that I was in the middle of a class day. That I had made no plans to go out, let alone with people I didn't expect or know. That being racially similar was no good reason for me to change how I conducted my social life. And then, for good measure, I informed them that the only reason I would change my mind was if they had been sent by my Venerable Parents. (Or—but I didn't say this—if their manners hadn't been so atrocious.) They slid off the couches and left to pass the word that I was, yuck, totally westernized and should henceforth be omitted from the booklet.

Looking at *Kwei-yee*, but discovering "Cathy," they were my introduction to the Chinese who viewed me with dissatisfaction and dismissal. I was one of "those" Chinese who was no longer "Chinese." I was not to their taste but then, initially, neither were they to mine. By the time I graduated from college, omission from their booklet was less a triumph of my American individuality than a failure to be inclusive. Had we been less quick to say "good riddance," to each other, we might have pooled our different perspectives and become better prepared for our futures, or those of our children. But our lack of mutual admiration was how I began to learn about myself and them, about how much I had oversimplified the matter of identity.

Of course it didn't help that many Caucasians expecting "Suzie Wong" or the "Flower Drum" girl, a daughter of Fu Manchu or Charlie Chan but meeting me instead were often as disappointed and confused as the Chinese. What did help was becoming an Older Sister. In 1962, *SanSan*—the baby I couldn't remember but never forgot—appeared from behind the Bamboo Curtain. Slowly at first, but then in flesh and blood, she got out because the communist bureaucracy couldn't resist my mother's fluttering hands and backbone of steel any more than those salesmen. Ten years before Nixon went to the People's Republic of China, and twenty-three years before Bette and Winston took up residence at the U.S. embassy in Beijing as "Ambassador and Madame Lord," my mother, with little more than an idea and airfare, went to Hong Kong and willed her daughter out. Cutting through all the reasons why it couldn't be done, she had parted the sea of Red tape with the strength of her endurance and overcame the sixteen years that had passed since the five of us had cried and laughed as one.

We spent *SanSan's* first days in America at the kitchen table, talking our lives together. We overwhelmed the long separation with stories, and the stranded intimacy with tears. And then I had to leave, to go back to school and be a college junior. I took with me only the momentous occasion of having a second sister but none of the daily reality. I was now an older sister but I had no homework or shopping trips to practice the role, no good advice for someone who had been starving while I was pouting over a birthday cake or too many peaches, no wisdom to understand that, when she looked at the finger bowl—juicy lemon aside clear water—she saw food, not an amenity. With barely enough Chinese to comprehend the magnitude of our difference, I spent those two days hating myself as much as the ideology that had made her go to bed hungry. Unable to express my anguish for her, I silently pledged to be for her always, a sister—not limited to being a Confucian "elder" or American "sibling," but someone who would relate to whoever she turned out to be after she learned English and could tell me.

Meanwhile, knowing what it had been like for her in China changed my own past; and knowing she was now in New Jersey did nothing and everything to change my future—more so when I realized that, legally, she and I were equally "alien." Until then, I, like Adee, believed we could do anything, whatever the outcome of the Civil Rights movement. Then I met the hobgoblin and found out otherwise. I had come to this country at the age of four but was still an alien. Until I was twenty, my status—or lack of it—had made no practical difference except that the Bendix Corporation couldn't hire me as a summer replacement, something about not having clearance. It didn't mean much to me. I thought all they did was manufacture washing machines. Right after that, just before I left for college, my father sat me down and told me the immigrant's facts of life, if I decided to become one. Up until then, I had no passport or visa of my own but was a dependent on my father's. Since he was a representative of the Republic of China at the International Sugar Council of the United Nations as well as the Vice President of the Taiwan Sugar Corporation, he was a foreign government official and, therefore, not an "immigrant" either. In other words,[6] we were in America only because "our" government renewed his year-to-year employment contract. By the

time I understood this, none of us considered transfer back to the East
a real possibility. Nevertheless, if I wanted to *stay* in this country on
my own, there were five alternatives:
- add my name to the end of a list of thousands who awaited
  immigrant status at the rate of 105 "Chinese" per year as determined by "race," not nationality;
- continue as an unmarried dependent of a foreign government
  official and "exempt" from the quota (as well as citizenship);
- marry a citizen;
- get a Special Bill of Congress passed; or
- obtain sponsorship by some institution that would attest to my
  being "necessary for the national security and defense of the
  country" like a medical researcher or rocket scientist might be.

It was my father's considered opinion that the last option was my best
bet, the one most within my control, despite the fact that I had failed
half my Chemistry tests and never got the hang of going from the two
dimensions of plane geometry to the three of trig. However, just
because one knows about "the birds and bees," doesn't mean one is
motivated to act responsibly. In college, I majored in History and
Government, and took no more science than what was required to
graduate. For, in the end, it wasn't my distaste for dissecting live animals (except the oyster, which I ate) that prevented me from trying to
be a pre-med major, or my aversion to the slide rule that kept me from
imagining a life as an astronaut, it was my utter familiarity with the
Declaration of Independence, the Bill of Rights, and the Emancipation
Proclamation, and my lack of identification with the Chinese
Exclusion Act or the McCarran-Walter Immigration and Nationality
Act.

For three years of college, my visa number was less significant to
me than "313," the room I shared with Adee in Hodgdon Hall. It was
her exclusion as a Black, not mine as an alien, that was more an issue
in my politically awakening mind.

Then I entered the Immigration and Naturalization Service building in Boston.

[6] When the People's Republic of China on "the Mainland" was internationally recognized in 1971 as "China," Taiwan needed my father to have the mobility that U.S. citizenship would afford, so he became naturalized. More than twenty years after that,
when an estate lawyer tried to show him how much more in estate taxes could be
saved, my father replied, "No. This country has been very good to my family."

I went in to seek information about joining Operation Crossroads Africa, a precursor to the Peace Corps. Its head, Dr. James H. Robinson had spoken to us in the school chapel. More accurately, he berated and inspired, dared and cajoled. He convinced me in a way Pastor couldn't. His challenge had to do with learning about sharing ourselves, not teaching "the truth."

Unsure what kind of a passport I should ask for, I decided to find out in person rather than telephone the INS. In the waiting room, during the two hours it took for my number to be called, I wondered if Dr. Robinson would assign me to an English-speaking area, or some place like Niger. If that happened, I hoped my French was not as bad as my professor thought it was. To pass the time, I practiced translating the bits of conversation I heard emerge from the low-level muttering that pervaded the air. Most of the voices were homogenized into indistinguishable sounds, so I was not overwhelmed with complex sentences. Finally, it was my turn. As I went up to the counter, I quickly reviewed the details of my request.

"Hello. My name is...."

Without bothering to look up, she interrupted, "What's your classification?"

"Excuse me?"

"What's your classification? Come on, come on, I don't have all day."

"A-2."

"Go to Room ___."

"Is that where I can get...."

"Room ___. All A-2s go there."

Locating the room, a large space partitioned into offices, each containing a desk and an I.N.S. official, I took a seat along the row of chairs near the door. Periodically, an officer would approach the one closest to the entryway, point at the occupant, and beckon the person to follow. This done, the rest of us would shift one chair toward the head of the line. Except for the same low level white noise in the background, there were no distinct sounds to break up the wall-to-wall tension evident in everyone's face, but mine. I was expectant but not worried. As far as I was concerned, the whole set-up reminded me of the Department of Motor Vehicles. Within half an hour, I was designated.

Seated in the cubby, he began as the other had, "What's your classification?"

"A-2."

"Let me see."

"Excuse me, sir?"

"Let me see your visa."

"I'm sorry. I don't have it."

"You don't have your identification papers?"

"No, sir. I don't carry them around. No one does. I mean, we might lose them. My father keeps our visa in the safe deposit box. At the bank. At home. In Teaneck. That's in New Jersey."

"How do I know that?"

"Excuse me?"

"How do I know what you say is true?"

Going into my purse, I took out my wallet and, after flipping through a dozen or more plastic inserts jammed with pictures of the family and shots of friends being silly in a Photo Booth, I found my driver's license. Laying it before him, I said, "See? That's me—Cathy Bao."

"Anybody can get a fake license." This he said as a matter of fact.

He showed no emotion of any kind. He barely looked at me. And the anxiety started to show in my voice and in my fumbling for some further verification of who I was.

"Here. How about this? It's my college i.d. card. I'm a junior."

"So?"

"You could call them."

"That wouldn't help your situation."

"You could call my father. I've got his number. He works for the Republic of China. That's why I'm an A-2, a dependent of a foreign government official."

"Look, Missy, without papers, you're nothing as far as I'm concerned. Put that stuff away. It's no good here."

"But it's all I have. I'm sorry about the visa. But I've never needed it before. At least not since 1946. I've been in this country since then, since I was four. I just came here to find out how I can go on Operation Crossroads Africa. Have you heard of it? It's like a student exchange program."

"The only place I'm interested in finding out about is your Port of Origin."

"What do you mean? *China*?!"

The pressure of being grilled with insinuations from a nightmare, of being a complete unknown, misunderstood, was too much. I started to cry. He was going to send me away—away from *Meiguo*, this "beautiful country" and back to *Da Lu*, "The Mainland," a place so foreign, I couldn't imagine me there.

Ignoring my tears, he picked up the phone. I became frantic to stop whatever next step he had in mind. Almost demanding, I asked, "What are you doing?"

Nonchalantly he said, "I've got to call upstairs to find out where to send you."

"'*Send* me?"

"Yes. We deport illegals," he responded with a bit of a grin.

He was enjoying himself. He had reduced me to a state of abject helplessness, and he thought it was funny. His half smile was the catalyst.

"No!"

Startled by the sound of a word he hadn't expected to hear, he looked at me, then lowered the phone back into its cradle as I lifted myself atop the high horse that seemed always to appear at my side at times like this.

"I came to you because I love this country. Because I hoped you would help me represent it with honor and grace. What you have just tried to do to me destroys what America stands for. You *knew* I was an innocent."

Without waiting for an answer, I walked out, self-righteous and vulnerable. He didn't stop me.

By the time I got off the M.T.A. at school, I was calm. I didn't go to Africa. I did go into Philosophy. My choice was not taking me any closer to being "necessary for the national security and defense of the country," but it would take me into a world of ideas so universal, that it had no legal boundaries, no prerequisites except methodical thinking—my specialty.

By the time I received my college degree, I had set my sights on doing graduate work in California, home to thousands of Chinese-Americans. There, I would be among those with backgrounds similar to my own, and with those accustomed to the different. There, I was sure the atmosphere would be less divisive for its greater diversity, the misalignments less noticeable.

To afford the trip and tuition, I took on four jobs. Among them was being a waitress in a Cantonese restaurant near my alma mater.

"How are you?"

"Dirty. Chicken."

That constituted 95% of my Cantonese. The owners, a family of recent immigrants, good-naturedly ribbed me about being so educated in all matters except my native tongues. The clientele, happily for me, usually ordered *Chop Suey*, *Chow Mein* or *Egg Foo Young*. If customers were hungry for *Moo Goo Gai Pan*, I could advise them that *gai* was "chicken." If they wanted to know about the *moo*, *goo*, or *pan*, I shrugged a "Your guess is as good as mine."

If patrons were former teachers, they glossed over their embarrassment in not recognizing me by inquiring about my future. I soon learned it was easier if I pretended not to see them, to be just another Chinese waitress in a Chinese restaurant, indistinguishable from the others without the distinction of an academic robe. I didn't get upset or think they were stupid or "racists" because, by then, I had realized it takes time to think, to make the foreign familiar. That lesson was learned within a year of *SanSan*'s arrival. Bette was getting married, and we were two of her four bridesmaids. However, there were eight ushers. The minister choreographed the recessional so that we four would each be escorted by one while the rest stood by, to follow after all the couples were paced uniformly down the aisle. The rehearsal took twice as long as usual because *SanSan* kept taking the wrong arm. As far as she could tell, each was attached to someone who looked just like the others. We cited all sorts of differences: eyeglasses, medium height, brown hair, brown eyes. None of it registered as sufficiently relevant to insure an orderly closing of the ceremonies. Not wishing to take any chances, we solved the identification problem by marking her escort with a red, instead of a white, *boutonnière*. By setting her sights on lapels instead of faces, she could find the right flower every time. Yes, to her White Folks all looked alike. Just as Asian and Black people can. Or men's suits and birds. Busy getting from the ABCs to college in less than three years, she hadn't had much opportunity to carefully look at a lot of samples and "see" the differences that mattered in America. Anyway, her difficulty has always been one good reason for me to be tolerant of my own and other's inexperience with certain human details.

Still, there are those who never try. At the restaurant, if customers looked up at all, they usually shouted their order in Broken English. That my diction was unaccented and my hearing normal were irrelevant for, despite what they heard from me, they believed I didn't speak English at the same time they believed I could understand it if they spoke slowly and loudly enough. One night, a group of psychology professors from Harvard gathered at the restaurant to celebrate some departmental victory. The task of ordering devolved quite naturally on the one female whose particular brand of leadership was by fiat. Seated next to her was her husband, made smaller and quieter than he already was by his role as the one outsider at the table of academics. She "strongly suggested" the best dishes to her colleagues and boomed and gesticulated instructions at me. She displayed her savvy by asking many "insider" questions about the menu, but heard none of my responses. Her husband seemed to shrink with each dish, a matter of self-protection lest his wife's formidable arm or voice swiped in his direction. His quick reflexes showed that he was inured to being treated this way, to being perceived as extraneous, inconsequential. I knew the feeling well.

He remained silent while I quiescently wrote down her final selections, delivered it to the kitchen, served the tea and, soon thereafter, the soup. Long finished with their first course, I announced to the table, by addressing her, "I apologize for the delay in serving the rest of your meal, but one of the cooks is ill and, with the Saturday crowd, the kitchen is like Bedlam."

She heard the last word and, startled by its sound coming from someone who couldn't possibly know that word (having just gotten off the boat from China), looked and said, "Bedlam?"

Leaning toward her for the first time, the husband, barely able to suppress a grin, quietly but firmly "helped" his noisome wife, "Yes, dear, 'Bed-lam.' I'm sure you know what that means."

She spat out, "Well, of course I do!" Turning her back to him and her face to me, she pulled a smile from her teeth that warned me to act as if the background clatter was the only reason why she had not heard me clearly and why I couldn't have heard her husband's remark.

"You're a student?"

"Yes." And then obliged her with a short conversation that demonstrated to her colleagues how perceptive and sensitive she was to connect me with the university. Maybe my ability to swallow the quick retort started with the hope that the Bedlam Woman was indeed more perceptive and sensitive after that dinner. That she was less grudging because she was not more embarrassed. That in her desire to avoid further interjection by her husband, she already had good reason to think twice and, therefore, I didn't need to add another. Since that night, being obliging often seems the better way to make a point.

By the end of the summer and dozens more like her, I was counting on the west coast. But soon after arriving in California, I realized that I had miscalculated the distance between where my new school was and where the Chinese were. I was 65 miles too far east of Los Angeles and 500 miles too far south of San Francisco. With a rueful smile to the geography teacher I had put down with a "Boring," I settled in until that time when I could make a move.

Meanwhile, I found out that my destination did boast the largest settlement of ex-China Missionaries in North America. With radar accuracy, they zeroed in. I was inundated with invitations from retirees starved for reminders of their ministry in Asia. Eventually, these petered out as word got around that I couldn't remember a thing about China and that their Mandarin was better than mine. The discomfort of not understanding so much of what they were saying to me in my native language goaded me in a way that imprecise communication with family never did. I made a resolution: I would learn how to write Chinese. This was one of my less brilliant decisions. With a vocabulary of a seven-year old, I should have concentrated on fine-tuning my ear for new words and bringing my conversation skills up to the pre-teen level.

Antidisestablishmentarianism...Amo, Amas, Amat...J'entre dans la salle de classe...Eins, zwei, drei. These could all be decoded. I could read any dictionary as long it was in alphabetical order. But Chinese doesn't come that way. Their written counterparts are symbols that are used to represent many spoken Asian languages. Like colors or gestures, seeing them brings no particular word to mind, they can't be "sounded out." Unable to decipher the hieroglyphs and connect them to the words I know, my Chinese is defined only by what I knew before I started to think in English. My mind attempts the richness of a Shakespearean play but my voice box comes out with nursery rhymes. As I got older, the discrepancy between what I could understand in English and what I could express in Mandarin became more pronounced. The more my education qualified me to say and hear words about the complex and deep in the classroom, the more deaf, mute, and shallow-sounding I was at home. The more educated my peers became, the less adequately I could respond when they asked, "How do you say '___' in Chinese?"

I remember dreams in which I "speak" English, Latin, French, German. I recollect none that are in Chinese. Although the brain experts now tell me that the benefit of being bilingual during early childhood lasts into adulthood even when the person can't remember, at the time I felt linguistically stunted and came to think of Chinese characters as the medicinal recipe for my symptoms. The Politically Correct may have thrown out the "melting pot," and replaced it with "tossed salad and dressing" or "smorgasbord" but, in their recommendations for society's diet, the menus never explain how we individual ingredients are to be grown and prepared. Somehow, writing the words would magically infuse my tongue with its native language and I would become more palatable. I envisioned the Scholastics of both traditions looking kindly upon my reverence for the written word and, therefore, helping me partake more fully of the feast that moved between East and West. That I could only hope to write the words of a child was inconsequential. This was a matter of *sense*, not sense.

Like the Straw Man in *The Wizard of Oz*, I was willing to believe that a "diploma," a piece of paper with writing, would qualify me to be who I was. Like the Witch, I was vulnerable to being watered down by life in the United States, recognizable only by the limp external trappings. The puddle underneath, a concoction of jasmine tea and cola, was not what people like the missionaries expected. Nor what I knew how to serve. Obviously, I had to write my own cookbook. In Chinese.

I made an appointment with the Chinese calligraphy professor. Stumbling over words and clay feet as if in the presence of the Yellow Emperor, I explained how I got to be so ignorant of my own language and in my most pardon-this-worthless-self mode asked, "Would you please help me. I need someone to check the strokes once a month lest I learn incorrectly."

He scrutinized me. I got smaller. He rose. I was an insect. He shook an accusatory finger at me and castigated me, "You are a disgrace."

I looked disgraced.

"You are shameful."

I looked ashamed.

"You are a dishonor to all Chinese."

"Now, hold it right there, Buster," I mentally gruffed the words in my best John-Wayne-Cowboy-Mode "You just went too far." Aloud, I

quietly reminded him that I had come to him, a Teacher, as a supplicating Student. That, obviously, he declined this Confucian relationship. That, respectfully, I withdrew my request. Before closing the
door, I saw him slump back into his chair, flushed with rage and, as it
turned out, pain.

Several weeks later, at a party, I met the first local Chinese woman
who was about my age. I introduced myself and, in my bilingual polyglot, asked for information about grocery stores and cheap restaurants
so I, starved for real food, might buy a bit of home. She replied in
English that these matters were of no interest whatsoever to her.
Turning abruptly, she joined a group at the other end of the room.
Making inquiries, I found out she was the professor's daughter.

For her, there was no "best" from the East, only the West. Her
roots, and her father, obstructed a joyless progress into the great melting pot. Hunched over by the burden of foreign ancestry and the ignorance of domestic bias, she was tripped as much by the real as the
shadowed, by others' callousness as her own hypersensitivity. I pictured
her sullenly picking at the scabs, the remains of injuries sustained for
not walking a clearer path. There may have been more to her but all
she and her father showed me were the whitish scars, an uneven skin
of bravado and disdain.

For myself, I had to face the fact that a desire to present linguistic
credentials and be accepted as legitimately "Chinese" had led me to
stereotype her as much as the Bedlam Woman had pigeon-holed me. I
had become so self-concerned that I was no longer mindful of what
variety there is among the diverse. Although I have since tried to
offend no one in this way, my own tenuous hold on a cultural past can
still be too important. As late as the '90s, I perpetrated my Chinese-
English Polyglot on a woman. Terrified, she fled. Rather than cope
with my presumptions, she abandoned her long-held place in the bathroom line. Her only defense was to run. Unlike the Professor's
Daughter, this one could not even shoot back with words from some
ideological arsenal, yet her retreat distressed me more.

When I related the story of the Professor's Daughter to my mother
the day after it happened, I wasn't yet sensitive to their viewpoint, but
only interpreted it in terms of my own perceived inadequacies. About
to go out again, and feeling hesitant about my decision to party
instead of study, I wanted to compensate for my lack of scholarly commitment by telling my mother, indirectly, how much more under-

standing she was than the professor and how much more "Chinese" I was than his daughter.

Clucking her rejection of their attitudes and, by implication, her confidence in my good judgment, I converted the telephone call into an approval of my social calendar. When I hung up, my date, obviously amused, said, "You talk to your mother in broken English."

"Don't be ridiculous."

"I'm not kidding. You do."

"No I don't."

"Oh yes, you do. Listen to yourself next time."

I did. And I do. At the age of twenty-two, I, for the first time, heard myself speak pidgin. Superficially, it was ludicrous— I'd scored in the top one percentile on the Graduate Record Exam for verbal competence!

After more extensive observation and analysis, I realized that, whenever I can't say all that I want because my Chinese is so limited, I arrange the English words I need according to Chinese grammar rules. It wasn't Broken English; it was Mended Chinese.

Motivated by a desire to be well-spoken yet not overreaching, my Double-Speak could express thoughts without flaunting either my education or ignorance when among those less conversant in English. The revelation came in handy soon after when, awarded a fellowship that would pay my way anywhere I enrolled, I hurriedly arranged admission into the University of California at Berkeley. Contacting Tom Nunes, a former schoolmate, for a place to stay the first night, I packed all that I owned into the used Mini Minor I bought for $300 when my parents thought that a graduate student on a bicycle was undignified, and drove nonstop to meet all those Chinese up in northern California.

Still between semesters, neither my friend nor his roommates were in town when I arrived. Their apartment, the second story of an old "Heights" house, was situated on a hill so steep that my tiny car nearly toppled over when I tried to make a U-turn at the crest. Shaken, I parked to review Tom's instructions:

- Arrive after midnight.
- Go directly to the outside stairway in the back.
- Avoid the piles of stuff stacked up against the house.
- Find the key under the mat.
- DO NOT MAKE ANY NOISE.

The cloak-and-dagger procedure was necessary because:

1. The lease specifically outlawed women on the premises; and

2. The landlady was deranged.

Having been one of the first females to receive tenure at a major university, the pressure to excel in a male environment had catapulted her from the English Department into Outer Space. After years of teaching, of hearing countless aspersions cast about the feminine gender ("Present company excepted, of course"), of being isolated by and reveling in her "exceptional" status, she retired early after suffering a complete nervous breakdown. Withdrawing to the sanctuary of what must have been an elegant house, she rarely went out. And neither did anything else she controlled. The piles around and in her house were her literary world gone literal. Stacks of "original resource material" filled the center of every room. This "library" of moldering and infested trash, garbage, canine and feline corpses, housed the life of a mind gone mad—as well as lives with six legs.

Unfortunately for me, not all her pets were dead. My stealth afforded one irresistible peek through the window at a filthy dining room but it couldn't get me past the sentry chained to the back steps. Once the barking alarm was sounded, I scrambled upwards, groped for the key, and made at least as much noise as the mangy guard dog. Within seconds of slamming the door, the telephone rang. For minutes the brrrringing kept me glued against the knob. It stopped. And then started again. I couldn't stand it. I picked it up, "Hello?" I whispered.

"Who's that? Who's up there? Tom?"

Unable to think of anything else, I again whispered. "Hello?"

"Is that a woman up there? Don't move! Stay right where you are!!"

The phone slammed down and then I heard her coming up the stairs. My thoughts thumped like her footsteps: What should I do? What will Tom and the others do if they're evicted on my account?

By the time she pounded her sixth knock, I had a plan.

Standing back as she pushed through the now unlocked door, I smiled brightly and said, "Allo."

"Who are you? What're you doing here? You're not allowed here! Where's Tom?"

"Ah so, Tom. Tom, gone." [Replace smile with frown.]

Advancing toward me, she demanded, "Whaddya mean? Who are you?"

I stood my ground. Then, like the cuckoo that doesn't have the brains to realize it's the middle of the night and should shut up, I popped out with a most cheery (though slightly idiotic) grin and, showing no sign of guilt, no awareness of being caught in the act, chirped, "I? I to be Tom's Younger Sister."

The Fury stopped; the fleas didn't.

"Sister?" Pushing her face closer to mine as if to give me a mirror in the glistening menace of her eyes, she snorted, "How can you be his sister?"

She had a point. After all, she was dotty, not blind.

Facing her, backlit by the aura of all the Innocents who ever suffered the consequences of human aggression, I explained how I, an orphan [eyes downcast, face mournful], was adopted by Tom's parents after "the war" [eyes wide, face contorted]. Stopped in her tracks by the tragedy of it all, she cooed, "Oooh, you poooor thing." When she then reached for my hand, I had to take it.

There was one hitch: I couldn't sustain the pidgin. I simply could not imitate myself talking to my mother. I tried to be all those "Chinese" characters from the movies. It was no use. I finished my fiction in regular English.

She never noticed the transition. Wondering to myself if the Bedlam Woman would have noticed if I had switched from "normal" to pidgin English, I concluded my dramatic monologue with details of a lonely trek across wide open spaces for the sole purpose of once again seeing my beloved Older Brother, Tom. By the time I finished, the landlady was in tears and brewing a pot of Chinese tea. By the time we sipped our first cup, her mood had changed. Now she was looking at me with an intensity equal to the one I gave the spot on my hand. With predatory readiness, she was poised to pounce. (Just like I was in the event the spot moved.)

"You say you drove here?"

"Yes."

"In your own car?"

"Yes."

"How long were you planning to stay with your brother?"

"Not long. After all, he has, ahem, roommates." [Eyes lowered, virginal face embarrassed and hurt with the suggestion of an immodesty.]

"You could stay downstairs with me."

("Oh my God. No!")

"You know, I'm old."

Without waiting to hear the protest about age that most Americans expected and gave, she continued, "It's not so easy getting around. If you lived with me, it wouldn't cost you a thing. Just run a few errands, maybe cook sometimes."

("Shall we have chocolate-covered fleas tonight, Dear?")

"Well, what do you think?"

"I think I must first ask my Honorable Mother."

"Of course, Dear. Tell her I'd treat you like my own granddaughter."

"I am overwhelmed with your kindness." [Hands clasped, deep bow.]

When she finally left, I showered until the water turned cold. Checking several times to make sure that I was alone in bed, I went to sleep with the hope that Tom would go along with the only scheme I could hatch for extricating me from her clutches without her retaliating and canceling his lease. Calling him the next morning, I explained what had transpired the night before and outlined the agenda for his return. At first Tom couldn't decide which was worse: the fact that he might lose the apartment or that he couldn't vacate immediately now that it was probably infested. And then it was a toss-up which was more funny: my attempt at pidgin or her plot to make me an indentured servant. In the end, he goodheartedly agreed to make it even easier than usual for his landlady to tamper with his mail. That settled, I called downstairs and, mysteriously vague, told his landlady that there was just one thing I had to do before moving in with her but that I would be back in a few days. Her joy was boundless. So was mine as I left to find my own apartment and register for classes.

Two weeks later, Tom called and told me, "It worked." The letter I had sent, with my name boldly printed on the "Return to" line, and the envelope unsealed, had arrived. On the same day, his landlady's daily inquiries regarding my whereabouts suddenly ceased. Thereafter, when he walked past her window, she would look out but only give a quiet wave from behind the glass—doubtless out of respect for Tom's feelings. She didn't want him to see her shudder and, then, sigh with relief. If they met by the back stairway, she would look at Tom with knowing eyes and a sad face but say nothing. There were no words in her for the Older Brother mourning his young sister's imminent and untimely demise due to the sudden onset of an incurable, fatal, and highly contagious disease.

With Tom's situation resolved, I asked around for the names of any psychologists interested in the relationship between language and memory. My inability to remember my childhood, coupled with my failure to speak pidgin at will, led me to wonder if hypnosis could "take me back." And, if so, would I relate my relived childhood in Chinese or English? Unsuccessful, I soon got more involved in the excitement of being in Berkeley. Aptly named after the philosopher, it was the first place where I felt "in the majority." But I did make a resolution: When the time came, I would speak Chinese to my child.

BETWEEN...AND FUTURE

During the earliest days of my acquaintance with the bees, I must confess there were moments of rebellion against the ordered routine of their lives.... But as I came, day after day, to know them better,...I grew to understand the respect and affection with which millions of human beings have regarded the honeybee....

But there is more than wonderment to be found in the commonwealth of the hive. Men today, as men of old, have discovered something calming, something reassuring in the solidarity of the swarm.

—Edwin Way Teale, A Book About Bees

William got English from his father and Chinese from me. At first it felt unnatural. And then it became habit: Put me in front of a baby and, no matter what it looked like, I would speak Chinese. No one seemed to mind, including William. So from the moment he was born, Bennett spoke one language to him while I used another. That was the simple rule. The reality was more complex: he got Chinese from my parents and most of their friends, English from my sisters, Bennett's family, and most passers-by. He overheard his parents converse only in English while witnessing his mother speak a polyglot to her parents and Chinese to the babies of those same passers-by.

It didn't occur to me to wonder what was going on in William's brain until one night, seated in his high chair at dinner, he asked for a *bing gan*. I explained in my usual Chinese that he could have "*a sweet biscuit*" after he ate his dinner. Dissatisfied with my response, he again said, "*Bing gan.*" And I again explained the procedure of first eating his meal before getting a treat. Another *bing gan* brought him yet another lesson on good nutrition.

Huffing a sigh of exasperation, he leaned his elbow on the high-chair tray and locked me in place with his eyes. Squaring his tiny jaw and concentrating his brow, he snorted out a quick puff of air, signaling to me that this was my last chance so I better pay close attention. Then he slowly, deliberately, and loudly sounded out, as if to some foreigner, "*Cook*-ie?"

Bennett remembers it differently. He says that William had asked his *BaBa* for the cookie after he realized the Chinese wasn't penetrating his mother's thick skull. And of course William doesn't remember it at all. Indeed, after he went to school, our Chinese sentences became isolated words or phrases, mostly about food and bathroom functions.

When he was ten, we started going to Chinese School on Sundays. The classes centered on calligraphy because the other children could already speak Chinese to their parents, English to each other. And then that too lapsed. By the time William was deciding which college to attend, I pushed the one with greater diversity. He preferred another.

"William, please tell me you aren't going to college in Maine just to be near L.L. Bean and J. Crew."

"No, but it can't hurt."

"Will you at least take Chinese? After four years of Latin, it'll be a snap—no conjugating, declining, genders…maybe some of it will come back to you."

"Okay, Mom. I think it's a bit far-fetched. But sure, I'll give it a try."

He did. By the end of his first year, it was evident that his linguistic DNA had come from me and tuition per word was $2.875 instead of $1.4375.

"How did you do on the final?"

"Hard to tell. I might have flunked. It depends on how gullible she is."

"Gullible?"

"The finals question was 'Write about how you can make better progress in Chinese'."

"Easy enough. What was the problem?"

"I got confused. I thought 'progress' was 'party' so I wrote: If you want to make a good party for Chinese, you need to invite a lot of people, play good music, and buy some beer and dumplings."

"What, no *bing-gan*?"

"I must say, Mom, you're taking this well."

What was the choice? If you want to hear as much of what your children are saying, it helps to have a sense of humor. And if you don't have one, *pretend*!! If the kid steps out the door, it's inevitable, they become at least "bi-lingual"—talking differently to different people, from body language to choice of words and grammar. Sometimes it's deliberate. In this country we have the ironic situation where parents want to afford a Junior Year Abroad for their college kids, that is, the *opportunity* to act like an immigrant and be a member of the minority in a "foreign" language, yet rarely encourage them to go across town or state lines to have the same kind of experience.

In William's case, he heard my many "voices"—Broken and

Mended, philosophical and emotional, subtle and in your face. From Bennett, he got a singular one—Bennett. William absorbed his extended family's way of talking and could catalog which topics were safe or explosive, trivial or momentous, sure-fire attention-getters or duds. He saw who thrived on the hand-grenade approach to conversation and who preferred slow osmosis. He could respond to who assumed *anything* they said *must* be of interest or to those who hesitated because they really weren't sure that spotting Lady Godiva on a *black* horse was significant. Like anyone with a family, we talked ourselves into the patterns that define, confine, and refine us. And, like most with a family, we have rarely talked about the ways we talk. I tried to break that pattern—as when I got back from my 25th college reunion.

I told William I had overheard two former classmates talking. The first, in Op Art clothes and dangly jewelry, said, "I don't understand it. My daughter's a bimbo, and my sons are trying to start a Young Republicans' Club at Berkeley." The other, wearing the same conservative blazer and pleated skirt in 1989 that she had on in 1964, nodded in sympathy, "I know what you mean. My hippie daughter is camped on some God-forsaken beach in Baja, selling seashell earrings for a living."

Not getting much of a response from William, I asked, "Do you remember what *BaBa* and I used to say we feared most?"

"Remind me, Mom."

"When you were born, *BaBa* decided that the most aesthetically offensive image he could conjure for his son was as a cigar-smoking rock star promoter. And I prepared myself for what he claimed would be your inevitable rebellion by joking that anything short of a born-again professional hockey player would be okay."

"Mom?"

"Yes?"

"That's not the message I got."

"What do you mean?"

"Marrying a stupid person was the worst. You said color and gender were my choice but you drew the line at stupid."

"All right, that too. Anyway, it occurs to me you may be planning to make us crazy some other way. Can you give me a clue? I hate surprises."

This was how I could not-quite subscribe to the American attitude about stages, especially "adolescence," while still practicing some of the Chinese approach of always assuming that no step in life's journey is inherently problematic. I hoped that presenting our son with a Worst that was beyond his wildest capability, and a Best that was within his grasp, would encourage him to fulfill all our respective dreams. To do this we had to avoid the extremes of self-destructive abandon on the one hand and, on the other, never-good-enough comparisons with non-existent rivals who do everything perfectly.

It was also my way of letting recent events slip into past history. We both knew how we'd spent the previous year. The arguments would start with him asking for something: designer name first, generic description second. Then me talking about the lean times—how we bought a car from gypsies for $75 by spending an hour talking it down from $80, only to end up crossing her palm with $6 worth of "silver" for a forecast of our future. Then William countering with how buying the best now would be money in the bank later, how this or that extra feature would save time or ensure safety. To which I would say things like "Back when I was your age...." and "You're too young to remember, but there was a time...." Over and over until I learned how to misuse my memories and he learned how to tune them out.

As William became increasingly interested in expensive labels and top-of-the-line accessories, Bennett revised his cautionary vision: William was going to be an expedition outfitter, someone more interested in getting the equipment than going on the trip. What I came up with was less forward-looking: William, the typical American teenager of the me-generation as portrayed in the *Readers' Digest*.

Had we inadvertently brought this on? As a young child, William thought it was part of the Christmas ritual to open the horde of presents with all the fanfare his Uncle Winston could muster, then store all except the books in my study closet, bringing them out one by one over the next few months. Half the money he got in red envelopes for Chinese New Year and birthdays went toward his college fund. He heard from us that watching too much television would result in Mush Brain so that too must be rationed.

"You've got 60 minutes left for the week. *Laurel and Hardy* was an hour."

"No, *MaMa*. I've got 76. I didn't watch the commercials."

Was the older William being driven by the accumulated yearning for the rest of the presents in the closet, the programs listed in the papers, the money in the bank? Had my mete-and-measure ploys bred a candidate for the Realm of the Hungry Ghosts where shmoo-like beings with huge stomachs but mouths no larger than the head of a pin roam, forever feeding, eternally wanting more?

Yet how do Bennett and I acknowledge our part in who he is without suffocating him with Idiot Compassion, turning his need for understanding into frivolous sympathy? On the other hand, how much wishing can a child hear about "turning over a new leaf" or what he "should have done" before he believes that you're really wishing for a different person altogether?

Most of this was no news to our friends whose children had preceded William into and out of the stage from hell. But my Chinese side only believed in stages to the extent they had to do with lectures about woolly bears and napping. Unlike my mother, I talked about them but, like my mother, stages weren't "to be expected." Then I looked at my study wall and it became clear that William was susceptible to more than the usual symptoms. I saw two pictures, one of Bennett when he was about seven, another of William at the same age. Each time someone else saw the resemblance of son and father in them, I retold how terrified Bennett had been by the Pinnochio story because he heard it around the same time the picture was taken, when his nose started to take on the formidable proportions of his paternal side. Looking for the hundredth time, I saw the same photos anew.

At birth, there's not much difference among the varieties of babies except for shading. Most grow out of that phase quickly. William's physiognomic changes took longer. In elementary school, William didn't look totally like a Bao, but people could detect something of me in him, especially when I stood next to him. As he got older, his features more resembled his father's and he was now frequently seen outside the context of my presence. With his dual heritage no longer self-evident, it would be up to William, not me, to announce his Chinese affiliation. Although I didn't wish for him the pain of being an American "minority," I didn't want him to be carefree about it for, often embedded in the segregated life is a cultural one. We just haven't learned how to preserve its virtues and be democratic simultaneously. By reducing intercultural differences and conflicts to political and economic issues, we haven't recognized the behavior that, rightly or wrongly, is our emotional glue. At the same time, the derogatory connotations of the terms we use to describe the cohesion—tribalism, territoriality, ethnocentricity, Old Boy network—have taken hold. Yet their everyday effects shouldn't all be obliterated. Our myriad of ghettos are communities. And leaving one can be a sorrow as well as a relief.

When William looked Chinese, chances were he would empathize. When he didn't, I wasn't sure. If no one could tell the difference between him and the teenage masses, all wearing the same logo on their jeans and shirts, would he make the effort? Or just "pass"? I was the one who taught him the Chopsticks-Fork Principle, who told him not to stick out like a sore thumb. What I had meant to do was promote careful observation, sensitivity to others' feelings, proficiency. Had I miscalculated? If the Principle is applied by someone who could blend in so easily, would it produce mere conformity? When I diverged from what my parents might have expected, I evoked mostly silence. When Bennett did, his mother immortalized her consternation in a poem she wrote,

> **Rite of Passage**
> It began with a slamming of doors,
> screech of locks, silences
> then after the barricades
> the deserted room.
> A scatter of insolent hats,
> pin-ups, two-tone boots
> should have warned me.
> While you put on the city
> like a bull-fighter's cape
> I follow, heart shriveling.
> Buildings jostle,
> streets tangle
> downhill to dead ends.
> All the alien feet
> run the other way.
> I haunt alleys and shadows,
> need no doors,
> pass through walls,
> hear the chatter
> of our teeth.
> In the halls the chandeliers,
> revolving, flash

> on hostilities abloom in alcoves
> and anywhere we step the floors
> may give way to oubliettes.
> I hang back fingering
> the chainmail in the cloakrooms
> while the same bird beats
> in my ribs as in yours
> and my throat aches
> with your aggrieved astonishment.

In a quieter moment, she saw him, "Grown tall and lonely, seeking Camelot..." and the stubborn visions that helped produce his artistic success. When William shriveled my hopes, Bennett was not overly concerned, joking that, regardless of culture, it's an anthropological truth that living with a teenager is guaranteed to make life change for whatever parents think is "worse."

I instead did my usual talking, to which William responded with a kind of "Who are you?" look that confirmed all his memory banks had been wiped clean. With that look, I was ready to disown him without another word. And then he'd give me another look to tell me he was willing to pay that price. This led to more talking, more silence, more looks.

From William's viewpoint, the period of warring states got as intense as it did because, unlike his friends who only had a United Front to rebel against, he had parents who were perfectly described by the bumper sticker, "Opposites Abstract." How to get us both riled at the same time was thus not readily apparent. Additionally, William and I were too close, he delivered arguments the same way that I argued mine, leaving no room for concession, connection, separation or satisfaction. It was exhausting but we kept at it because I was his mother, not his "friend," and he was becoming an adult, not a "*MaMa*'s Boy."

Finally he and I agreed that our extreme difference of opinion (regarding his ridiculous, unbridled and unconscionable desire to rush headlong into the immoral state of conspicuous consumption) wasn't personal, but hormonal and that, in essence, we were waging biological warfare brought on by adolescence and menopause occurring at the same time in the same household. Since neither of us wished to undergo a sex-change operation or move, we needed to do our utmost not to forget where we parked our sense of humor and call a truce.

Although we agreed to accept this theory, there were still more skirmishes that neither would concede were estrogen or testosterone-related. I think the real turning point occurred with the startling experience of sleeping next to some of my teeth. Performing the miracles of their respective specialties, the dentist, periodontist, oral surgeon, hygienist, and endodontist had all conspired to teach me that one doesn't have to be an octogenarian to be "long in the tooth." Menopause was "natural," this was not. Looking in the mirror, lips pulled back, I faced my mortality with an urgency that mere wrinkles couldn't produce. Coupled with my residual fear that, truce notwithstanding, William's memory banks might still be erased, I started to commit my—his—memories to paper.

By reading them to him, I could remind him without lecturing. Like Parables or Chinese operas, Memorial Day Parades or New Year Celebrations, the lessons on vices and virtues could be implied, discussed, criticized, revised, remembered anew, and edited without being too personal. We could talk about "characters" and "character" without talking about ourselves in particular (though, on a couple of occasions, I did mention a variation of my mother's Little Ambassador routine, "You know, William, if this gets published, there could be a lot of folks looking at you for proof that the Chopsticks-Fork stuff works."). This helped. Meanwhile, William put himself on a budget that set a cap on his spending but gave him greater discretion. This helped too.

His academic life also improved. This helped a lot.

For the glorious "A" in Religion notwithstanding, I had, despite our Montessori training, slipped back into the Bao habit of averting praise and dissecting failures. For years, William never got the kind of No-Comment Report Card I worked to give my mother. And when he added Standardized Test Scores to the roster, I had to say, "It's not possible, William. *No one* does worse the second time."

But when he finally could report respectable percentiles to Devin's mother, and Kate asked, "Was your mother ecstatic?" William's reply, "She'll take me back," was a milestone. He had learned how to make the past, however thick with cross-purposes and words, transparent with humor. My faith in his continued progress grew when William reported to me while attending Governor's School,

> Dear Mom,
> ...I met a girl whom you will be introduced to on

Saturday so be forewarned. She really likes you—at least
from your letters—and I'm sure you'll find her interesting.
She's of Russian heritage and is intelligent and all. We
have learned to despise the SATs as an instrument of the
"White Male System" to force all others who wish to
function in America to conform to our standards; but if
you are into it, she got a 1450. Intelligence is a spreading
disease at this place! Her name is _____ and you can act
"normal" because I met her parents and they're really
strange too....
Love, William   ((••))
                   ～
                 ➤◄

Governor's School was followed by telephone bills that were directly responsible for a sharp increase in the value of Bell Atlantic stock,
followed by his justification, "Mom, I'm doing that spiderweb net-
working thing you're always talking about."

Reassured there was nothing wrong with his memory cells, we
installed a second line. This investment paid off during his senior year
when he lived at school and his House Master told me that our son's
style of leadership as a Proctor was based on reaching consensus, not
enforcing rules. I was so gratified by this evident show of the Chinese
cum Rotomac manner, I began to think that William had no more
need for the outrageous, the outraging.

That's when he got a tattoo.

From William's standpoint, while there were a few drawbacks to
this—the aesthetic limitations of a deficit-spending budget and, of
course, the pain—tattooing was one of the few social taboos left on his
father's wish list of might-have-beens, and his mother's list of never-
should-be's. Thankfully, his teenage vitality hadn't mitigated his fairly
well-developed sense of self-preservation. Thus he chose the site carefully: the lower hip, a place to which neither grandmother would ever
be privy. Although he had some misgivings about the permanence of
this dermatological art form, he had heard the story of his father's
friend, the one who had his tattoo surgically removed and who thereafter carried the shriveled reminder of his youth in his wallet next to
his driver's license. With either outcome, he was counting on me to be
his audience, to "ooh," "aah," and gasp—mostly gasp—at the appropriate times. A rebel without a cause can get by undeterred, one without a good audience is hardly worthy of the name. In this regard, I

191

tried to be helpful. But the tattoo, so well situated, was nothing compared to the warring. I managed to wince and sigh several times before forgetting to remember that a blue lightning bolt now adorned the upper thigh of an otherwise perfectly nice second joint.

Devin's parents came to our aid. Unable to correlate the stigma of a drunken sailor with the pristine flesh of their children's friend, the unveiling of the discoloration stunned the Gallaghers into silence. Add their silence to my wincing, and the total should have been sufficient to mark the event as well as the leg. That's when I found out what really happened.

So William had to stand by, ignored, while I castigated, derided, fulminated, and thoroughly lambasted his father, "You *what*?! You *loaned* him the money to pay for it??!!?!"

Then we laughed and took the next step.

"I tried to reach you last night."

"Yeah, I got the message. A bunch of us went over to Emily's. We decided to bake cookies for the Desert Storm troops."

"I know. I tried calling you at her place too."

"K and I left early. Out to the golf course. It was incredible. She saw this shooting star and got all excited. I mean, jumping up and down. It was pretty romantic."

What I said was, "Oh? It must have been a clear night." What I almost blurted out was, "What the hell were you two doing?" knowing full well that "the golf course" was where Blair kids went to make out. Two weeks later, my prior restraint gave me the right to say to the both of them, "No more 'golfing' until after finals. This will be your last set of grades for college admissions."

They agreed and we took the next step after he got his driver's license and averaged $500 in repairs for every 700 miles he drove.

"William? I saw you and the exchange student from Czechoslovakia were parked in the driveway last night. I appreciate it."

"That's cool."

"Well, I can't sleep if I think you're driving these back roads in the middle of the night looking for a place to "watch the submarine races" as we used to call it. You could be in a ditch and nobody'd find you for days. I mean, it's a little disconcerting to start a new workday at 4:00 in the morning and find you haven't finished with the night before."

"Sure, Mom."

"You understand, don't you?"

"Yeah, it's simple: I can go on a date, I can have the car, I can stay out as late as I want…I just can't go anywhere."

"Thanks."

"No problem."

"William? I love you."

"Love you too, Mom."

Very early the next morning, before there was light enough to see the driveway, I found a post-it stuck to my computer monitor:

> When was the last time you saw the top of your desk? By the way, I'm in.

Then I turned for a moment and he took a giant step.

It was 7:30 in the morning. I was in the kitchen. William was in the shower. A young woman appeared without entering from the outside. I forced myself to ask her, as nonchalantly as I could, "You are using condoms, aren't you? Now, would you like coffee or tea with breakfast?"

She ran (back) upstairs. William came down, "What did you do to her, Mom?"

I told him. I also told him she was a wimp.

BETWEEN PAST AND FUTURE

When William was about to leave for college and I would have fewer opportunities to jog his memory without disturbing his mood, I put together a page for his yearbook: something he would look at periodically throughout his life. It would be my Time Capsule.

Searching the family album for material, I saw, still encased in plastic, the picture I gave him on that second day of school. For a moment I considered using it but realized that, even if he remembered it, the subtext couldn't be contained in a simple caption. As I flipped through, the photos still waiting to be placed in chronological order began to fall out. Setting it and me on the floor, I recalled the day he returned from grammar school and "liberated" a few pictures from their frames. Having decided I was deluded about the special status of humans, he had set them free, with plans to take care of the fenced-in cows later.

Turning each page, I was gratified at how many moments of his childhood had been captured on film. The album that resided in my parents' house had so few—and they were in Chinese when I can only remember in English. But there was one so vivid I could believe it was a reminder and not just evidence: in Brooklyn, seated under a Christmas tree, a little clown flanked by a ballerina, a cabaret singer, a cowboy, and Abraham Lincoln. Inspired, I created a leaf in the 1991 Blair Academy "ACTA." For weeks before its appearance, I resisted the temptation to show William the mock-up and receive the gratitude and benediction which I thought it and I deserved.

"Well, William, what did you think when you saw it?"

"Weird. But I guess you had fun doing it."

Then he did weirder. A year after he got the first tattoo, William got another. The encore succeeded where the first one failed—I was horrified.

It wasn't that he got one etched onto his forehead or anything like that (he still wanted to live). The site of the second was not the zinger as it appeared right next to the first. It was the subject matter. This time William was just a hair's breadth short of becoming a born-again professional hockey player with a stupid spouse. He had "ΔKE" permanently written on his body. As in *Delta Kappa Epsilon*. As in fraternity. Not just any fraternity but one that counts Dan Quayle and two Bushes amongst its brotherhood.

"How could you, William?"

Dear William,

As your possibilities and actualities develop and become part of you, keep in mind:

The Humor
which fosters
Perspective;
But, please,
not the circus—
your grandparents
would have a fit.

The Courage
which fosters
Strength;
But, please, not by
the sword—
lacrosse was bad
enough.

The Sympathy
which fosters
Pluralism;
But, not an Indian—
Too much genetic
engineering required.

The Imagination
which fosters
Invention;
But, not Superman—
Too much hubris and
ego.

The Wisdom which fosters a sense of the Whole.

"You joined a sorority once."

"That was high school."

"Then think of it as a web thing: I'm expanding my network. By the way, the Brothers are planning to go to Ft. Lauderdale over spring break."

I couldn't talk him out of it. But the Florida constabulary did—at a bar soon after William brandished his older cousin's driver's license. So William was outfitted in bright orange and, with a host of other too-young people, sentenced to three days of picking up litter off public roads.

"How was it, William?"

"Cold and wet."

"Does this mean you'll have a police record?"

"No record. But they don't want me in Florida again until I'm 21."

There is at least one god with a sense of humor.

PHOTOGRAPHIC MEMORIES

On the occasion of my parents' tenth anniversary, Brooklyn, NY, 1948.

SanSan between Teaneck High and Tufts University, mid '60s.

Bette, our parents & Cathy in Teaneck, NJ, late '50s.

Cathy, 1962 Tufts vs. Williams game, photo by A. Cooke for *Sports llustrated.*

Cathy, Bennett, Margaret, Mother, John and Father Bean, 1966.

Cathy, Bennett and William, early 1974.

Bennett and entrée, mid-1974.

Cathy, Bennett and William in front of tired door, late 1974.

Bennett, William and Cathy in the Columbine "ruin," 1986.

Cathy in all the hand-me-downs simultaneously, William in parochial shirt and tie with combat hat, 1985.

At the White House, 1993.

William in Levi's advertisement, *World Screen*, Taiwan, 1997.

Bennett with his work/play, 2002.

The Lees and Beans in My Living Room, 2001.

The wedding site on "the lawn," bifurcated by new sod and guarded by yard gods on columns to the right with L-shaped bridge spanning PondB in the background, 2001.

201

PART TWO

OLD AND NEW VOICES, A MEMOIR AND MANUAL

The summer after meeting Bennett, I returned east to help my parents move from Teaneck to their second, and last, New Jersey house. Alone in the attic, I sorted through the remaining odds and ends. Finding the diary I wrote when an adolescent, I read the opening line, "I write this so I'll *never* forget how it feels to be young when I'm a mother."

I was so embarrassed by the entries that I looked around, afraid a witness to my immaturity might appear from nowhere. After destroying it, I drove back to the new house in Englewood Cliffs. During lunch, the front doorbell rang. I went to see who it was. A boy of nine or ten was standing there, ball and bat in hand. Taking a second to make sure he was bigger than me, he said, "I know you just moved in but do you think your parents would let you play anyway?"

I replied, "Yes, I think that can be worked out."

It was almost like that day in 1951, when Jan and Claire appeared from across the street and we all asked for my mother's permission to play—that meant I probably already had it. This time I didn't ask though.

Only a few months earlier, I had. Going home from California for Christmas, I had ached with the possibility of everyone happily excited over my news of Bennett—a typical '50s sit-com scenario—as absurd a vision as me being blond and blue-eyed. If I were good. Culturally blindsided, I had cashed my parents' contribution to the next semester's tuition fund and boarded a bus for New Jersey. Carefully wrapped in my bag was one of Bennett's salt-glazed vessels. It would be their introduction to him.

Among family and close friends, Chinese say, "Don't be polite." They weren't. My mother said it reminded her of a beggar's bowl; Bette laughed uncontrollably; *SanSan* grimaced. My father, silent, just happened to be passing through California early the next spring to get a first-hand glimpse of Bennett though already of the mind that what I was seeing was not worth looking at. Bennett and I met him at the airport. Seated together at the restaurant, the conversation was as crumpled as the plaid tie Bennett wore. Its pattern, out of style for at least twenty years, was not helped by its recent stint as strapping for a knapsack. Afterward, too American, or too Chinese, or, maybe, simply too stupid, I formally asked my father for his opinion of Bennett. His response, date and number atop each of the ten pages, was an elaborate metaphor that took the reader through the rooms of a house, each room a setting for occasioning some virtue, each occasion providing an opportunity to excel or be deficient. Omitting only the bedroom (as "it is of no one's concern except the parties involved"), he concluded that "In the living room, Bennett would not be suitable."

I never again asked for their permission, although I did continue trying to please them. In my mother's case, with no abiding success until we found her burial spot.

As long as I could remember, my mother avoided funerals, maybe afraid the gods would prematurely associate her with the occasion. The one time when I was giving a talk in her neighborhood and she had a convenient chance to see her teacher-daughter in action, she nervously declined because there was a funeral home across the street. And when a guest at a holiday gathering entertained us with her fortune-telling, my mother adamantly refused to open her hand: after the age of sixty, she said, "There's only one prediction left." Then, in 1995, she did a 180° "swing," and cheerfully asked me to find a gravesite: a high, dry place where her descendants would visit.

High and dry were easy. But someone to visit after her daughters were gone? With my mother's aversion to funerals and our being the first generation of Fangs and Baos in the United States, we'd never built up any family traditions dealing with graves the way we did with other red-letter days. I was pretty confident that William would try if I asked him to visit his PoPo's grave after I was gone, yet I didn't want to push his filial devotion beyond credulity. So I decided there was only one place I could predict he would be forty or fifty years down the road: his high school reunion. I therefore checked out cemeteries within a five-mile radius of Blair Academy. When I told my mother the rationale of looking in our corner of New Jersey, she decided that it was more important to be visited by daughters and that her chances of this happening would increase if she wasn't interred so near the Mississippi. For several weekends, we shopped for a suitable plot—and "shop" was the operative word for we went from one cemetery to another in the same spirit as she used to go from Bergdorf to Bloomingdale's. Once we found a very high, very dry site that had the added benefit of being the once and future resting place of most of her mah-jongg friends, we then spent several more weekends showing it off. When all confirmed it was the very best, we took my father. At the time we all assumed he would be the first to go. That didn't happen.

Not long after we buried Mommy, Daddy and I were talking. One thing led to another and I finally lost control. But before the first tear formed or I could reinvigorate the memories he and I shared when she let loose her anger about the choices I made, he voiced the brutal truth and the soothing balm, "Don't worry about it. She's dead."

The only other time my father had used the words "Mommy" and "dead" in the same sentence was when he asked Chopsticks style as well as suggested in a Fork manner that I not publish my memoir until after she died. Sixteen months later, we were again sitting on the couch talking. This time Daddy brought forth a memory I would have shared had I not been only two and half years old at the time. Until then, we all knew the family story about how he had helped the midwife with *SanSan*'s delivery. We never read into it more than an understanding of what it was like "during the war" or "back in the old country." But he had been in America for sixty-four of his eighty-eight years and now he wanted to relate what happened after her birth.

> One of the neighbors came over and offered to do the dirty work—to bury the baby live under a certain tree. I told him, "No." He thought I didn't understand and explained that the tree was special and that, if he did this, I'd have a son within a year. I told him, "I like my daughters." Then [sixteen years later], when Mommy got *SanSan* out of China and the two were in Taiwan waiting for a visa, I got a call in Teaneck from that guy. He said he read about a "Bao Ching-yee" in the papers and wondered if she was the same daughter. When I said, "Yes,' he said he was calling to apologize. I told him, "You should," and hung up.

Before I could react, Daddy's voice went quiet and he, for the first time ever, asked for my advice. He wanted to know if I thought he should tell *SanSan* this rest of the story. Thinking of the harsh words that my father and younger sister had recently exchanged, I said, "Yes. And soon." Just in case he got tired of taking so many pills. Or just in case Freud was right and *SanSan* had subconscious thoughts about being a third daughter who was left in China for seventeen years.

Yes, the facts may be hard, but the brain doesn't haven't to be. Over time, we are related to more people than we know. The birth, marriage, divorce, and adoption certificates tell us who is legally related to whom. Our expectations tell us what those relationships should be like. But our experiences tell us "Get a life. And another. And another. And another." Over time, if you let them, a distant "parent" can become a close "child." Or a haphazard "sister" can become a great "second cousin." Thus we may need to grieve even though no one has died. Or give birth even though no one new has been conceived.

With so many lives to live and relate to and remember, there is no simple story line that can encompass the several directions we can travel, sometimes simultaneously. *Robert's Rules of Order* says in its *Hints to Inexperienced Chairmen,* "Notice that there are different ways of doing the same thing, all of which are allowable." However, if you want more guidance, one rule I have found useful when teaching the Chopsticks-Fork Principle is from Judith Martin's *Miss Manners Guide to Excruciatingly Correct Behavior,* "[When all the forks look alike], use the one farthest to the left."

If this is still not enough, I offer the following exercises. Together with General Robert and Miss Manners, they have given me a way to *re*-cognize "the facts" to get even more "stories." For when philosophers advise "Know thyself" and "Always in Moderation," it takes more than one retrospective glance to see how our modern and multicultural times give us at least two selves and several moderators.

Weddings are often the occasion for discovering just how culturally schizophrenic we can be. When one of our family marriages was viewed by the nuclear principals as a Declaration of Internecine War, the extended members were put into the terrible position of having to decide on which side of the loyalty line to place whatever identity was most at stake. Accepting the invitation was the "western" move—bearing witness to the idea that a wedding is, essentially, a union of two individuals and an absolute rejection of the "arranged marriage" concept that perceives the union as equally or more a matter of clan interests (as seen by the "better" eyes, usually of family elders).

My mother walked this matrimonial minefield with the authority of a Chinese matriarch, ruler of relationships, and the x-ray vision of a Superman, defender of The American Way. By not focusing on "acceptance," she applied some fuzzy logic to the notion of "absence." Thus the male partner of each couple attended, signaling "head of household" as well as recognizing the fact that the men in question also happened to be less sympathetic to the "arranged marriage" idea.

The female partners tendered their regrets. Not needing to specify an excuse, their absence signaled no particular message to the bridal couple but did tell the Other Side that the "maternal contingent" was abstaining from casting a vote but not from conveying how emotionally attuned they were to the pain caused by the bride's rebellion. Since *SanSan* was no longer partnered and, therefore, not in a position to split the symbolic difference, my mother neglected to forward my younger sister's invitation until two weeks after the nuptial fact. Though no one was delighted, it was a Chopsticks-Fork resolution.

One year before William's Nuptial Fact was the last year of Bennett's first full cycle. He spent this pre-60th time completing a Thirty Year Plan to take the concept of our home and make it reappear, intensified, as our house. The year of William's marriage was the last year of my first full cycle. So I spent my pre-60th year , trying to keep house and home together while planning a Chopsticks-Fork Wedding. We hoped for a celebration, not just a resolution.

CHAPTER 7

EXERCISE #1

Do this once a month, more often if a marriage or divorce, house sale or purchase, graduation or expulsion, birth or death, felony or pardon—some milestone—is scheduled:

> Sit cross-legged, face the East, then the West, and recite Jack Kornfield's reminder:
>> This life is a test—it is only a test.
>> If it had been an actual life,
>> you would have received further instructions
>> on where to go and what to do.
>> Remember this life is only a test.

Being Chinese in an area of New Jersey where we are few (but the Canada Geese are many), I pretty much got everybody's attention when I sauntered into the local sporting goods store. This one had an inventory to make Charlton Heston show even more teeth than usual. Anyway, there I stood, surrounded by an array of lethal weapons— some longer than I am—to inquire, "Do you carry those small marbles for slingshots? If you have white ones, I'd like those so I can find and use them again."

The owner puffed up to his full indignant height. Taking over, his wife and co-owner grunted her disdain for this would-be customer. I started to feel bad that I didn't want to buy something with more oomph—like an ICBM—but she interrupted my thought with the startling news that "Slingshots...[long pause]...are...[even longer pause]...*il-legal* in New Jersey."

Picking up my jaw, I backed out of this fortified Twilight Zone, doing what I do around here when unsure of viewpoints: wave but not smile. Proceeding to the Party Plus shoppe, I was able to buy a few favor bags of multi-colored aggies (at an exorbitant 10-cents apiece). Hoping these would last until the twenty-five hundred Trumark ½-inch "tracers" (on sale @ $.0192 per) were shipped, I went home armed—at least to the extent any Confucian Pragmatist can be armed while still married to a Jeffersonian Buddhist. On the other hand, my husband's respect for all sentient beings notwithstanding, it was he, not I, who landscaped our property with several acres of open field and two large ponds, both free of the tall grass that could help predators remain hidden until too late for the feathery wildlife. A real Nesting Nirvana.

For years I tolerated the dozens of geese that pooped up to 3 pounds each, per day. I tried to put them in the same category as the magnificent great blue heron that, morning and evening, elegantly waded our watery perimeters while performing a slow-motion *Tai Chi* dance with his neck—a warm-up before nailing a goldfish with its spear-like beak. Yes, goldfish. Although Chinese prefer edible carp, most folks in this county stock their ponds with bass for good eating. I would have fished either. However, my husband and father of the groom, who makes art for his living and breathing, chose beauty over feast.

But then our Only Son got engaged. And we all agreed to have a June wedding, on the open field, between the ponds, near the tree house. With that decision, I had two mating seasons to secure the premises for the celebration. Of those 16 months, I used less than fifteen minutes on the internet to order a LaserHawk 3070, equipped with a 3370 Slingshot Hyper-Velocity Band and, too optimistically, not enough marbles. (Soon thereafter, I received some of the strangest e-mails and catalogs advertising all sorts of weaponry as well as equipment for *Babes in Khaki* and *Camouflage Cuties*, whatever they are.)

Anyway, I easily won the first skirmishes against hordes of scouting geese—those still looking for a place to settle. With almost a Ph.D., nearly 60 years of life experiences, and enough skill to get the marbles in their general vicinity, I was more than a match against these geese, for when scouting, they get very, ve-ry suspicious of locations where hard little balls zing by out of nowhere. The tree house was especially useful to accomplish this because geese don't seem to look up. They can do left, right, and down, but not up. Or they are so flummoxed by the hyperactive air around them that they forget "up" is an option. By June 2000, our piece of the countryside was rid of all but one extremely stubborn pair that probably hatched on our property and were thereby programmed to return.

Canada geese may all look alike to us humans, but we do not all look alike to them. There can be a dozen humans milling around, but only when I step outside with a LaserHawk strapped halfway up my left arm, do the pair get agitated—proving that if geese can learn how to differentiate amongst the seemingly homogeneous, with effort and greater exposure, people can and, maybe, for more friendly reasons than fear of being hit. Not only could the geese pick me out of a crowd but they also learned to make less racket on their return landings after realizing I was less prone to rush out and harass them if they didn't honk their presence. Everyone who has lived north of Mexico in the Americas knows that even one honking Canada goose is sufficient to wake the dead. Given that geese are only a miniscule bit more intelligent than the dumber-than-a-rock swans, learning to be quiet is an incredible feat. The resident mallards—a *ménage à trois* consisting of two drakes and a duck—did even better. At first they would huddle near the geese like small fishing boats seeking protection from the mighty Canadian Armada, but they quickly concluded that I was only after the Invincible Pair and avoided proximity. By July, we all had worked out a routine that was repeated the following year (except for the scouting—that chapter is happily closed).

- The geese arrive from their southern purgatory and swim around together, being rather lovely except for dropping the telltale "cigars" every few minutes.
- As I or my missiles approach, they walk away, muttering to each other. Then they fly to the other side of the pond. I follow, they walk or fly again. Back and forth, around and between the ponds, over and over until I tire of teaching them the same lesson.
- Then I suddenly sprint fast enough to convince the pair they should spend a few hours where there are only foxes and dogs to worry about. This goes on for a couple of weeks, during which time the mallards learn discretion.
- Then, one warmish day, I see the male goose is swimming alone. When I target him, he becomes a lure and walks as far away from her as possible, this of course tells me exactly where she is hiding. At this point in the cycle, he never flies off but is cavalierly willing, even wishing, to endure my sling on behalf of his mate.
- Despite my admiration for his sacrifice, when she lays an egg, I steal it, whereupon he flies across the pond or field and tries to kill me.
- Every other day she lays another. I steal it. He tries to kill me.
- After I have collected about 5-6 eggs, they come to the brilliant conclusion that the nest is the problem. So they build another. She sits. I steal. He tries to kill me. But with less conviction. It may be that he is weighted by a downy resignation to so many failed attempts to put me out of his misery or, quite possibly, because I have perfected my imitation of Toshiro Mifune in *The Seven Samurai*, standing astride an imaginary steed, galloping with slingshot arm and marbled hands raised high above a head that is a-swirl with several feet of black hair whipping madly around it.

The first year I ended up with 19 eggs.[7] It was like being on a chicken farm except we only had to break one egg to make an omelet for three. When we got tired of omelets, I brined the eggs.[8]

---

[7] GENERIC EGG OMELET: Vigorously beat eggs in a bowl with a generous pinch of salt and minced leaves from "the stir fry" tree [*Toona* or *Cedrela sinensis*] or, if you don't have this wonderful bush in your yard, chopped scallions. Heat 1/3 cup of canola or peanut oil in a wok until just smoking. Pour in the beaten eggs. Allow them to sit afloat the oil for about 5 seconds, then quickly fold the oil into the fast-cooking mix so that, in less than a minute, it will be a multi-layered, fluffy, moist omelet.

The next season, by the time I stole omelets for nine people, I tried, for their sake and mine, a new stratagem—chasing her off the nest when I could practically see the egg on its way out, thus forcing her to finish the process somewhere else. Since geese mate for life, whither she goest, he follows. It didn't work. She ignored the marbles and left the nest only after laying another meal.[9] Meanwhile, of course, their digested food continued to soil the field where the bride and groom were to dance.

In an effort to be taken more seriously, I could have cinched up the 3370 Slingshot Band another notch in order to take greater advantage of its Hyper-Velocity capabilities. Or I could have given permission to the locals who have witnessed this *Crouching Goose, Slinging Dragon* saga, sometimes shaking their heads in disbelief, more often shouting, "GET A GUN!!"

Or after the wedding vows were exchanged, I could have invited everyone, but especially the bride, to get a drink, select an hors d'oeurvres, and then, taking care not to slip or slide, join me in what has turned out to be the most satisfying and winning aspect of preparing for their marriage: finding all those marbles I have seemingly lost.

[8]SALTED GOOSE EGG(S): Immediately after stealing the egg and dodging the gander, clean the egg by holding under running water that is slightly warmer than the egg. While doing so, use an all-surface scrubber with a dab of dish detergent to remove any mud etc. that might have hardened. Place the clean, raw egg in a large glass jar (smaller if you think you've won the war and not just the battle). Fill the jar with a cooled solution of boiled water saturated with salt. The egg(s) will keep for months, if not years, slowly absorbing the salt through the shell which acts as a preservative (and which is probably why you may not want to keep it for years). When you want to serve it -- hot or cold, as a condiment, garnish or straight up—cook the egg at least ten minutes until hard-boiled.

[9]AESTHETIC ALTERNATIVE: Prepare as usual for coloring or painting. Measuring about 3½" long and having a 7½" circumference, the size of goose eggs will impress children and adults alike as well as offer much more surface for elaborate designs. If organizing an Easter Hunt, I strongly suggest you hide them indoors rather than out—especially if you have an open field and pond in your backyard.

CHAPTER 8

EXERCISE #2

Is it a rabbit? A duck? A duck-billed platypus? A plucked daisy? Nude descending the staircase?

If you concentrate, one or the other comes into view. Or something no one else has seen.

But no matter how many you perceive, no matter how quickly you can switch from the "duck" to the "rabbit" and back again, the drawing can only be one thing at a time.

Carol Gilligan, Professor of Education at Harvard University, once likened this phenomenon to what (most) women and (some) men may experience when, for example, they render a verdict. They may first decide in terms of "the law," according to objective and impersonal standards and then, almost, but not quite, instantaneously view the same set of circumstances "in a different voice,"[10] in terms of the more subjective, personal and/or individual considerations.

The same kind of "cultural" double-take occurs when you go to the doctor's office: first seeing yourself as an "object," an anatomical specimen that is "examined," not touched; then seeing yourself as a subject, a person with history and worries, for whom the touching can be medical or sexual.

Background-foreground cartoons are often found in children's books. They can be more than a moment's entertainment. They can be a lesson in how to review our lives and our many cultures—as double visions, twice removed, by time and understanding. They can train us to admire the variety before deciding which, if any, is "better." They can remind us of what John Gillis has written, "We all have two families, one that we live with and another we live by."

---

[10] The title of Gilligan's ground-breaking book on "Psychological Theory and Women's Development."

When my mother still thought that I, "the practical one," had all my marbles and that I'd amount to something she could brag about to her mah-jongg friends, I told her, "I'm going to major in Philosophy." Although a science—any science except one with "psycho" in its name—would have been preferable, she recovered with the hope that I would yet fulfill her destiny by being the family scholar and getting a "Ph.D" after my name. Maybe even teach at Harvard.

Then, too soon afterward, I announced, "I'm going to marry an artist."

Although I tried to soften the blow by leaving out the part about being in a nudist colony and becoming a Democrat, there are some situations that, regardless of one's psychology, major, community or politics, can, all by themselves, convince the most optimistic of parents that their child is deranged. Marrying an artist is one of those situations. My courses in British Epistemology, French Phenomenology, and Comparative Eschatology notwithstanding, I had to disavow cultural relativism because I had found the impossible: a Universal Truth (almost an axiom if you live or want to live in a nice suburb). Then as now, Chinese or American, both or neither, normal parents don't jump for joy when their cheerleader daughter, former Junior Citizen of the Month, brings home someone whose career choice probably includes poverty. With so little time to nail down their vision of me in black academic robe and mortarboard, sedately walking in the hallowed footsteps of Hu Shi (China's version of John Dewey) and Confucius, my parents were now "seeing" me in hippie dress, off the beaten track, unable to keep my balance for all the marbles flying out of my head.

They didn't know the half of it. It was the sixties and we were in California, reinventing the world with a lot of swinging *shuai*. What I left out of the phone calls home wasn't just a matter of broken or mended language problems, though some of what I was doing could be disguised as another variation on the "me too, me too" syndrome. I did Modern Dance too—but Bette did it at Martha Graham's studio while I was prancing around barefoot in the library of the California State Women's Prison teaching "Mama," leader of the inmates, to lay down her crutches and, body racked with the pain of chronic bursitis, sashay across the floor in waltz time.

I wanted to get married too—but Bette found a future ambassador and I got me a potter. Life being so predictable in those days, I knew I'd probably meet my future husband in school. But life being so unpredictable in those days, I knew if I was going to stay married, it would be because I had a good matchmaker. Appointing myself, I made a list of my requirements. He should be:

- highly competitive—resonating with the American in me;
- domestically conservative—reassuring the Chinese in me;
- judiciously ethical—responding to the Self-righteous in me;
- impatient with stupidity though tolerant of ignorance— relieving the Educator in me;
- very picky about physical grace—pleasing the Athlete in me.

What I wanted was a relationship between two people who would

- complement each other with neither person dominant;
- compete with others but not each other so both could relax at home;
- have very different interests and talents in order to prevent boredom as well as bickering;
- regularly rock an' roll dance.

Except for the last, my Americanized version wasn't so different from what Confucius urged: Authority, ~~Obedience~~, Division of Labor, Affection. The object of my search would thus have to be

- confident, but capable of laughing at himself (and me if it were absolutely necessary);
- well-endowed with whatever it takes to excel in his field as well as the courage to venture into new territory like the kitchen;
- committed to The Chopsticks-Fork Principle;
- involved in Music or Art, that is, the only two disciplines in which I had no aptitude or expertise (maybe I should have added "Arrogant" to the first list);
- energetic (by Chuck Berry's, not Frank Sinatra's standards).

The American wrote "Being in Love"; the Chinese elaborated with "Sharing Good Experiences."

So I got a job in the music department. Finding no winners, I took to hanging around the art department. At its first party, I met Bennett Bean, the date who had dared tell me that I spoke pidgin English to my mother:

- We danced nonstop for two hours—"Stamina" and "Fluid Movements." ✓✓
- We talked about family—"Domestically Inclined." ✓
- We toured his pottery studio—"Productive." ✓
- We played jacks with my roommates—"Open-minded." ✓

217

- We laughed—"Witty." ✓
- And, oh yes, we kissed under the bamboo—"Good Experience." ✓

The "equality" factor was resolved on our first date. Taking me to see a movie, I was hoisted into Wallace, the Volkswagen bus that Bennett drove like a Ferrari. For two hours, I tried to make interesting conversation while groping for the leverage that would keep me in a narrow seat that was situated too high off the floor and too far from the dashboard to allow feet or hands to reach either. Between phrases of life history, my neck was whiplashing laterally each time another L.A. Freeway Driver passed us on the right. By the time we arrived in Little Tokyo, the two double features—quadruple doses of Toshiro Mifune and Shintaro Katsu—gave me enough time to recover. The swordplay was spectacular, the female characters were not. The men strode, the women shuffled. The men initiated, the women succumbed. The men barked, the women giggled. Whatever strength the latter exhibited was born of endurance, patience, resignation, and manipulation. The men acted, the women reacted. On the way home, I began, "Bennett, let me tell you about the difference between traditional Chinese and Japanese women. Better yet, let me tell you about the Fang and Bao women in the family." The news didn't seem to affect his mood, although he later admitted to being slightly crestfallen that I wouldn't walk three steps behind him.

Soon after that, the "competition" question was answered. After I judged a forensic debate in Santa Barbara, we had two options: see a movie for the second time or go bowling. As we both claimed not to have much experience, we got our shoes and score sheet. After a long search, we found a "children's" ball with a weight that wouldn't dislocate my shoulder but with holes sufficiently large for my fingers. Bennett went first. His form was flawless; he got a spare. He intended to win. So did I. Poised at the end of the lane, in pure Chinese-Will-Power-Mode, I relived that recess in 4th grade. Bennett: 86. Cathy: 204.

Once again his good mood was unaffected. Next, Bennett's Intelligence Quotient was tested. My inclination was to provoke a disagreement for no reason other than to see how well dates could argue. Refusing to fight, he left the room, but not before kissing me on the forehead. I was outflanked and didn't mind—it was such a gentle (cautious?) kiss. Content that the matchmaker had done well, I accepted

Bennett's proposal two weeks later. Of course the wedding would have to wait until our schooling was completed. There was also the matter of my parents—they who grew up on *The Sayings of Confucius*.

> Great Man does not have the edge of the collar of his
> garments colored either plum or deep red. The garments
> which he wears about the house are neither red nor violet.
> In summer he wears about the house a single gown of
> either fine or coarse hemp; when leaving the house he
> adds an additional gown. In winter his outer black gown
> is worn over a gown lined with lamb's wool; the outer
> undyed gown is worn over one lined with deer's fur; the
> outer yellow gown is worn over one lined with fox fur. At
> home he wears a lined gown which is longer than the one
> he would wear on ceremonial occasions; in addition the
> right sleeve is kept short at home for convenience in using
> the arm. He always wears a nightshirt, and it is half again
> as long as his body. For home wear his gowns are lined
> with thick fox or badger fur. Except for funerals, he
> always wears all his insignia hanging from his sash. Except
> for the skirt worn at sacrifices, his clothes always are cut
> and fitted. On visits of condolence he wears neither the
> wool-lined gown nor the dark hat. On the first day of the
> month he always attends upon his prince dressed in for-
> mal attire. When fasting, he always wears freshly laun-
> dered clothes made of hemp.

For whatever his inner qualifications, Bennett's packaging left something to be desired.

- His beard and hair were excessive.
- His angular "look" was not in vogue (actually, with so much hair, front and back, his features were barely detectable.).
- His clothes were very tired. Except for the socks—he didn't bother with those at all (or underwear, but they didn't know that at the time).
- His nails were clogged with dry clay.
- He wore cowboy boots.

And that was only what met the eye. What they didn't see was the "4-F" he framed from the Draft Board, supposedly for having been comatose after falling off a 40-foot cliff when he was a child, more likely because the Board psychiatrist wasn't overly confident that

Bennett, the only guy in line without skivvies, had fully recovered. His friends in the nudist colony congratulated him, his three-legged goat hobbled in joy, and his neighbors in the tree house made a tequila run to Tijuana.

My parents sat shivah. His, however, were ecstatic. Dr. William Bennett Bean wrote medical tomes as well as a 12-page limerick entitled

"Omphalosophy and Worst Verse,
An Inquiry into the Inner (and Outer) Significance
of the Belly Button"
(Not previewed, sanctioned, aided or undermined by
the Bureau of Navel Affairs)

And now he could start Sunday dinner conversations with questions like, "Cathy, what do you think is the greatest challenge facing our students in higher education?" Mrs. Bean, née Abigail Shepard of The National Society of the Colonial Dames of America,[11] who had been dreading the scenario of Bennett at the front door, introducing his barefoot wife to a surprised family, was relieved beyond measure when I appeared instead, shod. If immediately planning an engagement party didn't make her cup overflow, her mother's welcome did. Granny, née Margaret Churchward March of Cincinnati, although not quite all there in the living room, was sufficiently in her mind to ask that she and I be left alone while we got acquainted. For fifteen minutes she interviewed me, mostly about family. Sitting demurely on the edge of the couch, ankles crossed to the side, hands lightly folded, I responded directly to each question. With finality, she then instructed me "not to move" while she went upstairs. Returning a few minutes later, Bennett's grandmother carefully deposited an armload of antique silver spoons and jewelry into my lap, saying, "I wasn't sure you'd get these, but now I am." For some people, marbles aren't nearly as important as good manners.

We then proceeded to dinner which I ate without any visible qualms. When I had been fervently Lutheran because my mother had been too wise to forbid my dating and too smart to think Confucius couldn't use a little fire and brimstone to keep me physically strong,

[11] Unlike the **Daughters of the American Revolution** who could obtain membership by virtue of being related to soldiers, the Colonial Dames had to be descended from "leaders."

mentally awake, and morally straight, i.e., collectively virginal, I got to know all about Sunday Dinners and Potluck Suppers—tuna casserole, Jello with fruit cocktail and baby marshmallows, Swedish meatballs, and iceberg lettuce. By the time I met Granny, I could switch from a Chopsticks mode into a Fork frame of mind with hardly a slip of etiquette.

As I entered the dining room, I saw what I expected: napkins in silver rings, forks, knives, iced water, salt cellars, wine glasses, lots of plates and Father Bean standing before a chunk of meat no pair of chopsticks could disseminate. What I didn't notice was any apparent preparation. Then and since then, we would all be in the living room one minute, and ready to dine the next. At no time did I ever hear or see Mother Bean cooking, even when we stayed for a week. To someone who had been raised in the Vesuvius Culinary Institute, it didn't seem possible that dinner could appear without grumbling, spewing, quaking, smoking and searing. Bao kitchens were full of sound and furor with so much tasting, advising, and discussing that the many cooks (i.e., guests) ate half the meal before it was served (another reason for quantity). In contrast, Mother Bean's Abracadabra School of Cooking made dinner appear, gently. (Eventually, I opted for her "it was nothing" approach over the "much ado about everything" style. I made a lot of headway when I discovered the secret ingredient in her pantry—a freezer.)

After dinner, I saw Father Bean clear and wash the dishes. I suggested to Bennett that this was worthy of emulation. (Eventually, I found out how very much he thought otherwise when, soon after we married, I went to a weeklong conference. Upon returning, I saw every dish we owned in the sink, dirty. On top of those, also dirty, were new ones. No, he hadn't bought more. He had *made* more.)

Dishes done, the Beans initiated me into another family tradition - the sing-along. With heartfelt thanks to Florrie, music counselor at Camp Rotomac, this Chinese immigrant was able to cheer everyone immensely by also knowing and loving Songs from the African Veldt.

When we were married by the book in 1966, no one west of the Mississippi thought there was a problem, while everyone east of the Hackensack had misgivings. After my father broke out in hives when I said, "I do," I broke in several self-righteous high horses. For a long time, we were not "*not polite.*" My career choices didn't help ease the tension—teaching in the Black Studies Program, marching with students against the Vietnam War, quitting before my tenure took effect, and opening up an aerobics studio. Designing the logo to reflect my philosophy, I used the logical bi-conditional and created "Living Mind if and only if Body Works; Living Body if and only if Mind Works."

My mother was not amused. Her silence on how I spent most of my waking hours left little we could talk about that didn't remind her that she was "incomplete." She had one daughter who filled the public success slot and another who acquiesced to being their handmaid in this life and next but, increasingly, none who would be her kind of scholar.

Bennett came to the rescue. His life path had veered from *La Boheme* to having a career as a college professor and making sculpture shown in The Whitney Museum. He also put together their greenhouse. It was a present from Bette to our parents, given at the first family Christmas to which we were invited since we had married five years earlier. Bennett agreed to assemble it.

The work took a week. In freezing rain. Despite the lack of visibility, my father detected the meticulous work of hands disciplined by the materials of his art and hardened by winters on the steppes of Iowa— the equivalent of numbering and dating each page of a long letter. When it was ready for the plants, my mother saw the regard for beauty that kept this son-in-law out of the mainstream and in the studio. From then on, my mother for the most part accepted this surrogate for a disappointing daughter and created a space next to Bette's trophies in the family room for the show announcements, magazine articles and other visible evidence of his accomplishments. Things were looking up.

Although Bennett played the part, he still didn't look much like a Confucian "Great Man." Consistent with the personality profile I had outlined before meeting him, his view that the world was "delicious" led him to taste and invent concoctions most wouldn't conceive or consider. He trekked to Quartzsite, Arizona, for a "Rock Pow-wow and *Gem*boree." He raised hens that laid green eggs. He went to a Boston hospital where he had his brain waves recorded and a New Jersey one to x-ray his Buddha.

A casual onlooker like me saw nothing to justify the time and expense:
- a piece of rock labeled "Coprolite" but commonly known as dinosaur dung. (The petrified walrus penis came later);
- a chicken dinner that I calculated must have cost sixteen times

Would you believe:

BENJAMIN FRANKLIN WAS CHINESE?

Counting sheep causes feet to grow?
Cold germs can't exist in traffic?

Well, how about the idea that:

YOU CAN BE REALLY HEALTHY EVEN IF YOU DON'T EXERCISE?

*AEROBICS**MUSCLE-TONING**YOGA**DIET*
Jacksonburg Road near Blue Ridge Lumber

GIFT CERTIFICATES FROM THE HEART

FOR THE HEART, AND THE LUNGS, AND THE ARTERIES, AND THE GLUTEUS . . .

*If you answered "yes" to any of the above, please call 362-5622. We have a lovely bridge in just the right color that's on sale for a limited time only.

more to raise than to buy and twice as long to chew;
- a plastic frame encasing a long sheet of electroencephalograms with a few penciled arrows marking the points where aesthetic decisions had been made and where the doctor identified his waves as resembling an eight-year old's; and
- a quarter hour when every member of the Radiology Department, except one, watched the Buddha get scanned. The exception was the medic who had to check one woman for a possible subdural hematoma. Mesmerized by the vision of a bearded man carrying his Buddha through the hospital lobby, she had walked into a door and knocked herself out.

To Bennett, the fossil was beautiful, the dinner a feast, the sheet a piece of Conceptual Art, and the x-ray a means to diagnose why the statue—another Good Deal—had a dislocated head.

His flare for sartorial iconoclasm didn't diminish either. Summer and winter, he wore a long-sleeved turtleneck as the backdrop for whatever else he liked. Long before the "layered look" became fashionable, Bennett's style was its precursor including the down vest when only Eddie Bauer sold it to duck (and geese) hunters. Even his cousin's daughter, Alison, too young to know or care about "style," was impressed. Snugly seated on his lap while the adults conversed, she methodically counted the articles of clothing separating her from the buff chest of this "once-removed" relative. Reaching "five," she peered down the turtle's neck for more.

Unable to do the same as Alison, my mother ceased to comment on Bennett's wardrobe even while she rewrote the history of his beard. Having grown another after the wedding, he finally trimmed it closer to his chin. Taking me aside (which is the way a Chinese mother conveys personal information to a son-in-law), she said, "I'm so glad Bennett took my advice about growing a beard; he looks so much more, well..." Not wishing to overstate the improvement and seem boastful or strain all credibility, she groped for just the right word, "...so Professorial."

She also mentioned something about the whiskers hiding a few facial defects. This was auspicious indeed. For among Chinese, anything that can be cosmetically altered stops short of being a deformity, a mark of the gods' disfavor or of failure in a previous lifetime. With each spoken criticism, I became more relaxed. We were becoming comfortably "*not polite.*" Their image of us was further softened when we bought a house and I stopped taking birth control pills. Calculating that a year or two out of the classroom wouldn't be too much of a professional setback, I planned to care for a baby while writing the dissertation that still stood between me and a Ph.D. Our "family plan" was set back, however, when the effects of the pill didn't turn off until a few years after I went off. On the other hand, with a house of our own, only Bennett commuting, and hopes for a child, we had many more safe subjects to discuss and time to relax. The summer before our sixth anniversary, Mommy, Bette and Bette's two kids came to visit for the first time. They studied the route carefully, stocked the car with enough food to last days, agreed to allot time for several pit stops, and then proceeded from northeastern New Jersey to northwestern New Jersey.

After lunch, we went to a nearby glen. The brook, cutting through moss-covered rock banks, cascaded down a flat boulder into a pool of mountain coolness. My mother compared its beauty to places in China. Impulsively, Bette took off her shoes and glided down the natural stone slide, followed by Lisa. A few minutes elapsed before Bennett could get out of his many layers and jump in. Standing at the water's edge, with my young nephew and mother beside me, I was euphoric. Leaning toward me, looking perplexed, my mother remarked, "There's nothing wrong with his skin."

I asked, "What do you mean?"

"Bennett...his skin...his skin is fine."

Bewildered, I confirmed, "Yes," adding, "He still has that scar on his leg from falling off the cliff. But it's faded and hardly noticeable."

"No, no...his chest. It's okay."

"Of course it's okay. Why wouldn't it be?"

"His clothes—those turtlenecks....You mean, he doesn't *have* to dress that way?!!? He isn't *hiding* anything??! *Aiiya!*"

As her discovery sank in, I nearly joined the others for an unscheduled swim.

On the way home, tears of laughter mingled with the brook water as we told and retold the story of my mother's revelation and relief. Once home and showered, it was Bette's turn to take me aside. Using our bedroom to change, she pointed to Bennett's brain waves hanging on the wall.

"Cathy, we all know you've been trying to get pregnant, but do you really need to make a display of your rhythm charts?"

Eventually, I put away the rhythm charts and the "rhythm charts." Eventually, Bennett bought a regular suit, though he didn't wear it much. Or its successor. Then when he developed a bit of a middle-age sag, he happily outgrew them all. About the time we celebrated our Silver Anniversary, my parents stopped hoping he would dress like other people. I think that was also when his work first showed up in a national magazine.

Three years shy of our thirtieth anniversary, the issue surfaced again.

"Bennett, it's the *White House*. You've got to wear your suit."

"No I don't."

"Yes you do."

"No I don't."

"But Mommy wants a picture. Of you with Clinton. She can't know you went looking like, well, like you usually do!"

Responding to the magic word, "Mommy," Bennett, once again displaying the depth of his commitment to me, conceded, "I'll think about it."

Two days later, his head cleared the landing enough so that I could see from my desk.

"I did it."

"Did what?"

"Wrote a letter."

"A letter?"

"About getting a suit."

I love mail-order. I've even gotten dinner delivered UPS, but I wasn't delighted to hear I'd be escorted to my one, likely my only, White House reception by someone in an outfit from a catalog.

"Omigod."

"Don't worry—if this works, it'll be great!"

"What do you mean 'works'? What do you mean 'great'?"

And so he told me about the letter he 'd sent to one of the foremost fashion designers.

> I've been invited to the White House. I have nothing to wear. I think you make beautiful clothes. I think I make beautiful pots. Do you want to swap?

Or something like that. She's got the only copy. Why was I surprised? We had traded Bennett's pots for the jacuzzi tub in our bathroom and the caesarian operation that delivered William into this world. For two days I prayed to the Seventh Avenue God, "Please, please."

On the third day, he got a call to come in and pick out a suit.

Bringing in one of his pit-fired, painted, gilded earthenware vessels, he still had some credit.

"You look like a denim sort of a guy. We'll send you a shirt too."

When he told me, I urged him to call back, "My wife says she's tired of me being a 'denim sort of a guy'. Can you send the cashmere instead?"

Bennett ended up in a suit of elegant proportions and magnificent material. My mother was so pleased with the presidential picture, she didn't even mention the turtleneck he wore instead of the shirt and tie. In fact, it was only Hilary Rodham Clinton's appearance that puzzled her.

"What's that?"

"Christmas tree lights, Mommy."

"What are they doing there?"

"Well, it was the season."

"For a tree, yes. For around her neck? *Aiiya*!!"
"Aiiya—our first lady wore blinking lights in public!!"

We had been in the U.S. since 1946, but 1993 was the first time I heard my mother refer to someone in the White House as "our." We make many cultural journeys—into and out of schools, families, neighborhoods, moods, cliques, jobs, ideologies, countries, mindsets. My mother's journey began as a child living in a household with more servants than family members and culminated when she stood in line, in the rain, to cast her first vote as a U.S. citizen. I made a "duck-rabbit" tee-shirt to dramatize the "switching" she did with such proficiency and grace. On the front it reads, "Empress Dowager." On the back is "Just Another Immigrant."

CHAPTER 9

EXERCISE #3

In theory, education involves:
- learning from experience—when we go from particulars to generalizations;
- being rational—when we use the rules of logic to derive conclusions from assumptions that we may or may not have proven true;
- understanding paradigms—when we apply, analyze, or construct idealized physical, philosophical, or creative models.

In practice, teaching-learning-living is a lot messier.

For instance, we may generalize about Chinese based upon our experience with a few of the millions available, arrive at conclusions based on those generalizations, and then attribute them to a newcomer whom we have designated to be "Chinese." In essence, that's what my mother did when she conceptualized the model Confucian second daughter and rooted me in that image. For her this was not only "natural," but part of her responsibility—to give me a way for me to know who I am and how I was related to her.

Or we may stylize and characterize clothing into costumes, languages into lingoes, religions into fables, faces into cartoons, buildings into neighborhoods, activities into jobs, and attitudes into voting blocs in order to dress, communicate, legislate, advertise, plan, propagandize, include, exclude. We do some or all of this publicly and privately, consciously and unconsciously, in good faith and not, to or for ourselves and others. In other words, we generalize and expect. We have to if we are to learn anything about anything, let alone *do* anything with the knowledge.

In the process, however, chances are someone will think we're also "stereotyping." Exactly where and how we draw the line is critical and a lot less obvious than some of us have supposed.

It takes time to learn and then to think about what you think you have learned. So do yourself and others a favor by actually and metaphorically remembering to:

AVOID MASS CONFUSION
(or masked Confucian),
WEAR A NAME TAG
and HELP SAVE A FACE!!

Donny Decker called Bennett Bean "Burt" because no real man could possibly be named "Bennett." His home base was one of the three houses in the salt marshes of Travis on Staten Island, where his friends parked before motor launching to New Jersey, where they worked. We rented the house next door, once a tavern serving the wealthy who circled Staten Island as a summer excursion. The third was where Donny's wife lived with his mother. This put them about half a block away, close enough for a relationship, far enough so they wouldn't mess with his stuff—parts and wholes of trucks, machines, cranes, and sheds, along with parts and wholes of the equipment to keep it all in a constant state of repair and replacement. In the vicinity was a Con Ed smokestack. Around the clock, it spewed camouflage for the most vicious mosquitoes known to humankind that descended the chimneys nightly to devour what our corpuscles produced that day.

Donny didn't seem to know my name at all until the day his German Shepherd, #2, came up from behind and nudged me with its big scruffy shoulder. I nudged back with my smaller one. Then he lay down near me while I continued to pick through the broken glass and rocks in an attempt to find some dirt for a garden. When Donny came out of his back door, #2 didn't even try to be himself but stayed put. For the first time, I put my hand lightly on his back.

Looking up, I commented on the dog's lack of motion and my unprecedented one, "He's lonely."

Donny nodded. Neither of us mentioned #1—a big black mutt, leader of the pack, now dead. Neither of us wondered any more if #2 would take over the canine patrol—scaring the b'jeezus out of thieves who tried to break into the parked cars. The one time I witnessed the action was because the dogs had "treed" a man onto the roof of a sedan, collectively barking and foaming. When Donny appeared from nowhere to call them off, the would-be robber looked relieved—for about two seconds. Then he realized The Master of the Hounds was toting a shotgun.

It was reassuring to know that Donny liked us. We could tell because when we slept late, he didn't crank up his toys until he knew the noise wouldn't wake us. Or when a hung-over Bennett was trying to figure out how his VW bus got back in the middle of the night when, to the best of his memory, he had left it "parked" in a snow drift and staggered the mile home.

"But Donny, I'm sure I locked it."

"You did, Burt."

In return, we provided him with some entertainment—like shouting and waving our arms at his crane when he used it to move a truck from one part of his junkyard to another, passing over our house en route. And though he was mystified why "Burt" did chores around the house, or that he "allowed" me to buy a Morris Minor from gypsies without realizing that the bottom of the unibody vehicle was missing, he didn't openly mock Bennett. Instead, he took him to Stucky's, the largest foreign car dump on the east coast, and brought back a bottom, several tires, and an extra engine (just in case I drove as well as I bargained). Shaking his head a little sadly, Donny accepted that some men need more protection from wives than thieves. Shaking mine, I accepted that my backyard, now filled with spare parts, was starting to look like an extension of his.

When he wasn't rescuing cars and people, Donny was a Vanbro Cement truck driver on the weekdays and a mariner on the weekends. The first venture we heard about had to do with convincing his buddies to invest in a secret expedition to bring up, "tax free," the silver bullion from a ship that had sunk in one of the Great Lakes. They didn't believe he'd really figured out its location. After news reports of the find by licensed treasure hunters proved that Donny had been right, whatever else Donny thought up, from then on they were willing.

So when he bought a 96-foot freighter, no one hesitated to go for a maiden voyage, Bennett included. This also happened to be the same voyage that Donny discovered the intercom system was on the blink. This meant that when he wanted to go into reverse to avoid eating some of the Staten Island shoreline, no one in the engine room got the message. All they could hear was a lot of bell-clanging, that they interpreted as an expression of Donny's great joy at finally being a captain. Realizing they could sink, Bennett nonchalantly sidled to the lifeboats. There he met one of the crew's girlfriends, already primed for jumping ship. As the two watched landfall approaching too quickly, Bennett had the added problem of how to get into the lifeboat and not reveal the fact that, in his haste to obey Donny's yelling outside our window, "Time and tide wait for no man," he had pulled on a pair of jeans with its back seam split. Without any underwear on, Bennett weighed the consequences of letting her take the first lifeboat alone versus the chance her boyfriend would survive the shipwreck and decide that Bennett's exposure was intentional.

They all made it back, dry. Donny's reputation didn't suffer just because his "boat" had rearranged some of the beach. Hailing from early settlers of the area, his exploits only enhanced the Decker name. We had never thought of Staten Island as having natives or settlers. This was reinforced by the fact that when we first moved to Travis, reputedly integral to one of the five New York boroughs, Bennett and I couldn't believe that the only way we could subscribe to *The New York Times* was by mail. But then we looked outside one day to see Donny's cohorts huddled around him, looking down at something.

"What're you doing Donny?" Bennett called out the back door (as I would one day ask a child holding a compass in a Montessori hall-way).

Holding up something, he replied, "Trying to figure out how this works."

"What is it?"

"A sextant."

"What for?"

"To find out where I am."

Heck, if Donny needed a sextant, then we couldn't possibly expect the newspaper to find us without federal help.

Being located on Staten Island physically and psychologically, Donny would have found he was a chauvinist in at least five funda-mental ways, but he was generalizing, not stereotyping. Later, when we moved and arranged for one of Bennett's colleagues to "inherit" our rental, Donny became a good neighbor to a gay man. It took a few weeks, but how could Donny not learn to respect someone who stuck it out even when his air conditioner got stolen off the front steps on the day he moved in, and a huge compressor was installed right under his bedroom window the following week, and, finally, a pig was penned near his back door?

Going from renting in Travis to house-sitting on Grymes Hill took us from the lowest point in Staten Island to the highest. The altitudi-nal difference was purely geographical. The contrast between Donny and too many of our colleagues was stark, all the more so because they were members of "an institution of higher learning" who were sup-posed to know that there are worlds of difference—something Donny understood and respected without benefit of advanced degrees. Living on Staten Island kept us on our multicultural toes. Daily, it was like shopping for one experience and buying into something else altogether. The unpredictability was a crash course on our ethnic or "class" diversity and probably helped us shift from one set of values and assumptions to another more quickly than would have happened had the world behaved as we expected. Take one of the several deans at the college where Bennett taught. When I was introduced to him, he clicked his heels as he bowed and kissed the back of my hand. Without waiting for a return click, he stated, "We haven't seen you two at church yet."

In that millisecond, his bow went from a "duck" to a "rabbit," from Elizabethan courtier to Fascist general and I went from "new acquaintance" to "fair game," so I bypassed the "How do you do" and, without excuse or apology, stated back, "We don't go to church."

My answer, still true months later, didn't stop the same dean from asking Bennett and me to be human symbols of the theme chosen for the annual Faith and Life Week: East Meets West. Our only duty was to appear at the service prepared and conducted by students. We did. The kids, not unaffected by the folk music of the time, accompanied themselves on guitars and such other instruments as *Peter, Paul and Mary* would have used. After a lot of clapping and the joining of hands and swaying, a young man got up to deliver the sermon. In essence, his point was, "When, like Georgie Girl,[12] we come off the shelf, or come down from our LSD high, or get over our infatuation with Zen Buddhism, we must turn back to Christ who is The *real* Way, the *only* Truth, and the *brightest* Light."

I would have kept my mouth shut, but the Chaplain put me on the spot by introducing us and asking me to comment on the glory of God from "my" perspective. So I invited the kids to stay on for a discussion about the assumptions underlying the sermon and its effect on the sincerity of their "East Meets West" theme. Within minutes of my initial analysis, the Chaplain left in a fury, expecting his prize pupil, the sermonizer, to follow in his wake. But the boy stayed on through to the intellectually bloody end, through his anger, confusion, and finally, his tears.

Word got around. Invitations from students increased while those from the administration went down to zero, except those from The Faculty Wives Club who weekly sent me something—book covers

[12] Starring Lynn Redgrave, this hit movie of the time was about a painfully shy, physically dumpy girl who finds herself in the swinging London of the mid '60s because of —and despite—her exposure to the loose morals of her wild roommate.

with the college logo, recipes, calendars—and monthly requested my presence at their teas. Weekly, monthly, weekly, monthly, they wore me down. The following November, I finally went. It was a tea in honor of Miss New York State, "one of our very own coeds." Prior to the big date, another of the less avid tea-goers had warned me.

"Cathy, keep in mind something about this area."

Pointing to the street signs outside our house, she said, "See that? This used to be the intersection of Occident and Orient Avenues. After the Japanese bombed Pearl Harbor, the Borough council decided "Orient" wasn't patriotic. So they decided to rename the street. Considering the view of the harbor from this most high point of the island, they chose "Sunrise Terrace."

I laughed, "You're kidding. They never heard of 'The Land of the Rising Sun'?"

"Apparently not."

Still, I wasn't prepared for Tea with the Faculty Wives. Entering the President's residence, I was given a name tag, "Mrs. Bennett Bean, Art Department." I thought about flipping it over and writing "Cathy Bao Bean, Philosophy" but didn't. Sitting down, I was treated to an operatic solo by the guest of honor and then a talk on the spiritual uplift she got from participating in the Atlantic City *Miss America* pageant. As soon as etiquette would permit, I located "Mrs. President" and tried to leave.

"Oh, Mrs. Bean, we are so delighted you could *finally* join us."

"Yes, thank you. It's been very interesting."

"Really, you must come again next month when we have our Christmas Tea. We're asking all our foreign students to talk to us about Christmas in their home countries, and wouldn't it be lovely if one of our very own Faculty Wives could lead the discussion by talking about Christmas in China."

I didn't miss a beat, "We don't celebrate Christmas in China."

She didn't either, "Well, make something up—it'll be *so* nice."

Thinking I could escape her state of mind, I worked on getting my own "name tag" by signing up to be a volunteer interviewer in a campus governance study on how decisions are really made. Going up to the front desk of a big New York hotel, I asked for the American Association for Higher Education's room number. The concierge took one look at me and said, in a voice not designed for confidentiality, "This is a respectable place, we do not allow prostitutes on the premises."

Stunned, I sputtered "campus," "education," and the Project Director's name—everything to assure this man of who I was. Without another word, he telephoned the A.A.H.E. suite and told the Director that, "a person" was in the lobby claiming to have legitimate business with him. Asking for my name, he spoke it into the receiver. Obviously hearing confirmation of the nature of my "appointment," but still believing that I was trying to "improve" myself by going from streetwalker to call girl, he insisted the Director come downstairs. When he did, the concierge, unwilling to impugn a "regular" guest's reputation outright, instructed the Director that he must personally escort me upstairs *and down*. Which he did, seemingly unaware and unperturbed that I had just been humiliated. Deflated in a way Mrs. President couldn't manage, I followed, wondering what had been the deciding factor. I thought of the Bag Lady on the Staten Island Ferry. Had she cut my hair, the concierge may have let me pass for a decent sort. The next morning, getting ready to canvass students about who they thought makes the crucial decisions on campus, I considered wearing my hair up. Then I got angry and let it flow.

I should've worn it up. In the crowded cafeteria, while scribbling notes on why most kids thought departmental secretaries were the real decision-makers (no surprise to me), a nearby student, wearing gloves, put his hand in his pocket, along with my hair. Not realizing I was scuffling behind him tethered to his jacket, I was led backwards through the room. Once we cleared the door and the noise, I finally got his attention and, to his surprise, retrieved the lower two feet. Soon after that, I closed the refrigerator on it and then got it caught in the rollers of a copier machine and had to hold on while its delay system took its time to turn off. With so much hair history—and that's not counting the time I set it on fire—I decided that, as a rule, wearing it up at work was the better part of valor and, if I met another concierge from hell, I'd mention something about bedbugs in a very loud voice. [13]

> When I got my first teaching job, I self-censored my attire as well.
> "Mrs. Bean."
> "Yes?"

[13] The 1990 film, *Pretty Woman*, is one of the most popular movies in Asia. About a prostitute with principles who marries a millionaire who gets them as a result of falling in love with her, I especially liked the scenes when the concierge learns a few lessons.

"People are saying you've been wearing slacks to class."

"Excuse me?"

"I said, it's been rumored that your mode of dress is not, shall we say, customary for women faculty."

"And mini skirts are?"

"Well, that *is* the style these days. And we *do* try and stay current."

"Yes, so do I. Unfortunately, classes only last fifty minutes and I'm only five feet tall."

"I don't understand. What does that have to do with dressing properly?"

"For me, everything. In a mini, I would not be able to raise my arm to reach the upper half of the blackboard without exposing a great deal more than I'm willing to show. And because I would just as soon use class time for teaching rather than for erasing, I dress myself accordingly."

She didn't respond well to my rationale or my tone. It seemed to be coming from someone who appeared to be about the same age as her still-dependent daughter, someone who had no right to argue with her. The fact that most Chinese look relatively immature until well into their forties may be a social asset in a youth-oriented culture, but it can be a professional liability in a business setting.

There were others who thought I should be seen if properly attired but not heard. During the first faculty meeting where students were given a place on the agenda to present their requests for expanding the curriculum and gaining greater access to the facilities, no one could help noticing the antics of one geography professor. Besides sitting at the executive table in front, he was still wearing a heavy layer of pancake makeup—something he often did to call attention to the fact that he had just "rushed" from the TV studio where he was a commentator representing the conservative view of any issue. Every time a student got up to speak, he would "casually" turn his back on him or her and noisily flip his newspaper in front of his face. If the floor was taken by a colleague, he would put down the paper and give his full attention to the proceedings. When I got up to voice my support for establishing an interdisciplinary Black Studies Program, he began to read the papers again. At that, one of the students addressed him by name and asked why he was not paying attention to me.

He replied, "Students are empty vessels into which we, the teachers, have the sole duty of cramming as much information as possible. I have no obligation to listen to this…this," And while he shooed his hand in my direction, he struggled to find the words that would match his dismissive gesture, "this fffluff of fffeathers."

Held in awe by many who considered him a celebrity, his contempt would have solicited more favor than laughter had he not been so alliterative. As it was, he came very close to sounding like Daffy Duck. TV personality notwithstanding, he spoke with a what Chinese call a "big tongue."

It didn't take long to realize that getting my own teaching position cited on my own name tag wasn't going to resolve the real identity issues. Although learning how and what to teach required a lot of *shuai*, this kind of swinging was energizing. However, getting along with some of my colleagues put me into a tailspin, especially the new chair of the philosophy department. Regularly he left scribbled notes on my desk with instructions on whether they were to be typed or mimeographed. With equal regularity, I put them back on his desk in the same condition as I received them, often attached to elaborate and lengthy instructions on how to operate the office machines and an offer to help if he were inclined to learn. At first, I reminded him that I was his colleague, not his typist. When that did nothing to reorganize his set mind, I got on my high teaching horse and spent hours perfecting snide memos, and then hours more thinking about them. He never acknowledged my responses but added other kinds of notes to me asking that I justify the inclusion of "novelists" like Dostoevsky and Camus in a "philosophy" course on existentialism. After suggesting that he read a few books, I pretended to ignore his other forays into a life of the mind. The more he belittled me, the more I fought to appreciate my worth. Finally, at the first departmental meeting after we had relocated in a small house acquired by the school, the chairman sat at the head of the table and, looking only at me, said, "I've scheduled a little Open House to let students know where we are and to see if we can convince a few to enroll as majors. Cathy, how about baking some cookies for the occasion?"

"Chinese don't bake. We steam. Why don't you ask one of the men here?"

He didn't, but offered his wife for the job. Another did the same, after shaking his head at me to underscore that, once again, I had proven myself unable to be a team player. The chairman coughed politely, signaling his willingness to overlook my childish/female recalcitrance, then made a flourish of checking his agenda for the next item. He had a way of using our meetings as an opportunity to announce all the many many deeds he had accomplished since we last sat together, like negotiating the correct change with several tollbooth operators and successfully performing his morning ablutions. By the time we neared the end of his long list, I was barely paying attention.

"Wouldn't it be nice if you made curtains for our new home here." It was not a question.

Hearing the silence, I looked up, then followed his line of sight to see who was standing behind me. Obviously someone must have entered the room while I was too busy with my doodling to notice. Finding no one, and seeing all the men around the table looking at me, expectantly, I asked him, "Do you mean me?"

"Of course, Cathy."

"You're kidding, right?"

"It would add a nice touch, don't you think?"

I declined the honor and proposed, instead, that he perform a rather tricky biological maneuver with the rods. The belligerence intensified further. I was up for tenure. If offered a fourth-year contract, the job was mine forever. Throughout the review process, the chairman countered every move I made. Though I got tenure anyway, I was exhausted, burned out. For months he had controlled my mood. I didn't know how not to hate him and, therefore, myself, for letting him get to me every time. My ignorance ran amok at the last gathering before the summer break. We were discussing the role our department should play in the Black Studies Program, a project that did materialize despite Daffy's objections. To my somewhat radical outline of how to support the program, the chairman retorted, "You can say that. You can say anything you want. You've got tenure. Most of us don't."

To which I snapped, "Since when have you known me to refrain from saying anything because I was afraid of the administration? It's you who think that tenure is the road to free speech, not me. And to show you just what I think of your precious tenure, I resign."

Seeing his disbelief was incredibly gratifying. For a while. But his astonishment was all that resulted. It wasn't a "bonus." With everyone playing a different game, there was no home run, no point to be made. Later, someone told me that all I had needed to do to fulfill my part of the fourth-year contract was show up for the new academic year. Evidently, I had enough sick-leave accumulated to have gone in

for the first day of the fall semester, and not show up until most of it
was over. I could have made the Chairman's life miserable and fulfill
the tenure contract. I didn't know that at the time. It may have made a
difference but, more surely, it would have prolonged the misery and
delayed the transformation of a "little ambassador" into a "double
agent."

The husband who had offered his wife's cookies asked me, "What's
your beef? You got re-hired, then tenure—everything you wanted."
Maybe not until many more women and men went public about this
did he get the beef. After I left that job, I often recalled my friend's
landlady back in Berkeley. And felt more than sympathy for her when
I did. She hadn't quit. But then, I didn't go mad. Instead, I went home
to make a baby (as well as curtains) for the nursery, to become open
again, to recognize myself.

This was possible because we had become homeowners. When we
first started house-hunting, I had nowhere in particular in mind for
what difference would it make? As long as we could commute, location wasn't relevant—memories and furniture were portable, and modern communication would keep us connected with family, friends and
colleagues. The important factors at the time were quantifiable: price
to accommodate my budget and height to accommodate Bennett's
sculpture.

We started looking on Staten Island, but the only places we could
afford among those we were shown were buildings on streets judged
"unacceptable" by the written and unwritten criteria of insurance
agents. One place might have been okay once we took out all the
beaded curtains, the many marbleized mirrors (hung in the most peculiar places), and the heavy chains. However, the sheer numbers of half-
dressed men running into and out of the rooms just after and before
we inspected them, convinced me that going from the red-lined to the
red light district was probably not far enough.

Then we looked in Manhattan. This was where Bennett thought
we ought to be. And I agreed. At first. Where else could I take a modern dance class in the same room as Twyla Tharp, change, discuss the
phenomenological reductionism of Merleau-Ponty an hour later, and
then spend the evening skipping a Swedish *schottis* at the Jewish
Community Center? In this universe, the logical choice for us would
have been to buy a loft in SoHo, and hang up an AIR sign to alert fire
fighters that an Artist-In-Residence would be roasted if flames weren't

quenched forthwith. Several of our friends had done this. Like pioneers, they had settled in abandoned warehouses, finding one of these floors more spacious than any comparably priced apartment, and more convenient than "living" in one place, and "working" in another. Faced with this, I pictured my typewriter in the same room as Bennett's table saw. My imagination balked. Then I tried to envision my mother coming up a freight elevator and sitting between the two machines to eat Thanksgiving dinner. My mind refused. I told Bennett he could not be an AIR. He couldn't ask me to invest our savings in such an uncategorized space. He couldn't ask me to ask my mother to eat in a room where he sliced plexiglas as well as turkey.

Gradually, I was realizing that a "place of our own" wasn't just owning a house or even being "where my heart is."[14] Like all the Chinese I knew, there was a part of me that could close the front door, leave the American ways outside, and never consider asking permission before opening another's mail or knocking before entering someone else's room. In this home, it made perfect sense for my mother to conclude that *SanSan* must be sick if her daughter was in a room, alone, with the door closed but not studying. Needing doors for quiet was one thing; needing them for privacy was something that happened only if there was a house guest or plumber roaming around. Yet in my Teaneck house, the Bao walls that separated the rooms had not been torn down. For to the extent we could afford them, each set of walls helped demarcate a way of being, and not just being private. They each held furnishings that helped facilitate and impose order, status, and function in a country where so many seemed confused about who was guilty, or the respect due to elders, or what the back seats of cars were for. More important than being a signal of our individuality or assurance of our privacy, these "Chinese walls" reminded us of what was appropriate.

Maybe this is why Beijing can now think its people can be capitalists without also being our version of liberal. Or why so many Asian countries have had a female head of state when we can still count state governors with one or two hands. When Americans are still struggling

[14] In Chinese, one word—*jia*—is used to mean either, or both. I used to feel disloyal if, in planning the logistics of getting together with my parents, I had to say, for the sake of clarity "your" house as distinct from "my" house or home. When forced to imply, grammatically, that there were two different *jia*, the statement wasn't merely inaccurate, it hinted of disloyalty.

with the transition of taking a "housewife" out of the kitchen and putting her in the capital as a "president," countries where sexuality is not
pervasive but limited to the bedroom, can regard females as being in
the office without worrying about some guy down the hall mistaking
her for a Playmate Bunny. Where people know who they are by what
they are *supposed* to do, they are able to play their roles well. The
Constitution has assured me of American privacy but I needed walls to
maintain certain distinctions and deter Chinese chaos. No loft in
SoHo was cheap enough to overcome the panic I felt at the thought of
living in some holistic, all-purpose, space where only my mind drew
the boundaries.

Next stop: New Jersey.

Looking at the chicken coop, we told the realtor we weren't interested, that the previous tenants had been too short. He pointed out
that the back wall where the nesting boxes had been stacked was tall
enough for any human. Which led us to point out that the front wall
was so low that even I, one of the shorter versions of our species, had
to stoop to get in. And then he explained that a coop was about all our
budget could handle. Which led us to explain that we needed thirteen-
foot ceilings on all sides, not just the one for, even if we could bend,
Bennett's sculpture couldn't. Made of big sheets of plexiglas, yes, they
could be constructed in the back, but getting them out the door to a
gallery or museum would require a flexibility they didn't possess.

So he showed us a cottage with a huge garage. Built to store very
tall machinery, it could easily accommodate the sculpture, in process
and in transit. I was satisfied. Bennett wasn't. Going through the house
a second time, he pointed out that there was only a three-inch clearance between him and the top of the doorways. Which led me to suggest that it could be as much as four or five if he cut his hair. Which
encouraged the realtor to remind him that he wasn't made out of plexiglas and could bend. Bennett then explained that it would be somewhat disconcerting to live in constant fear of being knocked uncon-
scious. To which I responded that, if he did sustain any injuries, we
would be able to afford the best in medical care because we would
have saved hundreds on utilities, the place being so cozy and all.
Stooping his way out, Bennett mumbled something about it being so
cozy that room temperature could be maintained by body heat alone.
Climbing into the bus, I grumbled that he was being just a mite too
picky and his complaining was nothing more than a campaign to try

the city again.

By crossing the river, we had solved the insurance problem. If we also wanted thirteen-foot ceilings at six and a half-foot prices, we would have to go further west and fast. I had worked out a timetable: the first month of our summer vacation, we would find a house, move, and send out our change of address cards. That would leave me July and August to be thoroughly neurotic about what we had accomplished in June. Done well, I could be acclimated to my new surroundings by Labor Day with a week to spare before students laid claim to my time and attention. Anxious to stay on schedule, I talked Bennett into making an offer on an elegant house located in what was once an elegant part of Trenton. There was just enough of a back yard to build a small studio for Bennett. He relented. We offered to buy, contingent upon our getting a mortgage.

Looking up "banks" in the Yellow Pages, we picked one for its brand name. Believing that it was important to make a good impression, I put on my blue suit and left the bearded one at home. Introducing myself to the loan officer, I described the property, and with as much a show of pride as a Chinese can muster without offending the gods, I informed him that we had been conscientious about paying our bills as we incurred them and had, thereby, proven our ability to act responsibly. He responded by telling me that we had also, thereby, no credit rating. Not sure if that was good or bad, I nodded my concurrence. Speechifying about "balloon payments," "title insurance," "points," I did hear an understandable "...$50.00 to apply for a loan." Trying not to gasp, I again nodded, content that the enormous fee would be money well spent if it enabled him to bring us closer to a home. Taking out a form of many pages and colors, he wrote down the preliminaries that I dictated. Asking about our sources of income, I told him where we worked.

"The *art* department?"

Shaking his head as if this was sad indeed, he sighed, put down the pen, and predicted that the most I could hope for was a very small, short-term loan, not enough to warrant the application fee. Rising, he was already looking beyond me to the next person in line. Not rising, I insisted he explain how it could be that a couple, both healthy, well educated and employed, were considered a bad risk. Looming over his desk, his condescension was so burdensome that he had to drawl, "What your husband does is not, shall we say, very stable. And according to the formula, you can't afford this house."

"Why not? What 'formula'?"

"The one we use to determine your budget potential." Pointing to his calculations, he said, "See for yourself."

"We've been paying more than that for rent. Look. You've got the numbers wrong. You've figured this using only my husband's salary."

"That's right. Your job doesn't count."

"Doesn't count? That's absurd. How can it not count?"

"Because you're too...you're still...you're still too...young."

Not waiting for another question, he gave a "come hither" wave to someone in the waiting queue. Dismissed, I picked up my purse and started to walk away, wearing my I-am-so-puzzled look. Then, with an oh-I-get-it snap of the fingers, I turned abruptly and, in a voice that carried well beyond the vicinity of his desk, exclaimed, "Are you trying to tell me you're afraid I'm going to breed?!" Not as good as bedbugs, but good enough when there was no law yet to back up my threat to sue for the unequal treatment due to gender. (As to laws protecting artists, that'll be when hell freezes over.)

When we did find a house and home in rural New Jersey, my appearance in our new neighbors' lives was less expected than the albino deer pictured on the front page story of the hunting season stats. Without too many of us around to learn from, the local populace had the same difficulty placing a Chinese teacher of philosophy in their midst as I had putting my mother in a freight elevator. Which is why I ran the Laundromat. The place could be packed but, whenever people needed help or wanted to complain, they would come clear across the room, dodging armfuls of clothing and open dryer doors to seek me out. More telling was that, despite hearing, "No, I don't work here," they would ask me their questions or lodge their protests anyway, without any doubt of my expertise. I did the best I could—sharing my dimes and quarters, or lending them pen and paper for jotting down to whom a refund should be sent.

It was also during those first years in rural America that I let the pharmacist believe that I had been a bride even before being eligible for the first grade. With no "name tag" except my face, I responded to his questions: "Chinese or Japanese?" and "How come you don't have an accent?" But he had already decided who I had to be before knowing so, when I said that I had come over from China in 1946, when I was four, he still gave me a knowing look and commented, "I see. A war bride." If he couldn't see the difference that a dozen or so chromosomes and years could make, then there was probably very little I could say that would. Like so many distinctions, it takes time and experience to learn them. And some people just don't have enough of either, as *SanSan* hadn't when she couldn't tell which usher was hers at Bette's wedding.

It also takes time to teach: witness the day I became a Filipina for a man at the service station. Seated in the waiting room while our cars were being fixed, we were both flipping through magazines. Although my eyes were cast downward, I was aware of the man's glances. After a few minutes, he leaned toward me and said timidly, "Excuse me. Are you from the Philippines?"

"No. From China."

"Oh." The man sat back into his seat.

Not seeming to require more from me, I didn't follow up with any more. Continuing my search for a good article, I could hear the rate of his flipping increase and then, "Are you sure you're not Filipino?"

"Quite sure."

"Oh. That's too bad."

I tried to read, but there was no way I could ignore his comment or his agitation: fingers drumming, foot tapping, chest heaving with shallow breaths. Finally, with a sigh of resolve, he clapped his magazine to a close, reseated himself at the edge of the chair, stretched in my direction, and said, "I know a Filipino."

"That's nice."

"Maybe you know him too. He lives in Manila. Name is __."

"Doesn't sound familiar. But then, there're a lot of people in Manila."

"Yeah. I guess so." This time he was deflated.

I could feel his disappointment and, with a sigh of my own, I gave in. "My father-in-law was born in the Philippines."

"Gee, that's great." He gathered momentum, there was no stopping him now. "You see, __ and I are pen pals. We collect stamps. It musta been ten years ago when we first...."

Had my car needed more attention, I'm sure the man would have gone on for more than the hour he had already spent giving me a finely tuned account of each philatelic exchange the two had conducted by mail and all the hot dogs they ate while "seeing America" when their correspondence culminated in his friend's visit. By the time my name was called, he was still in overdrive, pulling me after him, a willing but now overloaded trailer. I got up, "Well, that's me. I better go and see how much they're going to charge me for fixing the ol' clunker. It was nice talking with you. Bye."

"Yeah. It was nice. Really nice. Thanks. Thanks...a lot. Uh, I guess I did most of the talking...." his voice trailed off with a touch of embarrassment in it.

"It was my pleasure. I've learned a lot about stamps. Maybe some day your friend will visit again or, better yet, you might go to see him in the Philippines. Have a good day now."

Confident again, he finally cut me loose with "Sure. Yeah. You too."

Although his story was not the usual, and it took longer than most, his need to relate it to me was the same as any one of the many ex-GIs who have stopped me in the streets or by the check-out counter, and announced, apropos to absolutely nothing happening at the time, that he had been in the East during the war. "The war" could have been any of the three from WW II to Vietnam. It didn't seem to matter that the country from which I came could have been the enemy, or the issues over which nations had fought were still being debated. He would simply see my face and nostalgia for those "glory days" would stoke memories of a Time of His Life when he was somewhere different, doing something of national importance.

The little ambassador may have taken a back seat to the double agent but it's still my policy to help preserve any capacity to think kindly. Really, that's what the "politically correct" movement attempted—a little sensitivity and good manners. And because supplanting good will with an informed opinion takes a lot of time, if a passer's-by main connection to a global outlook is rooted in some mythological but well thought of setting that exists only in his or her mind, then my penchant for accuracy or reality won't weaken it. The rewards of living in a more sensitive and well-mannered world are worth the ambiguity. If, however, the myth is of some nightmare place, then I will do my best to cut its tie to whatever peoples are being slandered by the association. For instance, take the time I became a Korean.

I started out the afternoon as simply being "Bennett's wife." We had been invited to attend an opening sponsored by the arts council of an adjacent county when its members found out that he was a "real" artist. One of its board members introduced himself and his colleagues to me with great fanfare and self-importance. After the preliminaries and a short discussion about the value of promoting the aesthetic sensibilities of the people in the area, he asked, "Are you Korean?"

I replied, "No, Chinese." With the stamp collector so fresh in my mind, I quickly added, "From the north. Racially speaking, people from Tientsin and Beijing are probably more closely related to the Koreans than the southern Chinese or Cantonese."

"But you're really Chinese, right?"

"Yes. I was born there."

"Well, thank goodness!

"I beg your pardon?" I thought he might be a different kind of veteran, one with painful memories, and not like the usual check-out counter GI. Of an age that could have put him in front of North Korean guns, he might have been one of their emotional casualties. I would proceed with care. Listening, I heard him say, "You know, those Korean women are the ugliest in the world."

While my vanity wondered which aspect of my appearance had caused him to think that I might have come from the Peninsula instead of the Mainland, and my arrogance marveled at the prestige of an arts council with such a horse's ass on its board, I managed to remain cautious: "On what do you base your opinion?"

"Pictures. I've got some friends stationed over there, and they're always sending me snapshots. You know, some of them are pretty wild."

Stopping long enough to deliver an exaggerated wink and poke an elbow in my direction, he continued, "Y'know."

When I didn't react to the innuendo, he elaborated, "You know. Guys on R & R have only one thing in mind."

"Oh. I see."

Satisfied that I now shared the secrets of understanding Korea and his friends, his grin grew broader but then slowly waned as I arched one brow as far as it could go and went on, mirthless: "That's like my going to New York, taking pictures of the most worn hookers I can find, and showing them to Koreans with a note that says 'These are typical American women.'"

"Uh?"

As I abruptly turned away from the subject and him, I continued to engage the others in the group. They looked as surprised as he. And I wondered whether it was because of what I said. Were they startled that a Chinese would defend a Korean? Or even that a female would disagree so openly with a "gentleman" of his standing? Maybe it was the combination. Or maybe his behavior. But since we were never invited back, I guess it was mine.

I rarely heard my parents tell stories about the people who actually lived around them, who were related to them for no other reason than they shared some proximate space. And if they ever "taught a lesson" to a stranger, the stranger probably didn't realize. I can't decide if this means they were more or less Americanized, less or more Chinese because the moment I can see a resemblance to one or the other stereotype, the less I'm convinced of the generalization. When Bennett and I first married, our union was illegal in several southern states, Strangers in New York felt free to approach us and say, "You should stick with your own kind," and a Nevada storekeeper refused service based on my long "Indian" braids. Though I never really suffered as a result of their prejudice, I identified these incidents with the African American struggle rather than the one endured by descendents of Chinese who built the transcontinental railroad. When "Chinaman" was banned from polite conversation along with "Chink," my father insisted with his above-the-fray wryness, "But I *am* a 'China Man' if you translate literally from the Chinese. There is no insult."

"Insults," like "scolding" are culturally relative. When I was younger and the Chinese hardly qualified as a "minority," I could explain in a few words why Daddy and I never held hands as we walked up Cranford Place from the bus stop on Teaneck Road. But when *SanSan* got divorced, explaining the incident became a lot messier. Five years after marrying a brown-haired, brown-eyed man, of medium height who wears glasses, they went on a trip to Europe. Apropos of nothing going on at the time, he informed her, over dinner in a restaurant, of his wish to end their marriage. When she returned to the States, there were many sisterly calls and hours of trying to console her for a loss no one is prepared for, however common. Finally, two weeks later, she called home. My mother answered.

"*SanSan?* What's the matter? I can't understand you. Are you crying?"

Handing the phone to my father, my mother worried. Was it cancer? Why else would a daughter of hers cry long distance?

"*SanSan?* What's wrong? Oh? At a restaurant? Why didn't you come home right away? Why didn't you tell us? It's been half a month since you got back. What? You thought Mommy would faint?!"

Changing his tone from the inquisitive to the informative, my father continued, "*SanSan*, I think you've gotten us confused with the Japanese. In Japan, when a husband wants a divorce, he takes the woman back to the family. And while the mother weeps, the father apologizes for his daughter's failing...."

Hearing only one side of the conversation, my mother figured out the rest. Grabbing the phone, she demanded, "Why are you crying? Every tear you shed, I lose face. Where's your pride? Don't you know who you are?!"

Explaining how my mother was being "motherly" with such a seemingly harsh reminder of *SanSan*'s familial identity when her personal one was so wounded has been only one notch easier than trying to explain to William's teacher how he could be five years old and never hear me say "I love you." Or why, when my father started to hold my hand even when he didn't need my younger arm to steady his older feet, I was warmed; but when my mother started to say "Thank you" politely when I fulfilled my daughterly duties at her deathbed, I was chilled. Not to the bone however, for when William was three, in *duankuzi*, at school and I was free to work outside the house again, I sent out a pile of job applications. Successful, I called my mother to share my excitement. I told tell her I'd be teaching two courses, meeting the classes twice a week in the evening, from 6:30 to 10:00, and that I'd be getting help with the housework because I'd found Miss Place who, despite being too aptly named, would come in twice a month. My mother's response confirmed what I knew but didn't know.

She lamented that it was only a part-time position. She was sorry that I would have to commute so far from home. She thought it was a shame Miss Place couldn't work full-time and take care of William so I could concentrate on my career. She claimed never to have heard of Montclair State. What kind of a school was it? Did I really have to work at night? In the dark? She considered it a good idea if I immediately applied for a full-time position at Princeton or Rutgers instead—some place with a recognizable name. She worried that William wouldn't get as much attention from me as he needed now that I was going to spend so much time away from home. She wondered if I couldn't get a job at that place in Teaneck—what's it called?—so that I'd be even closer to her house and could have dinner there before class, maybe stay overnight. She suggested I get a later schedule—then

I wouldn't have to leave home until after William was in bed. By the time she was nearing the end of her list, I was laughing at her ideas. Openly and for the first time.

"What's so funny?"

"I can't help it, Mommy. You want me to get a full-time part-time job at a college you have and haven't heard of but is nearer your house and mine, with a schedule that meets earlier and later so that Miss Place and I can both take care of William all the time for part of the time. Yes???"

By the time I finished, my mother was giggling. For weeks I wrapped my future in her response. And when I got the phone bill, I couldn't wait to immortalize The Call with a story about how its cost was well worth the conversation.

"What call?"

"You remember. About my teaching."

I heard her all too familiar silence and rushed to fill it with details about William's latest triumph and Bennett's upcoming show—words she would understand and remember.

I've heard people vow, "I'll never make the same mistakes with my kids that my parents made with me." My standard response is, "Probably not. You'll think up new ones." And then we laugh—a nervous incantation to quell the fear that our children will say the same about us. In the case of the totally Americanized, this is often followed by an enumeration of grievances, the short list of woes written with too many tears to be forgiven or forgotten. The still-Chinese tend not to put these into words which the deities can hear for inattention, however painful, is no excuse for ingratitude. After all, one could have remained in oblivion and never been born. This silence is sometimes construed as filial piety.

As my mother's smiles for me alone found a final resting place in more distant memories, I felt a deep nostalgia for those days when I worked for, but rarely got a "No Comment" report card. And though I might have brought them forth again with confessions of a shame I did not feel for failing to do the work that would have better blended with the patterns woven on the family heirloom, I chose instead to reserve my stories and most of my laughter for the people who could love me because I had them. On the other hand, I chose never to stop listening to my mother for William's sake, no matter what was said in words and silence. To have done otherwise would have ripped me apart and sundered William from possibilities which he, not me, should decide. Meanwhile, I would remember the smiles once given to me and make new ones where I could.

Sometimes, re-cognizing the emotions that attach to the stories can cut through the complexity, like the times after my mother died when my father took to reminiscing in English about old hardships. He did this in part to hear them himself and to ensure his immortality through my memory and, in part, to put into perspective any self-pity I might have felt because my mother had left this world less American than I had hoped for. He told me one story about how, after a Japanese attack, he had collected the dead, sometimes charred, bodies of civilian casualties. Whether previous tellings had been less gory or I just hadn't understood, this time I got all the gruesome details he could muster, including the corpses that refused to stay prone but would sit up with such force that they'd break through the thin wood-en coffins. When he finished, he sat back in his chair, tired from the effort. Instead of seeing my father with a lesson to teach, I thought of all those veterans who talked to me. I blurted out, "Daddy, it sounds like you had a great time!!"

He looked at me, about to self-censor but, instead, exclaimed glow-ingly, "I did!"

.

CHAPTER 10

EXERCISE #4

The Rule of Thumb: Open both your eyes. Cover the left eye with your left hand. Line up your right thumb with a straight edge like the corner of the room or a doorway. Uncover the left eye and see how much the thumb remains aligned with the straight edge. Now open both eyes again and do the same thing but, this time, with your right eye covered.

Most people have a dominant eye which means that, when looking through it, there will be a less perceptible shift in the alignment of thumb to straight edge. Eye dominance doesn't always match hand dominance so some people have "mixed dominance"—they're right-handed but left-eyed or vice versa.

So far, no one knows to what extent dominance is determined by genes, or what your mother ate for breakfast, or how many kids attended your birthday party. What one can conclude, however, is that the same person can focus on the same thing and see it differently. This "bifocal" capability happens when vision is "normal." Similar variations occur in the other senses depending on such factors as age, environment, experience, and even expectations. For example, if you go to a brewery, the typical tour ends in the tasting room for free samples. Now, if you actually care about tasting what you're drinking, you would start with the more bitter (usually the light) and go to the (ordinarily darker) sweeter brews because, if you do it the other way around, your tongue will have been overwhelmed by the malt sugar and unable to fully appreciate the quality of the hops. Those who slip a sample to their children, find that the toddler will want more while the fourth-grader thinks it's all pretty awful. This is because the toddler's taste buds aren't yet fully developed and don't register "bitter," while the older child's palate has a wider range and he or she will have to "acquire a taste" for the stuff (or its social implications) to consider the experience a good one. Meanwhile, older folks will probably prefer the sweeter, for the ability to taste degenerates with age, a process that can be accelerated by other factors, like smoking. Since the sweet receptors are the last to go as a rule, the choice also "makes sense."

So if what you see, hear, smell, taste and feel depends on what you "get," it's not hard to understand why police investigators often complain that eye-witness or first-hand reports are unreliable. Yet if you think about it, the discrepancy and difference help make the "ordinary" and "extraordinary" turn into each other. With more viewpoints than people, our universe is doubly rich. And probably doubly troublesome. But that's the price of getting an education.

When Soho lofts and New Jersey chicken coops left so much to be desired, we met Billie Burke. Somehow she had gone from travelling in a *Wizard of Oz* bubble as the Good Witch Glinda with a magic wand to driving a station wagon around Warren County as a real estate agent with a basement office.[15] Still prescient though, she pointed us toward the eastern equivalent of Kansas, northwestern New Jersey, where we bought an old farmhouse and barn on 5.7 acres of poison ivy vines the size of my leg. There was no heat in either building; the rusty silo had caved in; and a lot of the grass around both structures remained unmowed—some sections for another ten years. Despite the shabbiness, a few neighbors still managed to conclude that I was the maid or whatever you'd call the female equivalent of the Bachelor Father "houseboy" on TV. Goodness knows what they thought Bennett was. He'd grown back his beard and hair, and seemed never without an entourage of buxom apprentices who were learning how to work with clay, without bras. It didn't take long for the Township Council to go into executive session in order to reconvene in our barn for the purpose of shutting us down.

Once the councilmen realized that Bennett was "a college professor doing research," and I was his lawfully wedded wife (who, more important than also being "a college professor," knew the apprentices by name), they advised us to apply for a Change of Use Variance to convert the barn into a "studio." With lots of nodding, we thanked them mightily, walked them to their cars, and then looked up "variance" in the dictionary.

> An official permit to do something normally forbidden by
> regulations, esp. by building in a way or for a purpose
> normally forbidden by a zoning law or a building code.

With two "forbiddens" we were crestfallen. Until then, we had equated "living in the country" with "not bothering or being bothered," with escaping the expensive regulations of the city and the oppressive expectations of the suburbs, with the fresh yellow line going down the center of the road—painted right over the middle of a very large cow pie. Not quite. People out here don't want to interfere with other people's business as long as no one is getting hurt, but they still want to know *what* the business is. And they sure as hell don't like being ignored. So we quickly filled out the forms, published our intentions in the local paper, and groveled before the appropriate

[15] Really. I didn't make this up.

Committee at the Town Hall. After they got a handle on us, we got our variance and were able to live and let live like everybody else for almost thirty years. This meant that "Washington" was the town situated near Belvidere, the County Seat, "the market" wasn't on Wall Street but where local farmers go to negotiate a good "stock exchange" at the auction; and "Charlie" meant the mayor.

Nevertheless, "politics" remained a national and sometimes statewide matter. For Bennett, it was nowhere[16] and he wouldn't have even registered to vote if I hadn't insisted. So when Charlie faced a challenger for the mayoralty, Bennett didn't know or care, and I wasn't paying much attention, having been too busy trying to convince the Immigration and Naturalization Service to grant me American citizenship and the right to vote at all.

With Permanent Residency or a "Green Card" by virtue of marrying a citizen, getting "naturalized" after a three-year waiting period was a bit more complicated. First the I.N.S. wanted to know where I had been since 1946. Not a problem since I had kept all my report cards from grammar school on. In addition, I could produce the Junior Citizen of the Month certificate, tax returns since high school, and all the utility bills from my California stint. Maintaining a paper trail was mandatory for any alien. Staying in North America was not a bad idea either. I not only didn't join the Operation Crossroads Africa program, but I also took no chances on our honeymoon and cancelled a trip to the Bahamas in favor of Florida. When I was finally eligible to apply for citizenship, I was very careful to avoid perjury by elaborating on several of the "yes or no" questions. For instance, "Yes, I have 'taught' communism, but no I have not proselytized." Admittedly, I was Thumbing my Nose by Thumbing my Knows a little bit. More problematic was getting mail from The Black Panther Party. I did wonder to myself how they knew since it was delivered in a plain brown wrapper with only an anonymous return address visible. After the F.B.I. conducted several probes for UnAmerican activities but found nothing, the I.N.S. simply asked me why I hadn't mentioned this. My answer was equally simple: no one had asked me to list my "subscriptions," let alone my research. The man agreed. Unlike the hobgoblin

---

[16] This attitude developed in college when he and others drove from Iowa to the White House in donated cars. Picketing and fasting, they hoped to pressure President Kennedy and his Special Assistant, McGeorge Bundy, into a unilateral cessation of nuclear testing. They failed.

in Boston when I was a college junior, this one was doing his job.

By the time of the Watergate Hearings, I was a citizen. And I was pregnant. While fixing up the room that would soon be a nursery, I was glued to the television, taking a break only when I needed fresh air to clear my system of the fumes from the floor stripper. Sitting on the back steps, I thought about casting a ballot for the first time, hoping for an era without "dirty tricks." A car drove up just as I was going back in. A stranger got out. I called my "Hello," and met him halfway. He responded, "Hi. Is Mr. Bean at home?"

"No, he's at the dump. May I help you? I'm Mrs. Bean."

"Well, no. Do you know when he'll be back?"

Looking at my watch, I said, "He's been gone about 45 minutes. So unless there's a lot of good gossip, he should be driving up soon." We both laughed—everybody knew the unofficial and illegal dump was the social gathering place. "Would you like to wait?"

"Sure, if that's okay with you."

"Of course. Would you like some lemonade or iced tea?"

"No thanks. I'll just wait."

Which is exactly what he did. No introduction. No chitchat. When Bennett drove in, the van more loaded down with treasures he had retrieved than garbage he had left, our guest was so anxious to greet him that he blocked the door and ended up shaking hands through the open window. I had followed at my slower, pregnant pace. I couldn't believe what I heard: the man was campaigning against Charlie. Now a citizen, I was doubly sensitive to his slight and to a spiel directed solely to the ostensible "American" or "the man of the house" or both. After he left, I told Bennett about what didn't happen while he was at the dump.

The next day, Charlie came by to campaign. For an assortment of reasons, he didn't bother with Bennett but immediately put his arm around my shoulder and told me how much he'd appreciate having my vote. Later, Bennett and I agreed that Charlie might still prefer ignoring the Nineteenth Amendment, but at least he had the smarts to realize that women do vote regardless.

Some twenty-six years after falling in love with Gil Hodges and pretending I was Jackie Robinson in the sand lot, I felt the power: Charlie won reelection by *two* votes. While I took personal credit for his political future, he appropriated my past and decided that I was the closest he'd get to a Lenape Indian and asked if I'd dress in buckskins and long braids for the town's 1974 Bicentennial Parade.

Soon after I told Charlie, "No thank you," William was born. Before HMOs, caesarian deliveries mandated I stay in the hospital for a week. One day, the nursery ran out of blue blankets. When the nurse tried to hand me William in a pink one, I told her, "That's not mine." She insisted he was. I only believed her when she showed me his tag. Who knows what I would have done had she brought him in buck-skins. Later I told Charlie he could borrow William if he needed a papoose for the next parade.

From then until his marriage in 2001, William has appeared in many guises and many lands, but this has been William's only family home. It's not quite a "chair of roots," but it is hard to believe that we live an hour's drive west of New York. The morning after going into profound debt to pay for the unheated house, undisguised barn, and unmowed six acres, I looked out the back window and saw Bennett and our dog, Po Bean, cheerfully chasing a bunch of deer up the hill-side. Neither had a stitch of clothing on and no one but me seemed to mind. The deer gone, the two then "marked" our property. I crossed my suburban fingers that they'd run out of bodily fluids before the cops arrived.

It turned out we had no cops: our township borrows them from other jurisdictions. We didn't have any banks either. The closest one, six miles away, happened to be the one that gave us a mortgage. When no big-time creditor was legally obligated to finance an artist and/or a woman of breeding age and/or an inter-racial pair, none did. Yet here all it took was the realtor picking up the phone and telling Mr. Beatty, president of The First (and then only) National Bank of Hope, that "A couple o' teachers want to buy the ol' Yunker house." Without an interview, application form, or fee, we were "approved" by the end of the week. At the closing, we walked into a stone building built almost 200 years earlier by the Moravians, and faced the tellers standing behind a glass partition held together by a few posts stuck into the counter. Across the top was strung a series of very dusty wires that constituted the alarm system. Beyond the tellers was the vault. Its door of gears and wheels was kept ajar by a rolling stand piled high with ledgers and an ancient typewriter with gold-rimmed keys. Inside the safe were scattered a bunch of cigar boxes, each overflowing with papers, rolls of coins, and such other things a bank might find handy. The first time I went to make a "night" deposit on a Sunday, I went to the drive-up window. Opening the drawer, I saw Mr. Beatty inside. He waved me to the front door, unlocked it, took my deposit and gave me a hand-written receipt. Then, ready to count out lollipops as he slipped them under the glass, he asked how many kids we had. When I replied, "None, only a dog." He returned the candy to the box and gave me a dog biscuit instead. Before I could adjust to that, he came out from behind the counter and handed me a bunch of carrots. From the kindly look on his face, I decided this was a gift—not quite a free toaster, but definitely benign. So I thanked him.

Later I learned more about the ranking of home-grown vegetables and felt downright flattered that it was carrots and not zucchini. The first time I opened my back door and found a bag of zucchini from an anonymous donor, I was so touched by the generosity that I asked at Chrusz's store whom he thought I should thank. The gentle shop-keeper gave me a "Too bad about those marbles" look, then chuckled and said he'd ask around. Within a week or two, the donor was leaving zucchini the size of bowling pins. Soon we got baseball bats. After zuc-chini season, we got tomatoes. First a couple for a generous salad. Then spaghetti sauce. Then enough to supply a crowd of mad fans wanting to throw something.

The following year Bennett planted his own garden. Amnesiac, we practically named the first zucchini. Soon the row of plants did its exponential thing and we felt the panic of being unable to eat them all or cope with wasting them. Like so many before us, we started carry-ing all the extras in the car just in case we spotted a doorstep without a zucchini. The next summer, Bennett planted half a row. The next, only one plant. After that, we'd smile like Mr. Chrusz, every time another "back to nature lover" moved in from the east and circled the display of Burpee Seeds.

In the aftermath of our ignorance, Bennett fell in love with How-to books. First it was the bees.

"Hello, Mrs. Bean?"

"Yes."

"This is the Post Office. Can you send Mr. Bean out here right away?"

"Why? What's the matter?"

"It seems the Queen got loose. And the bees are going berserk try-ing to find her. We had to evacuate the building. If he could come over and help us out we'd appreciate that."

Bennett was convinced we could make money selling honey, get reassessed as a farm, and lower our taxes. I knew he was serious when he framed the certificate. His university degrees were stuffed in a drawer, but evidence of taking a three-day beekeeper course was displayed for all to see. Then he showed up in my study dressed in a pair of old painter coveralls. Without a word, he laid open his latest How-to book on my desk and pointed with one hand to the picture in his manual. Still mum, his other hand came from behind his back to present me with the summer hat I had made when I was going through my English lawn dress phase. After putting that down, he slapped his hands together in a pleading gesture and gave me a smile—something between infantile and demonic. Then he batted his eyelashes. Unable to refuse, I tacked a mosquito net veil on the embroidered brim. He put it on, slid his hands into a pair of oversized asbestos gloves, and modeled the results. I could find no exposed skin. So he marched out of the house toward the hives. Watching from the back steps, I too felt confident: one look at him and any bee in its right mind would move to the next county. Back upstairs for about ten minutes, I heard a slam of the door and then kitchen cabinets being ripped from their hinges. Running downstairs, I saw him rubbing his stomach.

"What're you doing?"

Pushing one hand into a pocket and down the leg, it emerged near his shoe top and waved at me, "I forgot about this. Anyway, the book says to put meat tenderizer on the sting: it breaks down the protein that causes the bad reaction."

"What you're doing isn't going to work."

"Why not? It's in the book."

"I'm sure it is. But you should also have read the label on the shaker—similar packaging but wrong stuff. You've got the MSG, not the Adolph's."

The incident left me no choice.

"What're you doing, Cath? Where'd you get that stuff?"

Brandishing the rubber hose, I said, "I'm practicing with this kit your father sent me."

"What kind of kit?"

"The one that's going to save your life. Since you insist on keeping bees despite being highly allergic to them, I'm going to learn how to give you injections."

A stinger is one thing, a needle quite another. After he sold the hives for less than we made due to a sudden drop in their market value, Bennett got chickens.

"Hello—Mrs. Bean?"

"Yes."

"This is the Post Office. Do you want us to deliver these chicks or will you pick them up?"

"Chicks? What chicks?"

"We've got fifty chicks here from Murray McMurray."

"Who's Murray McMurray?"

"Looks like some kind of mail-order place."

"Are you sure they're addressed to me?"

"Well, actually, they're for Bennett. Does he want to pick them up?"

"He's out of town. I'll be right over."

I unpacked the box in the kitchen. Reading the directions, I was told in no uncertain terms that if I didn't follow the instructions within 24 hours of their shipment, they'd die. Since Bennett wasn't due home until the next day, I blocked off the fireplace, hung a 100-watt bulb over a makeshift hen made out of an old blanket. That done, I grabbed them one by one, stuck its beak in a pan of water, then in the special feed Mr. McMurray was kind enough to send, then back in the water. I found out the dunking procedure turns them on. They processed the water and meal in a matter of seconds, dropped what they didn't need on the floor, and then went into some kind of frantic stage, except one who decided I was her mother. I named her Sarah and she was the only one that died of old age.

When Bennett got back, he had the good sense to look sheepish and to apologize for neglecting to tell me about this latest scheme to cut our costs. Normal people put statues or clay flamingos on their lawns. Our decorations could walk and crow at all hours of the day and night. Normal farmers breed chickens to sell. Ours were for looking at. Mr. McMurray sent us fowl with feathers where they shouldn't be, skin where the feathers should be, and tails that were so long they dragged on the ground. If they were pretty, the future groom, William, got to play with them. If they were ugly, mean or neurotic, I got to cook them.

In addition to the bees and chickens Bennett has read about and we have raised: snakes, cats, geese, mice, swans, fish, and varieties of fruit known only to medievalists and Sinologists. And dogs, except for the one we let somebody else raise. That was the Rhodesian Ridgeback the shopkeeper gave to Bennett when he walked into her antique store and she saw instantly he was a sucker for freebies. What did he care that the characteristic ridge of hair along the dog's back went in too many directions for showing. I was in the yard watching William toddle when Bennett returned. He opened the VW bus with a "Ta-da" gesture, and a 3-foot "puppy" streaked out. As it galumphed around the yard, it started to circle closer and closer to young William. That's when Bennett informed me that the beast he'd brought home was also known as the African Lion Hound. Picking up William who was about the size of a cub, I went directly into the house, called the local paper, and placed a "Free to a Good Home" ad. Obviously not as lucky as the shopkeeper, this elicited no response from the readership. I placed another the following week, "Rhodesian Ridgeback $25.00." We got several calls within hours of the paper hitting the streets.

But it's the ducks I remember most fondly. This project we actually discussed beforehand.

"Bennett, is this really necessary? They're so expensive. More than that, I hate the idea of clipping wings."

"Don't worry, Cath, we won't have to."

"How come, *BaBa*?"

"You'll see, William. It'll be great, we can brine the eggs they lay and give them to *PoPo* and *KungKung*."

Bennett knew that if he mentioned any kind of advantage to my parents, I could be persuaded.

This time, before the four Muscovy ducks arrived, he had built their housing, using some of the giant radar installation he got from the army for only $30.00—a "good deal."

"Okay, Cath. The book says we've got to leave them in the cage for three days. That way they have time to get oriented. Once they know this is their home, they won't leave."

"You're sure about this?"

"Of course. It's in the book."

So on the third evening, the three of us went out. The light reflecting off the trees was both soft and brilliant. The autumn weather had been perfect for producing just the right amount of rain and frost to turn the leaves their most colorful. William and I stood back, holding hands, while Bennett lifted open one side of the cage. Then he stepped back and we waited together. The prisoners, though free, took a few minutes to realize it. After all four were out, they flapped their wings a few times. It looked suspiciously like a warm-up. It was.

They took off, into the sky, toward the orange rose clouds. As I watched our investment fly over the horizon, I started to say something sarcastic but stopped when I saw the look of utter disbelief on Bennett's face.

And because William asked, bewildered, "*MaMa*, where are they going?"

Grimly, "Southeast."

"I think they didn't like that cage."

Softening, "You're probably right. Maybe they just needed to be on their own."

"But *MaMa*, aren't they ours?"

"Not really, William. Still, didn't they look beautiful?"

They did. And with that vision, we were content.

I started toward the house while Bennett turned to make his way to the studio. Then we heard William, "*MaMa, BaBa*, look! They're coming back!!"

Twenty years after we ate them, William got married near where they and a few of my marbles landed.

In the meantime, there was so much to do. Never did it cross my mind to wonder, "If it took four years to comprehend zucchini and creatures with brains no bigger than the head of a pin, how long will it take to deal with a whole house? What we bought wasn't quite a "handyman special" but it also wasn't the sort of place my mother could boast about. In the scheme of things, she took all comers to her newly purchased cemetery plot when the grass wasn't yet green but only brought to our 18th century house those who had just arrived from places like Hong Kong and Beijing where the overcrowding was so oppressive that our acreage, mowed or unmowed, was equivalent to a king's ransom. But as we completed each stage of renovation and each appeared in magazines and books as a backdrop to Bennett's recognized work and our self-supporting lifestyle, my mother seemed more willing to explain the peculiarities to her mah-jong friends with, "He's an artist."

And there were peculiarities—the ones that came with the house, and then the ones that Bennett perpetrated. Among the former was an array of wallpaper that was not to be believed—huge cardinals flying through kelly-green foliage, and white swans amid pink fans floating on a black pond. Thus, thirty-one years before William married Lisa on the back acre, I spent the summer painting. By the time classes started, I had great deltoids and it was possible to go into several rooms without being visually assaulted. However, by the time we finished the first Thanksgiving turkey, more important than decor was staying warm. Commuting from work, we'd rush from our heated cars to huddle and sleep in the one room with a functional fireplace. That the walls were covered with columns of gold chains woven around red roses against a purple sunset had ceased to be important. Nevertheless, we weren't upset when, two weeks before Christmas, a museum in San Francisco shipped back too many pieces of Bennett's monolithic sculpture and we collected enough insurance money to install ducts and a furnace. When we turned it on, we found out what happens to the interior of a 250-year old house that gets central heating for the first time: it dries out and the walls shrink. A lot.

I spent the second summer painting the shrunken walls. Standing on a ladder at the northwest corner of one room, I noticed a crusty bulge in the corner. I picked at it with one finger. Then I pulled it with two. Big Mistake. The previous residents had "caulked" with toilet paper and this was now glued solid with the paint from the first summer. Muttering "crazy" and "stupid," I circled the top of the room, then down the corners, finishing in the southeast. Looking at the equivalent of several rolls littering the floor, I backed into the doorway for the full effect and then apologized to the Yunkers *in absentia*. What had been manageable cracks before central heating, were now gaping ravines.

The next summer I devoted to the floors. The Yunkers would buy a rug, center it in the room, then paint the floor where it didn't cover. If another, larger, rug showed up, it was laid over the first and a little less of the floor around it would get another coat of paint. Some rooms had three or four rugs and as many colors around the perimeter. Looking at the selection, I figured the system had to do with keeping warm, certainly not aesthetics. With stripper, knife, steel wool, and denatured alcohol, I worked through the layers to get to the natural beauty of the wide floorboards. Some were loose. Under one was an old whiskey bottle. Under another was an area about the size of a shoebox. In one corner was a neat pile of fluffy white stuff with a slight indentation on the top. In a second was a smaller but just as tidy pile of husks from seeds. And adjacent to that was a tiny leather bootie filled to the brim with mouse droppings. It was so perfectly organized, I expected to see *The Good Housekeeping Seal of Approval* displayed in the remaining corner.

My delight notwithstanding, I didn't think about how easily the boards had come up until we turned on the heat that winter, and I realized that, d'oh,[17] if walls can shrink, so can floors. By removing the rugs, I had uncovered an obstacle course for human toes and, simultaneously, unblocked the equivalent of the L.A. Freeway system for mice. Our heated house had attracted dozens of mice in from the cold—and they needed a way to get from the leftover popcorn in the kitchen to the peanuts in my study. I declared war. Bennett, on the other hand, declared his increasing respect for all sentient beings. As he found more and more of his Buddha nature, I became more and more like Shiva, "the Destroyer." At first Bennett was willing to bait, set and clean the traps as long as I laid them on the floor. In this way, I stood between him and the corpses and he couldn't be held accountable for robbing the universe of sentience. After more classes at the Dharmadhatu, however, he announced that when it came to killing, I had to bait, set *and* lay the trap. Evidently, there had to be "three hands" between him and death, that is, three people. Thus, for example, he could eat meat as long as the driver drove, the slaughterhouse slaughtered, and the butcher butchered. For a while longer, he continued to get rid of the bodies. But then that ceased and I ended up having to bait, set, lay, and clean the trap. I never did get why. Nowhere in his How-to-be-Buddhist books did I ever find reference to the untouchability of dead mice. Since William had the only other set of hands in our household but couldn't yet sit, let alone hunt, I was solely responsible for exterminating unwanted tenants.[18]

In any case, aiming our eyes more down than up when walking around the house was good for a reason not having to do with preserving toes and spotting prey: it prevented vertigo. Although the painted walls and unpainted floors looked better than before, the overall effect was not reassuring for, without the many clashing colors, it became

[17] Having learned my interjections prior to *The Simpsons*, I first wrote "duh." Then I read an article in *The New York Times' Week in Review* (9/9/01) citing *The Simpsons and Philosophy: The D'oh! of Homer*. Then I emailed several friends and relatives of all ages, polling their opinions about the difference. Then I tossed a coin. Then I decided to go for the more up-to-date expression.

[18] When William could sit up by himself, even play lacrosse, he still didn't catch mice —by virtue of attending a single class at the *Dharmadhatu*.

very evident to even a casual onlooker that our house would never be in danger of passing the "level" or the "square" tests. If one held up a thumb to check out corners, the only way the two would line up was if the thumb was broken. But we lived with the minimal first round of "improvements" because William needed a lot more than paint. Thus, living his first years in an uneven house, he thought it was normal to sit in the middle of the kitchen floor, roll a ball toward the wall, and then watch it circle round and round and round, only to end up back where he sat. Or he would toddle in my study, where Bennett had built-in bookcases installed. Starting at one end, William would steady himself by holding on to one shelf. At the other end, he could barely reach the same shelf because it remained level when the floor did not. I suspect this early childhood experience was why William never got the hang of geometry or billiards. On the other hand, he has proved to be an adept navigator of Fun Houses.

"Charming" as this was, when we had saved enough, we brought in professionals for some structural changes in the older half of our half-hall colonial—mostly making a large kitchen and, above it, a master bedroom out of several smaller rooms. Previously, Bennett pretty much had a free hand when it came to the right brain activities like decorating. Even when he would flagrantly exceed the monthly budget set by my left brain, the potential argument often ceased to be important by the time our two brains converged—as when he rearranged the living room around a too-expensive chair. Three weeks later when I noticed the change, we were into a different quarter and financially flush again and the chair seemed to fit right in. Now, however, this round of renovating was "structural"—as in "built-in" and "permanent"—so he drew up plans and showed them to me. Knowing I wasn't very good at visuals, he demonstrated,

"Okay, Cath, the chopping block..."

"...For short people...."

"...Okay. The chopping block for short people will go out from here, next to the greenhouse door."

"Greenhouse?"

"Yes. To keep all your mother's plants."

Responding to the magic word, "mother," I asked, "The ones I've already killed or the ones that she has yet to give me?"

"Hmmm. Anyway, under the chopping block for short people we'll have cupboards on the one side. The other will hold my cookbooks.

And I'm putting in shelves all along this wall for the funeral urns.[19]
The fireplace will stay the same but this wall will come out. Over here
will be a counter of Peruvian black granite, and...."

"Bennett?"

"Hmmm?"

"Where's the stove going?"

"Stove?"

"Yes, 'stove'—the device that spews fire when you turn the knob."

"Stoves are ugly."

"Nonetheless, this is our kitchen, yes?"

"Yes."

"All kitchens have stoves. Ergo, according to the rules of logic, this
kitchen must have a stove."

"I'll think about it."

"You do that."

And he did. For days. Which also gave me time to calculate the
benefits of not having one. Which is why he let stand the little room
next to the kitchen and made it The Stove Room. And why our new
kitchen easily became our main gathering place even as dinner was
being prepared for guests. And why, in retrospect, our guests didn't
crowd into our living room and end up, broken, in the basement.

This bit of hindsight occurred in 1990, eleven years before the
wedding when we had saved enough to renovate the other half of the
downstairs. And a good thing too for, after the contractor finished esti-
mating the job, he gave us the disturbing news that the living room,
dining room and front hall floors were, like our uni-body Morris
Minor, being held up by nothing except habit. After his crew tossed
out half the downstairs, he also showed us how the front door was
being held up by the wall *over* it. Somehow—probably after we turned
on the heat—the doorframe lost contact with the sill below it and had
been hanging by witchcraft from the second story. With several
advanced degrees between us, we did find it hard to comprehend how
it was we never wondered why the front of the house reacted so badly
whenever this door was slammed.

---

[19] When Bennett was fired the second time, he got a few issues of *American Cemetery*
and *Casket and Sunnyside* with the hope of breaking into the funeral urn business
which, unlike higher education, was more inevitable. When none of the funeral homes
were interested because, basically, the bronze lobby had monopolized this niche, we
used the samples to store tea.

Around this time, I began to express my desire for a steel and glass condo with built-in hoses and tile floors slanting, like our original kitchen but to a central drain hole. Bennett's response was to replace the floors with exotic rosewood raised from some jungle bog and inlay blocks gilded like the gold-leafed interiors of his vessels. As to walls that had suffered greatly for having the floor pulled out from under them, Bennett patched the cracks, then painted. With a sponge. He would start with one color, do the entire room, then decide it wasn't quite right. He would then sponge on another color so the two would form a mottled third color. When that wasn't quite right, he sponged yet another layer. Normal people would have done a small patch as a test area. Bennett had to do the whole room—henceforth referred to as Living RoomA—to get the full wrong effect. A total of twenty-five applications and two months later, I developed a severe allergy to paint and he had to stop.

Outside the house, however, Bennett kept his free rein. He made things. Some he sold, others he kept. Not distinguishing between "work" and "play," what he made to make a living was almost synony-mous with living with what he made. When he wanted a ruin and couldn't find one at the flea market, he invented a machine that squeezed out terra cotta forms like toothpaste. Mixing and matching, he put them together to make columns. Taking down the two-seater outhouse, he built a pergola that was reminiscent of the coliseum, just not as big. Liking what he saw, Bennett took the next leap of logic, "If I want a ruin, others will too." So he sent a picture of ours to *House and Garden* and the magazine published it as the product of a new business, "Columbine." The play on words was not unrelated to the fact that he had planted columbine flowers all over the property.

Similarly, when Bennett needed a piece of marble for a project, he found a monument maker in the Bronx. Touring the premises, he couldn't help but notice the "trash heap": one pile of all the pieces that got cut off in order to make the grave marker square or rectangular according to the customer's choice, another pile of rejects with mis-spelled names or wrong dates, and yet another of the no-longer-good-enough—those replaced by predominantly Asian loved ones who could now afford something bigger and more elaborate for the dear departed. Storing the stone vision in his brain, he brought it forth after a show where his work was displayed on less-than-optimal bases. Desiring to control the height at which people viewed his ceramics as

well as make a statement about the hierarchy of materials, he conceived the "dolmen series," that is, a sculpture composed of his signa-
ture work—painted and gilded clay vessels[20]—on top of a 4-5 foot
stand consisting of semi-precious stone, polished aluminum and large
chunks of granite. Going back to the Bronx, he struck a deal: for the
cost of hiring a truck to remove the "trash heap," Bennett would get to
keep the granite and the monument-maker would get to clear his back
lot. At most Bennett used a few dozen pieces for dolmens. In other
words, one, maybe two, truckloads @ eleven tons per would have been
more than sufficient to convince the art world that there is, indeed, a
hierarchy of materials. But Bennett couldn't get the stone vision to go
away. So, between 1989 and 2000, we accumulated about one hundred truckloads of granite—that's roughly two million, one hundred
seventy-nine thousand, five hundred pounds more than he needed.

"But Cath, it's such a Good Deal."

So by the time the limousine brought the bridal party to our
doorstep, we had a granite driveway, stepping stones to and from here
and there, as well as the Great Wall of China fronting the house and
barn, with a lesser wall around the vegetable garden. The only draw-
back were the epitaphs. In English and Chinese.

This was not a problem with the rocks. Unlike the granite, none
were inscribed. None were free either. Whether a piece of jade that fit
in the hand or a 3000 pound boulder, Bennett collected them all. As
with his other obsessions, they appeared in his work/play. The one I
couldn't help but notice was installed by a gigantic forklift device.
Hearing something very mechanical trudging through the side field, I
looked out the window and saw it stop at the base of HillockB.[21] By
the end of the morning, a limestone slab (52" wide x 94" long x 7"
thick x 1.5 tons heavy) sat on two granite leftovers. When Bennett
asked what I thought about it, I found a huge chain in the woodshed,
laid it on top of the limestone, and put a schedule next to it:

- *Week One: Vestal Virgins*
- *Week Two: Isaac, Son of Abraham*
- *Week Three: Lambs*
- *Week Four: to be announced*

[20] If you'd like to see what I can't begin to describe, go to www.bennettbean.com.
[21] HillockA had been situated too close to the pond out of which it was made.
Aesthetically unacceptable, Bennett dismantled and reassembled it at its current and,
hopefully, final location.

I hoped that, one day, flowers would give the altar a more matrimonial, as opposed to sacrificial, aura—as well as help counteract the effect of the gravestones around the lettuce.

As objects and stories spilled on and over the property lines into grapevines, people heard about what we did. Though few would consider moving hills or buying rocks, they accepted the information and passed it on to the next guy while pumping gas or buying the Sunday paper at Chrusz's. Once, when the florist didn't find anyone home to take delivery, she spotted me seven miles away at the A&P. I'd never met her before, only her husband, Peter, at a meeting to plan how the area schools could celebrate Math-Science Week. So while her daughter took the flowers out to my unlocked car, we stood by our grocery carts and exchanged a five-minute installment in a conversation that referred to the talk that took place when Peter told me what he thought about what I said to someone else a few months before, someone I had gotten to know because Barbara, who works at the travel agency, thought I might be interested. She had concluded this after reading what I wrote in a Letter to the Editor when the local weekly paper published yet another diatribe from a resident who regularly made public his scorn for feminist or liberal politics.

These long conversations create a web of casual truths. It is small talk, but not unimportant. It's how we become a community, and how the community becomes us. In our case, it was the transition from "the ol' Yunker house" to "that artist's place." Then, after Bennett was recruited to produce the town's bicentennial picnic and didn't poison anyone, I was referred to as the "Wife of the Pig Roast guy."

And then I got the keys to the church. Of the public buildings on Main Street—Chrusz's General Store, the gas station, Stella's bar, and the post office where we also got our chairs caned and bought Halloween pumpkins—the church was the only one large enough for me to hold classes. It didn't much resemble Merce Cunningham's studio in New York but Bertha, Helen, Nancy, and the others didn't seem to mind. We put on our leotards, took off our shoes, and leaped around. Some people weren't too sure about us doing *modern* dance. On the other hand, the name notwithstanding, it couldn't be too risqué, being so close to the church an' all. A couple of the dancers wondered if we shouldn't give a performance so the folks could better understand. I nixed that idea—what with the leotards an' all.

Once we did have an audience. When the kerosene heater went off.

Although the man responded immediately to my call, it took him an inordinate amount of time to refill such a small tank. Whatever he said about what he saw through the window began to appear elsewhere.

"I guess you ladies have pretty tough feet. That floor's just one big splinter."

"Saw that Russian guy on TV last night. Dijya catch it? He gets right up there. Whadya think? He any good?"

People started to know that I lived here. Not the Filipina or the war bride, but Mrs. Bean, sometimes Cathy.

"Some dandelions you growin' there. Got some stuff can take care of 'em. You oughta try it...For the bees, you say? Yeah, guess they gotta eat too. Don't much like the stuff myself. The honey, I mean. Heheh."

Like me, they sized up Bennett's work more in terms of how hard he worked to make things happen than because we understood why his clay vessel—with a lid the size of my thumbnail, and a spout that led nowhere—was "art," let alone a "teapot." And when Wagner College kept firing him but our name didn't show up in the "For Sale For Taxes" list, neighbors were also impressed with the fact that, whatever it was he made, someone was willing to pay good money for it.

His landscaping was barely more comprehensible. For the first ten years we lived here, the lawn never wholly appeared at once because it got mowed only where Bennett happened to walk while pushing the mower. Similarly the first pond he dug had no continuous existence. Situated and shaped by Bennett's eye for beauty not his knowledge of geology, the water that appeared in April sank through the cracks to China by July because half our property sits over the Federal Springs Thrust Fault. After HillockA became HillockB (see previous footnote), Bennett hired back the dozer and dug out PondB. Happily, this second body of water was fed by a spring and remained year-round in this hemisphere. Bennett then stocked it with fish—another "good deal" because the minimum of 100 at wholesale cost less than 50 at retail—and fed them Rise @ $17.99 per 50 pounds. Aptly named, the stuff stayed afloat so we could watch the feeding frenzy while we ate chopped chuck @ 99¢. Meanwhile, he buried pilings so that, when the pond froze, he could walk on the ice and build an L-shaped bridge to span the middle. Unfortunately, the weather warmed before he could finish so neither end of the structure reached either shore. Not wanting to lease a lot of expensive equipment again (thank goodness), he decided to wait for the next winter freeze—until an attentive neighbor stopped by.

"Nice piece of sculpture, that. Kinda like the way it floats on the water."

"Oh? A 'bridge' you say? Well, yeah, I guess you could call it that."

It had never been easy explaining Bennett's art; it was harder explaining what it wasn't. Bennett didn't wait for winter. He hired the bulldozer back to push the land to meet each end of the bridge. By midsummer, the new grass extended to the new shoreline. By the next summer, the whole thing blended into the landscape and a picture of it ended up on the cover of a *Smith and Hawken* catalog. Daily, Bennett would walk out to the middle, a bowl of Rise in hand, taking with him whoever was visiting at the time.

"Sure, we can talk while you feed the fish."

"Well, I'll be god-damned. Must be thousands of 'em. Much of a market for that kind?"

"You don't sell 'em? You just *look* at em?"

"Ever try catchin' em?"

"You sure? The kids would like that. Yeah, that'd be nice, real nice. No, no. I'll call before showin' up."

Over the years, fathers and grandfathers left off calling before bringing their kids to fish off our bridge. The scene is pure Norman Rockwell—children dangling their feet off the edge, the sunlight reflecting on the water and the tops of their heads—except these kids grow up thinking it's perfectly normal to reel in great big goldfish out of a country pond. And if that isn't enough reward, I informed one of those fathers two weeks before the wedding that there might be some extra noise around 9:45 p.m. on June 2nd, but not to worry because it was probably some superstitious but otherwise harmless Chinese scaring off evil spirits. Since none of his fellow state troopers showed up before or after the illegal fireworks display, I have to conclude that the skyrockets and goldfish did their job.

Or it could be that the mischievous demons were exhausted after two years of building My Living Room: some place besides the kitchen where we and more than four guests could sit at the same time. Approaching his 60th birthday, Bennett had promised never to stop taking my aerobics classes if I gave up all talk of buying an ugly condo in a retirement village. With this, we committed to one last round of construction. Since William still had no fiancée, we figured we had plenty of time to get it done by the time he and whoever would need a place to marry. This was early in 1999, before I knew that "contractor" and "evil spirit" were overlapping categories.

By the end of that spring, Bennett had lots of drawings from which Al, the architect, could draft plans. I scanned them long enough for my left brain to glean the basic information: four walls, a floor, a ceiling, three windows and two ways to get in and out. Not long after that, I heard Bennett make mention of drawings from which Bill, the architect, could draft plans. Looking at these, even my left brain noticed that Bill was not Al and, while there was still a floor, ceiling, and four walls, just about everything else was different, including the location. Somehow, My Living Room had moved about 160 feet down the road into the barn next to a little box marked "Green House." Inquiring, I was informed by Bennett that before My Living Room could be built with ArchitectA, he would have to "practice" the curved ceiling technique he conceived on a new office in his barn with ArchitectB. I reminded him that our tax assessor already dubbed the barn-cum-studio "The White Elephant." And Bennett reminded me that I had agreed we'd die here after taking the last of another three or so decades of my aerobics classes.

"And the little box labeled "Greenhouse"?

"Oh that. It's not really a greenhouse. But it'll have big windows and heat so that your fig trees can get through the winter."

"You're going to build this whole room so I can eat the annual fig?"

That day our "White Elephant" turned pink.

I didn't argue too vigorously. One, because the greenhouse near the butcher block for short people was left unheated and, therefore, not very hospitable for either my mother's hand-me-down plants or Bennett's burgeoning collection of potted tropical fruits. And two, because the second greenhouse could double up as a lunchroom for the studio assistants, I would have the kitchen to myself. Naïvely submitting the barn plans to get the requisite building permit, we thought, "no problem" since ArchitectB was experienced in local ordinances and we already had the change of use variance we got in the early '70s. That was good for as long as we owned the barn. In the end, however, we again had to grovel in the Town Hall. Six months later, we attained the dubious distinction of holding a second variance exactly like the first. And the building permit.

In the interim, William got engaged and, fourteen months before the agreed-upon wedding date, the final count-down began. The office and lunchroom were started but the new addition to the house, My Living Room, was postponed. The first reason why this made sense was that half the upstairs flooring and their adjacent walls had to be ripped out and replaced. Having held up the front door and my books for all those years, they were tired. Unfortunately, the contractor-cum-evil spirit also got tired. As we waited for his return from a lunch that lasted several weeks, Bennett figured that, as long as we were no longer saving up for an ugly retirement in a nursing home:

- we might as well go all out on the new walls. No sponges here. Instead, let's hire Ann Marie, an Italian hair stylist who was bored with permanents, and teach her how to apply layers upon layers of colored goo with a spatula;
- and if the result isn't sufficiently subtle, let's make it chatoyant—glow from within—by smearing hot beeswax over the result;
- and if we want the exterior of the house to look uniform, we'll have to pry the old siding off (along with any telephone and electrical wires that are in the way) and put the same stuff that was going on the outside of My Living Room on the old part of the house.

I got to within six months of the wedding by donning a face mask against the dust and proceeding through curtains of plastic to get to my office that had to be relocated in the attic, just above the tired floors and walls. During these promenades and nightly clean-ups, I dealt with the underlying truth of our colonial house: mud walls packed with horsehair and straw containing two centuries' worth of black walnut shells from generations of squirrels and, occasionally, their skeletal remains. Our walls were ostensibly cleaner, straighter, and fancier but my x-ray vision knew this appearance was only one of the realities.

Four months before the wedding, I went from my newly renovated upstairs to my already renovated kitchen. It took a moment to realize what was wrong with the picture: there was nothing but two windows and wainscoting between me and the county road outside. Some time between breakfast and lunch, the walls had disappeared. When I stopped screaming, Bennett muttered something about new insulation,

"…As long as we were siding…."

Two months before the wedding, we had unremitting rain. This turned the dirt road that all the construction trucks had carved into our yard into a long mud pit. Since the wedding invitation requested the honour of a lot of presence at "the lawn," this was not good. When it finally stopped, we had weeks of drought. This dried up the road but turned "the lawn" into an unpleasant yellow as well as put a further drain on PondA.

On the other hand, four weeks before the wedding, we had an Art Object, a.k.a. My Living Room, with a curved ceiling and four skylights suspended so high that all creatures residing up there will never know the terror of being swept or dusted. One wall consists of eighty-one steel rods screwed into the wall for an elaborate display and shelving system for Bennett's art. Another wall is faced with about 3500 pounds of limestone, sandblasted with his pottery motifs. A third has lots of windows to match the style of the original house; and the fourth has a set of high-tech glass doors leading out to a sweeping stairway to "the lawn." And the whole is lighted with a panel of sixteen switches that I can't begin to master without labels.

Three weeks before the wedding, Bennett decided the rusty top of the silo would be an eyesore. After intimating that he'd mail order a (cheap) standardized "cap," he built a red pagoda instead. One week before the wedding, sod was laid over that part of the back yard that reminded me of Mr. Claiborne's icing on William's birthday cake. I had thought astroturf made more sense because, sigh, sod needs a minimum of *two* weeks of soaking to become one with its new environment. To remedy this oversight, Bennett set up an elaborate system of hoses and pipes across "the lawn" to water the sod and to pump water from PondB to PondA which content was wending its inexorable way to China.

Three days before the wedding, I insisted that we'd freak out all our Chinese guests and most of the others unless Bennett torched the granite so the epitaphs were no longer legible. Running out of time, he made a judgment call and left the funereal messages on the stones facing the lettuce figuring this was a wedding and guests had no business walking into our vegetable garden. Two days before the wedding, unremitting rain returned as Ann Marie's scaffolding in My Living Room came down. (Two days after the wedding, it went back up so she could apply the umpteenth layer of goo with the spatula.)

One day before the wedding, we conducted a garden tour for folks from Philadelphia who'd heard about the pagoda in northwestern NJ.

They didn't seem to mind the last minute touches being made to the shed that now had PorchA and PorchB extending from opposite sides in case the firewood inside needed a place to drink mint juleps, a grape arbor, DeckA and DeckB, a walled garden, a total of three greenhouses, and a tree house—all of which had been, somehow, related to building My Living Room.

Half a day before the wedding, no longer able to afford new furniture, we carried chairs from Living Room1 to the new one—just in case four people wanted to sit down at the same time. Three hours before the wedding, the rain stopped and we rejoiced. This was short-lived because, two hours before the wedding, we discovered the limousine driver had parked down the road after delivering the groom and his party but, for reasons yet to be determined, had neglected to fetch the bride and her entourage. Around this same time, the oyster shucker informed me that he couldn't possibly set up under the tree house.

"Why?"

"It stinks."

"What stinks?"

"The cat."

"What cat?"

"The dead one."

"What dead one?"

"The one under the tree house stairs."

"Oh."

Actually, it wasn't a *whole* dead cat anymore. Which is why, dressed in our Parents of the Groom finery, we were relieved to learn that Maggie, wife of Little Bobby Hanson, our friend and wedding photographer, didn't mind reaching under with a hand slipped into a garbage bag, pulling it over what was left of the cat and what was the beginning of more flies. After she smothered the stench with ashes and baking soda, a host of Chinese ancestors and Colonial Dames came down from the heavens to kowtow and kneel at Maggie's feet.

Relieved, Bennett took the first guests to the house. Encouraged by the Ooohs and Aaaahs, he led them upstairs to sniff the bees-waxed wall, asking each newcomer, Twenty Questions style, to guess what it was. I couldn't stop him but was glad he restricted this game to the groom's side of the family—those who knew what it had been like for William and me to have Bennett for a father and husband: someone who made a god to sit under a child's bed and birthday parties in the streets of New York; someone who had once been unsuitable for my father's living room but was now the creator of my own.

By early evening, the sun shone on the bridal couple. Later, the moonlight glowed from the top of so very many extraneous structures as the fireworks highlighted my first white hairs.

CHAPTER 11

EXERCISE #5

Exercises to condition our minds for recognizing, handling, seeking, and even enjoying the diverse potential imbedded in our experiences are not unlike those that promote physical fitness. Most important, it's the doing that counts. Furthermore, what happens as a result will depend on genetic disposition, what shape we're in when starting, and the availability of facilities and faculties, as well as the amount of time devoted to practicing them. Throughout, everyone of all ages should keep in mind:

- We ought never be so out of breath that we can't sing.
- Both feet should fully and firmly touch the ground at regular and frequent intervals.
- Delayed soreness occurs within 24-48 hours of working and stretching an aspect of ourselves that has been dormant. The discomfort is an indication of progress and will soon dissipate. The key is to continue, not stop.
- Muscle weighs more than fat and requires more energy to exist. However, because muscle is denser, it takes up less space. Thus we each can become a relative heavyweight.
- As we safely increase strength, endurance and flexibility, we will be gratified to hear from the experts that doing so at any age is beneficial.
- Vigorous exercise increases circulation to, from, and around the heart and the sweat has some power to immunize.

If you exercise vigorously, you may get naturally "high" on endorphins, the brain chemical that induces a sense of well-being. This "jumping for joy" should not, however, be confused with "happiness," a condition that has many different meanings depending on the cultural dictionary used. Also, having a constitutional "right" to pursue the happiness you define is no excuse for excessive pouting when you don't "get" it. On the other hand, some crying can be helpful because tears contain the adrenaline that causes stress that can lead to high blood pressure as well as heart attacks.

William bonded with his Best Man, Archie Lin, at Bowdoin College every Friday over a hot stove. The two, and Alan Liang, took turns creating a gourmet menu, then preparing it for the three to share. Given my sign on the microwave at home, "It's 10:00 p.m. Do you know where your dinner is?" it made perfect sense that the way to William's heart was through his stomach—a route that rarely suffered from traffic jams at home after high school when he was pretty much full-grown.

Bennett did try to fill in the dietary gaps by becoming an especially alert driver. I encouraged him as road kill requires no shopping or cooking by me. The rule was that if Bennett, or someone we knew and trusted, personally witnessed or accidentally perpetrated the demise of the pheasant/turkey/deer/snake, he could bring it home. Once in the kitchen, Bennett would become so intrigued with how to translate it into dinner that William and I only had to appear when whatever it was was "done." This was not always self-evident because Bennett's favorite How-to cookbook for these occasions was, *Bull Cook and Authentic Historical Recipes and Practices* by Berthe E. and George Leonard Herter. Besides advice from George on how to survive in the wilderness in case of a hydrogen bomb attack, there was advice on making authentic mayonnaise: "If you are a woman, do not attempt to make mayonnaise during menstruating time as the mayonnaise will simply not blend together at all well. This is not superstition but a well established fact well known to all women cooks." (Sounds to me like Berthe was setting the stage for The Menopausal Theory of Cooking.)

There was only one time I got worried—when I went into our tiny freezer for some ice cubes and found an owl, feathered and whole, bolt upright and eyes wide open in a plastic bag. Fresh kill is one thing, storing for future consumption is quite another. Happily, Bennett wanted to stuff it—with cotton. Unhappily, the taxidermist said it was an endangered species so he had to report it. As we were now the registered keepers of this owl, it had to remain frozen until someone from the U.S. Fish and Wildlife Service picked it up. At first I thought the service would arrive momentarily. Then tomorrow. Then next week. Then next month. I've made many adjustments—from China to here, from childhood to motherhood—but I never did get used to that owl in my freezer. After it had spent about a year next to the same ice cubes, I put the bag in a cooler, drove it and William to school, handed it over to his friend's mother who happened to be a part-time Park

Ranger, and made her sign a receipt.

There was only one time that William got worried—when his
father brought home the eels. Skinned, gutted, reduced to 2" pieces,
they continued to move on their own for several minutes after being
sautéed. Otherwise, William, raised on the Menopausal Theory of
Cooking, was so grateful for nourishment of any kind, he ate whatever
appeared on his plate. By the time he was in college, it was clear that
he had adapted very nicely. "You know, Mom, I'm the only kid at college who goes back to campus after a vacation weighing less than
before going home. I'm not complaining. I just wanted you to understand why picking a school for its excellent cafeteria service was not
unreasonable."

"I understand. And you might be pleased to hear that because your
father can now get kangaroo, beaver tail, snake, lion burgers, and elk
steak delivered in a box, he's not so intrigued with ordinary New Jersey
road kill."

"Can he buy that mead stuff too?"

"I'm not sure he even tried after tasting the batch he offered your
friends. I had hopes that it would be better than bad red wine for
catching fruit flies, but I was scared to go near the stuff—it kept making noises at me."

"Is that what's in the jar on the counter—drunk bugs?"

"They died happy."

Whether he learned by nature to "dine" and not just "eat," or by
nurture to forever cancel the effects of oatmeal dinners and frozen sandwiches, William had followed a direct line from Eric's carrots to the
Archie-Alan-William Dinner Club at college. At first I wasn't delighted
to see my credit card charged for ingredients, let alone equipment like a
Bernz-o-matic torch to carmelize the crème brûlée, or the cost of
another pie tin. Pointing out that we'd already paid for "the excellent
cafeteria service," William responded to my complaint by using the
"civilized date" fund I had created.[22] However, by the end of the semester, I'd heard enough about William's culinary successes and failures to
realize that what he learned about putting together a meal—subdivid-
ing the project into components and executing each such that they
formed a whole event that satisfied all the senses in four dimensions—

[22] After he joined the fraternity, I offered to underwrite one date a month if he took
her to a civilized setting lest he forget how to converse and be social outside the
Animal House setting.

was basic to any job he might get that could make him financially independent of us in the very-near-future. Compared to what we had paid in tuition, these kitchen courses were an incredible bargain.

On graduation day, I met and liked Archie. However, the next month I decided he was the best thing since Eight Treasure Rice came ready-made in cans.[23] William had already returned to Taipei for an extended education in Chinese working, conversing and, of course, eating, when a large envelope addressed to him arrived from Archie. Opening it, I found a note to me, asking that I, after looking at them, forward the graduation day pictures to William. When I showed it all to Bennett, he looked at the outer envelope and started to tell me that William was no longer a child so I shouldn't open his mail anymore. Married to me, he had gotten used to my reading any mail that looked interesting, but he thought he should stand up for William's constitutional rights. Then, looking at Archie's note to me, Bennett realized that, in the case of mail, federal law and The Enlightenment had lost this round to the Chinese penchant for defining "privacy" in terms of "family," not the "individual." What I realized was that the Chinese-American hybridizing was not peculiar to the Bao-Beans but that William's Best Man was also a product of dual, though sometimes dueling, cultures and that both are generally pleased to be who they are. This was good news as I was preparing for the next big step. Having pretty much figured out the basics of being a Chinese-American daughter, wife and mother, I was ready to focus on being a grandmother. (Later, I back-tracked a bit and put in "mother-in-law" before the "grandmother.")

Bennett had already started—by pinning up drawings of little girls—chubby-faced cuties advertising something wholesome in long-ago magazines. I thought this was bizarre but harmless. Though I did remind him that, given William's penchant for Asian girlfriends, he shouldn't count on our grandchildren looking quite so blond. A few months later, I had a dream about having a baby, like William but not quite. In the dream, a friend came over to show me how to diaper. When she finished demonstrating, I asked, incredulous, "Really? I only

[23] Traditionally, it took one or two days to make this steamed dessert from scratch. When somebody decided to package it in something like a Bumble Bee Tuna can, my mother and her friends took the result one step further by not bothering to open the can before heating the contents in boiling water. It hasn't exploded yet and we save washing an extra dish. I've never gotten the nerve to boil an American can.

have to do this once every six months?" Then, still asleep, I got the joke, started laughing, woke myself up and, full of residual mirth, announced to myself, "A Grandparent Dream." Fully awake, I pictured William's offspring scrambling up Bennett's knee, then maneuvering into the soft part of his lap to plead, "Please, *KungKung*, more about the stinging bees and flying ducks." Or running into the kitchen to cajole, "*PoPo*, if you tell me again how you beat the I.R.S. with the logic of bi-conditional clauses, I'll cook dinner."

It must be hormonal, for why else would our Stone Age ancestors tolerate, let alone nurture, a potential rival? In any case, we started to look at William the way our parents looked at us during the seven years before I got pregnant—for indications of Bean Futures. Our friends from the "Respect Our Children's Privacy" school of thought gasp when they hear how up-front I am about my agenda for his life (and they don't even know about my opening his mail.) I try to explain that my Chinese side considers anything that has family repercussions to be fair game. Like the fly that lands on a spider web: If it's big enough to cause reverberations throughout the web, then it's a potential subject for open discussion. With a little ingenuity, this can justify talking about anything as long as one tries to elicit a smile and not just give information.

From the time William's Hybrid Vigor made him 2" taller than his projections based upon "normal" growth patterns, he heard me telling him that his SAT Math score, DKE membership, and bunions could be attributed to a shameful lack of Chinese will power to study more, resist peer pressure, and wear socks. If this made him take some responsibility for bad choices that would increase his chances of being reincarnated as an earthworm, fine. But if this made him feel powerless in the face of conditions beyond his control, we cheered him up with the thought that we are all similarly composed. Therefore, be patient because, at each stage of life, young and old will undoubtedly react to the other with the same disdain/horror/disbelief that was or will be felt by the other, sooner or later, and vice versa. Meanwhile, we should all keep in mind that lifestyle genes seem to skip a generation. Thus, while Bennett "rebelled" by becoming an artist (and I did so by marrying him), William only dressed like his father on Halloween and never wrote important dates on the furniture, liking the more portable Palm Pilot better. However, one day, William's Grandparent Hormone would turn on and he'll look at his progeny as a breeding ground for a bundle of semi-annual joy who, in turn, will grow up thinking that the only justification for wearing a suit is to go to the White House. In other words, "stages" are a family affair. Since we were programmed to be grandparents, it would help if he found a wife and, sigh, I learned to be a Mother-in-law.

He met Lisa. Right off the bat we could see her through William's eyes: not only did they share the same birthday and therefore double the chances of getting a cake annually, but she was about to attend the French Culinary Institute of New York. That I also saw her through my father's eyes happened six months after they started dating, about a month after my mother's passing, when friends of the family were going to be in New Jersey from Florida.

Auntie and Uncle Wang had known my parents in China and were an integral part of my life and psyche. Having taken up exercising after their retirement, they were more sprightly than many much younger than they. I saw their visit as a chance to surround my father with young spirits to help him look forward, not just back. I asked William and Lisa, as well as my "*dry daughter*"[24] and her boyfriend to meet at my father's house after work. Had my mother been alive, I wouldn't have considered presenting a mere "girlfriend" to their grandparental gaze. Her opinion of my too "modern" ways—including my "liberal" philosophy of child-rearing—had barely been mitigated by the fact that William, like my father and all her friends, worked in an office and not a barn, or that William could, thanks to two years in Taiwan, converse in Chinese, and loved shopping as much as she. But she was gone and my father and I were in the process of establishing a new kind of relationship where approval was far less relevant than attention and kindness.

I arrived at my father's house after his nap, before any guests appeared. He had not yet gotten out of the habit of wearing his pajamas and robe throughout the day, so he looked very much like an invalid. Auntie and Uncle Wang arrived. Then the kids. Opening the door, William was in front, looking very corporate in his dark suit. Behind him was Lisa in a miniskirt, showing legs that didn't stop. With my gut constricting into the kind of knot I felt when I first told my mother I was marrying an artist, the "Omigod" that was my immediate reaction did an about-face and I instead pictured my father

[24] Like a "godchild," but without any "god" obligations, this relationship is by mutual choice and consent.

as a teller of "good ol' days" stories and thought, "He's going to love this!!" And he did. Or at least he had said nothing to take anything away from our enjoyment of a huge pot of delicious lamb stew Lisa made and the Chinese take-out I ordered. Toward the end of the evening, the Wangs asked if I would like them to be my "dry" parents, my *Kan MaMa* and *Kan BaBa*. It wasn't a question so much as a confirmation of our relationship since I could remember. It was an expansive evening, extending "family" in several directions, by blood and choice, with lots of chances to "walk and talk" our different ways.

That was the theory. The reality was that the more Bennett and I said, the less Lisa did. After a few misunderstandings, I let it be known that, if this relationship was to have a smooth future, it would help to have a heart-to-heart talk. When William passed on this exciting news to Lisa, she acquiesced and a date was set for them to spend a weekend with us. When they arrived for what he and Bennett were now calling The Summit Meeting, Lisa stepped out of the car, Bennett jumped in, mumbling something about having to go shopping with William. By the time they returned, Lisa and I had covered a lot of territory, mostly stories about values. When William stepped out of the car, I informed him, "You and *BaBa* are wimps. Lisa isn't."

Even so, she didn't jump into the conversational fray. Maybe there was a translation problem similar to the one William had in his high-chair. Instead of getting traditional "*bing gan*" from the woman who was born in China around the same time as her parents, who looked Chinese and spoke Chinese (sort of), Lisa heard me talk about computer cookies at web sites in the speedy, unaccented contemporary English of her peers. Maybe it was that she too dressed like a hippie for Halloween. Makes sense—if lifestyle genes skip a generation, of course William would marry someone who fit into his future, not our past.

Like so many of their female friends who had careers in what used to be male-dominated professions, Lisa worked with men whose mothers were feminists or whose fathers had been sued for asking female colleagues to make curtains for the office. They were raised on articles about biological clocks running out and being married to a job, about trying to have it all and being exhausted. Most had fun running the corporate maze of 12-hour days and 6½-day weeks, but few would have sacrificed not ever having a family for the pleasure. They are cultural hybrids with an emphasis on business, not social and political policy. Many, if not most, of their friends are Asian, but more like me than the ones I had met in college or had seen in their 1960"face book." By the time I had their sophistication and travel experience, as many Asian peers or discretionary income, I was much older than they and had more time and inclination to ponder and play with ideas as a form of family entertainment.

It couldn't have been easy for Lisa to learn how to be conversational and still be polite in the way she had always associated with the older generation. And that was just me. Bennett provided his own challenges. His love affair with the beautiful involved objects that often had no label or price tag. To know what to say can be daunting. Not to know what to say it *about*, doubles the difficulty, like when she first looked at Bennett's furniture series—mantels and screens made of wood that he chose from a small local mill that only cut fallen trees. Heating moveable type from sets he bought at flea markets, Bennett imprinted the story of the wood. On three sides of one was:

NO MORE AN-
ONYMOUS WOOD
SWAMP MAPLE
IT WAS NINTY
FIVE DEGREES
WHEN WE SAW-
ED THIS LOG
IT WAS THE
FIRST THAT
CASTNERS
HAD CUT FOR ME...
AND RODNEY
WAS SURE THAT
I WOULD LIKE
IT I DIDN'T
NO KNOTS
NO STAINS
NO TIGER
NO STUFF
ID HAVE TO
DO IT MYSELF...
IT TOOK A

> *DAY FOR HIM*
> *TO LEARN I*
> *WANTED THE*
> *WOOD WITH*
> *THINGS THAT*
> *NO ONE ELSE*
> *WANTED...*
> *B BEAN 1998*

Trying to respond to a future father-in-law who didn't at all mind that "ninety" had become "ninty," I was afraid Lisa might feel compelled to say something nice, like the neighbor who had looked at the bridge that didn't reach either shore and concluded it had to be sculpture, "Nice spelling, that word. Kinda reminds me of what Picasso did to that woman's face." Or like me when I finally saw something I liked in Bennett's California studio and managed to do a critique of why. (Later, he agreed it wasn't bad—for a three-legged goat that happened to step on some clay.)

Neither Lisa nor I had grown up with Bennett's aesthetic the way William had. Our idea of "nice" was mostly a matter of "new and shiny,"[25] self-evident at a glance. William, however, had learned otherwise. From the time he could stand up in the giant Chinese pickle pot in the middle of the studio floor, he knew his father revered nothing absolutely. Whether it was the tradition that said a the potter can shape, mark and glaze but in the end must yield to the Fire God the final say on what was produced, or the modern standard set by the Dishwasher God, everything Bennett touched was sure to contain at least one anomaly if the viewer looked again or heard the "no more anonymous" story behind it. Making few distinctions between producing "art" or "garden" or "salad" or "room," Bennett regarded every surface under his control as potentially beautiful, or at least interesting. After dinner one night, I went upstairs to write. I presumed Bennett had returned to his studio. When William called from college, he asked what we were doing. After I responded, Bennett said that he was in the kitchen, painting it red and green. I ran downstairs. Yup, red and green.

[25] Like so many of my parents' generation who left ancestral homes in China which housed "real antiques," they were uninterested in purchasing "used" items in the States. After all, one didn't want to chance "inheriting" any bad kharma from the unknown previous owner.

From the beginning, I'd rather be upstairs looking at words and numbers than downstairs painting. Judging from what one of the bridesmaids said at their wedding, "William, I know you'll want to pick out all the furniture but, trust me, Lisa will be home a lot more than you will," they may take a bit longer to figure out their trade-offs. What is fascinating about the process is that William has probably inherited both his parents' respective penchant to hold nothing sacred except perhaps their own opinions which they are more than willing to express with hardly a "by your leave." The only saving grace to believing in them with all our hearts and minds is that the world changes and it usually doesn't take long before many of them have ceased to be important. Nevertheless, since William is our son and the primary repository of what was and is important to us, we couldn't help but root for the home team when it came to immortalizing our style. However, when Lisa's father visited us during their engagement, I saw in their relationship the Chinese part of my past. After he left, I told her, "No wonder you were caught short when you met us. Your father was here for three days and expressed only one opinion! Still, it was one that will be important for a long time."

It'll take a while to fully reinterpret the "home team" concept to include someone not raised in this house that Bennett built and I recorded. With each visit we will continue to familiarize Lisa with the setting out of which William evolved so she can understand what kind of trade-offs he might have in mind. This never-ending tour of the house is done in the same spirit as one might go to a museum (or excavate a ruin as is the case with my study.)

On her first tour, Lisa had noticed the sixteen 3½" by 3½"gold squares embedded in the rosewood floor—a suggestion by the carpenter after he saw Bennett's gilded ceramics. "If you put gold on the floor," he said, "I'll cut $500 from my installation price." My kind of Good Deal. We ended up with a unique and elegant floor, he ended up with bragging rights among colleagues who did boring gymnasiums. The story told Lisa how an ordinary workman can respond to extraordinary beauty.

Between the candlesticks on the dining room mantle are several pieces of Bennett's work, somewhat in a line, looking very much like what he calls them: "The Drunken Lily" series. Lisa was hesitant to touch these precariously situated vessels but she now saw how objects can dance for being barely able to stand up.

She then looked at another series altogether, a dozen garden trowels on a small table by the window so the surfaces gleamed in the natural light. As Bennett explains it, the day he wanted to plant some tulip bulbs and found nothing but pieces of trowels left by overly exuberant teenage boys who have worked here, he decided to do something about it. For the next year or two, he designed the quintessential trowel—not only unbreakable, but exquisite. In fact, the design is so stunning that Bennett had it fabricated in silver from ingots and coins he just happened to have acquired from several "good deals." With a wife who often pushed the politically correct agenda, he used micarta instead of ivory for the handle. The result was gorgeous and, of course, totally useless. Another cost-accounting nightmare. Another reason I would never be bored married to BennettA, BennettB, BennettC, et al. But the trowel did end up in a *Time* magazine feature on "the business of gardening." When it was published, I was miffed because the article only identified a picture of the object as a "$2000 silver trowel," with no mention of the artist.

Thank goodness. For two weeks later, in the "Letters" section, it was reported that there had been so many irate notes to the Editor from "real" gardeners who love the earth and who are offended by those who are only interested in fancy equipment as well as those who make millions pandering to this despicable market that *Time* summarized their gist in a special "box" under a drawing of Bennett's trowel on a black velvet pillow with tassels. And the moral for my future daughter-in-law? Hide the silver.

By the time Lisa heard about Bennett's latest project, she didn't blink an eye upon hearing that he's making sculptures composed of designs on goatskin encased in spinning metal frames—"self-portraits" because the designs are his dna codes.

A different challenge for a potential family member is the book on our coffee table in Living RoomA,

Racial Anatomy of the Philippine Islanders,
Introducing New Methods of Anthropology
and showing their application to the Filipinos
with a classification
of human ears and a scheme for the heredity of
anatomical characters in man
by Robert Bennett Bean, B.S., M.D., 1910

Surprisingly, it wasn't that long ago when William felt the same qualms even though he knew so well one of the more bizarre bits of Bean lore—that his grandfather had been born in Manila while his great grandfather was there measuring Igorot ears. Upon returning to the States with a collection of pickled ears, someone stole the suitcases containing them. These were eventually returned by an anonymous and probably horrified thief. Yet the humor of family lore in the context of history can only be funny in retrospect.

Despite knowing that his father had been named after a noted anthropologist, it was only when William was a college senior and taking a course on racism that his ancestor's work became a social reality. During the first week of the course, William was appropriately vocal. Then, during the second week, he read about some misguided scientist who "proved" that the brains of blacks were smaller than those of whites, or that factors such as ears could be used to differentiate one "race"[26] from another. Calling home, he asked, "Mom, the text quotes Great Grandfather. Do I own up to this one?"

I replied, "Sure. You're our best revenge."

If William was still processing the hundreds of thousands of opinions he has heard from his parents since he was born, then Lisa could never be expected to catch up. On the other hand, if I played with numbers in the same spirit as Professor Marvin Minsky at M.I.T., there was much hope in that,

> If a master skill requires 20,000 "units" of knowledge or process but you also need, say, 100 'decisions' or experiments to acquire each such "unit," then you would get a number like 2 million 'thinking events'. If each of these requires the order of a minute of waking time, that would require about 6 years.

If achieving stasis among in-laws can be considered a "skill," then Lisa and I are doing quite well for, having made almost one million seven hundred fifty thousand decisions to put on the wedding, we need less than a year of active relating to pretty much know what we're doing—about the time it takes to make a grandchild.

[26] For a refutation of the hypothesis, see Stephen Jay Gould's *The Mismeasure of Man.* 2nd edition. New York, Penguin, 1996, as well as an article entitled, *Research Methods In Primary Care, Article One,* by T. Greenhalgh, *British Journal of General Practice* 1998; 48(431): 1356-1357 (June).

CHAPTER 12

EXERCISE #6

Celebrate Bean Throwing Night

Every February 3rd, the last day of winter and the eve of spring, when people are particularly susceptible to bad air and misfortune, do as the Japanese do: scatter beans at family altars, the front door and in each room, saying *Oni wa soto, fuku wa uchi*—Out with demons! In with good luck! If you eat the same number of roasted soy beans as your age, you shall increase your chances of good health in that upcoming year.[27]

Also on this day, hold gatherings to throw lucky beans, lucky rice-cakes, lucky coins, candies and sweets for (grand)children to catch and enjoy.

---

[27] As with some folk remedies, there is substantial scientific evidence that isoflavones, only found in soy beans, is effective in preventing and suppressing prostate, colon and breast cancer cells.

William and Lisa met at a dinner party hosted by a mutual friend. They spoke because they were both born on Bean-throwing night, February 3rd—William in 1974, Year of the Tiger, Lisa in 1971, Year of the Boar (or Dog...we're still negotiating this difference of opinion). The discrepancy is not crucial because, according to Chinese astrology, the Tiger-Boar and Tiger-Dog match are both destined to be extremely compatible and successful. When the news is good, I can be very superstitious.

About two years after they met, I gave them Granny's mother's diamond ring to symbolize their engagement. With no discussion that I can recall, William and Bennett assumed the wedding would take place at the stone altar, between PondA and PondB. Lisa accepted this inevitability. Her parents, divorced and in transit, would take part in whatever we four devised.

"How about the first week in June when we usually have our annual Pig Roast? We've had very good luck with the weather then."

Lisa hedged, "I'll have to check with the astrologer."

"Astrologer?"

"Yes, in Taiwan."

"Taiwan?"

"Yes—he's my grandmother's."

"Has he ever been to New Jersey?"

"No."

"What if he picks February??"

At this point, Lisa says nothing, but I can tell from the shape of her backbone that this is not because she has suddenly become a wimp. So I urge her to e-mail her cousin in Taipei as soon as possible so the latter can talk to the grandmother about how to consult with the astrologer. For days I crossed my fingers and toes in between sending prayers to the God of Common Sense. How, I wondered, could I, whose son could sew, iron and cook, be getting a daughter-in-law who was more traditional than I *and* not persuaded by my impeccable reasoning? Keeping silent about my fears lest the gods hear me and get ideas they hadn't thought up themselves, I tried to imagine her postfeminist world where a woman could shatter glass ceilings and still make curtains for the office. A few days later, I received from Lisa her cousin's message, "Grandma says to go for the weather, she isn't that superstitious." Yes! My kind of grandma.

Throughout the year of wedding preparations, I made daily forays all over the future wedding site, shooting my marbles at Canada geese. By the next May, I and my trusty slingshot had succeeded in getting rid of them in time for their last droppings to be washed away by one of the wettest spring seasons in living memory. Then, when the rain stopped and we entered a dry spell just in time to kill the sod laid to disguise the road that the construction trucks had dug across the back yard, I looked out from GreenhouseC one morning and was horrified to see a large pair leading five goslings out from the trees that line the back of "the lawn" between PondA and PondB. Evidently they had hatched at the Presbyterian camp located across the road beyond the tree line. Although our Christian neighbors have lots of fresh water, the land is dense with trees and tall grass that is camouflage for predators. So the feathered parents braved the asphalt and traffic in search of safer accommodations at the Bean's. With a pocket full of marbles, I rushed out to convince them otherwise. For several hours and a lot more filling of pockets, we played Seek and Hide. I would herd them into the trees in an attempt to make them cross back over the road but they would hide in the underbrush, laced with poison ivy until I went back into the house. Already scarred by a short, but intense, stint as a gardener, murdering thorns and thistles that can grow several feet in one day, I had no desire to dress in long sleeves at a June wedding. But by mid-afternoon, I was running out of ammunition, and had to brave the poison ivy. This final maneuver did the trick and I had the great pleasure of seeing the geese head back to the camp.

In my office, I returned to cataloguing wedding presents that had been shipped to New Jersey rather than San Francisco where William and Lisa were living. My two-line phone rang and I could tell it was the studio line ringing mine. Picking up, I expected to hear the most annoying combination of words in the English language, "What's for dinner?"

Instead, Bennett said, "The Fed Ex guy came—can you come down?" Thinking it was another present, I smiled at the image of "our Fed Ex guy." The first one, Niko, had the route when it stopped at the M&M factory in Hackettstown before arriving here. This resulted in enough freebies to give everybody in the studio a sugar rush on a regular basis. As Niko got to know Bennett's work, he expressed admiration for it and envy for the energy that emanated from the studio—two reactions that are sure to get Bennett's attention. But even he was surprised when our Fed Ex guy asked if he could buy one of the vessels. With coaxing, we learned that he wanted to give it to a high school buddy he was going to visit in Canada. It seems the buddy had achieved financial success and our guy was feeling self-conscious about the discrepancy and wanted his gift to be "impressive." We understood immediately.

"Where in Canada?" Bennett asked.

"Toronto."

"Well, it happens I have a show opening there."

So our Fed Ex guy bought a vessel with the help of a very large "PPD" (or Perfect Person Discount). This he presented to his buddy whom he then took to the gallery where the proportion of size to price may have been noticed.

Our current Fed Ex guy, Larry, was a Classics major in college and currently a Keystone State martial arts champion. When I asked the studio folk what he's like, they chorused, "Kinda crazy," with the implication that he fits into Bennett's world. When I introduced myself to confirm their impression, it took only one minute from the first handshake to an animated lesson on why Latin is so much easier than ancient Greek. I liked him immediately. Getting excited about ideas is still what I do best.

Remembering there was a reason for my reminiscing about the Fed Ex crew, I went downstairs and out the back door to see what Larry had delivered for the kids. Surveying our land, I was gratified to see no geese. Dodging the sprinklers pumping water from PondB to the struggling sod, I admired the parts of the garden that were weed-free and then went in to the studio. The downstairs of the barn is so full of stuff that, visually, it always takes me a few seconds to locate a human against the background of pottery equipment, works in progress, bags of clay, water cooler, packing material, refrigerator, microwave, pails of mysterious liquids, work tables, storage racks, bottles of what was supposed to be home brew, desiccated animal parts, gardening tools, fish food, and, in the middle of the floor, a drawing of a bed where the cat likes to lounge. The view is further complicated by walls filled with show announcements, baby pictures, Buddhist artifacts, magazine clippings, letters and postcards from galleries reminding Bennett of what they want, a giant calendar with three months of his life mapped out, an elephant foot, and photographs of William, me, the many assistants who have been employed here, and Toshiro Mifune.

When my eyes adjusted to the chaos, I found Bennett sadly point-

ing to a box on the floor. I looked and immediately felt sick to my
stomach. He explained that our Fed Ex guy had driven his van up the
hill behind our property after the goose and gander were well on their
way back to the Presbyterians. Unfortunately, a couple of the goslings
were too slow. Confused by the traffic, they meandered back and forth
over the yellow line until they were exhausted. Whether or not Larry
knew Bennett was now using the studio freezer to keep the road kill he
intended to photograph (not eat) when he was older but they weren't,
he did know enough about the goings-on at the Bean residence that he
didn't hesitate before stopping to pick up them up. I couldn't believe
it—after all those wild goose chases, Fed Ex had delivered them back.
Alive and well.

The next day, one day before the wedding, after the rehearsal took
place in a drizzle, more than ninety out-of-town guests attended the
Bridal Dinner in the barn. Remembering a younger William driving
his dates on roads that were still narrow, with few lights and many
ditches, I was afraid that if we didn't provide a fun place, folks would
go to search for our only local entertainment—"Whiskey Pete's" or
"The Chew 'n Brew"—and never find their way back to their hotel or
inn. So we cleared out the upstairs of the barn, filled the large gallery
with harvest tables, and opened the double doors to the main entrance
and its newly partitioned GreenhouseB. Without wanting to tax people's patience with too much dressing up in one weekend, I suggested
that everyone, especially Bennett, come in casual, comfortable clothing. No one was too surprised when I suggested we order in ribs from
Porky's take-out service. At first Bennett agreed only if I made a vat of
my own special barbecue sauce. I thought this was a miserable idea. I
also reminded him that Adee was coming. She had already caught me
once committing a culinary felony—when I got back from my first
trip to her home town, Atlanta, and tried to reproduce Alex's barbecue
sauce for the best ribs I'd ever tasted. What I achieved satisfied Bennett
but I wanted perfection. So I called Georgia and asked my college
roommate for help.

"Cathy, I bet you put in soy sauce."

"Just a little."

"Think 'slave'—no soy sauce!"

To balance out the effect of 'no soy sauce,' Lisa had the idea of
serving Chinese noodles, symbolizing long life, in bright red "take-out"
containers. And since we ordered and made enough to feed everyone

for another week, the Friday dinner satisfied the need for overabundance. This, added to the sound and motion from Little Sammy Davis' 3-piece rock 'n roll band, we managed to produce enough of a "Chopsticks" style that the gods could see and hear that this was a household of "great wealth" and communal joy.

By noon the next day, what had become a drenching rain overnight had stopped, leaving the sod very happy but with enough time to dry. By five o'clock all the wedding party had arrived and were having their pictures taken in front of a colonnade composed of Bennett's terra cotta columns, each topped with a Yard God.[28] By six-fifteen, one hundred sixty guests were seated in a semi-circle around the base of HillockB, to watch seven groomsmen, William and the minister place themselves at the top and along the right slope. As the serene majesty of Brahms' first *Variation on a Theme* by Haydn could be heard, seven bridesmaids placed themselves on the left slope.

Finally Lisa, escorted by her father and mother, came into view and was met by William at the bottom of the wide stone steps. He greeted each Lee and then walked with Lisa to face the stone slab now turned into an altar by virtue of the robed figure standing in front of it and the huge bouquet of red roses on top of it. Had Uncle George, formerly chaplain of the United States Military Academy at West Point, not taken ill that week, the man who had co-officiated at our wedding would have performed the same ceremony for William and Lisa. Instead, our friend Allison conducted *The Celebration and Blessing of a Marriage* alone. Later she confessed, "I cut out a few 'Jesus'es." Before an assembly of Buddhists, Taoists, Jews, *Falun Gong*, Uncommitted, and so few Episcopalians, this seemed appropriate. After a triumphal recessional to Brahms' last *Variation*, a few of us formed a reception line while an array of exquisitely fashioned hors d'oeuvres by Peter Callahan appeared. A New York caterer, William, Bennett and Lisa chose his cuisine from "a tasting" that I didn't attend. I didn't need to, feeling already blessed that someone—anyone—would cook in my stead. Getting a drink and a small plate of oysters, I climbed the cat-free stairs and passed between the multiple trunks of what had been a massive willow that we had planted when we first moved to New

---

[28] When a batch of porcelain clay got too dry to throw on the wheel, he carved, sometimes hacked, these Bodhisattvas. Quick and direct, they were made in honor of Enku, a Japanese monk who dedicated himself to creating 100,000 statues of Buddha. He almost did before he died. He, too, must have been a cost-accounting nightmare.

Jersey, to join others who were already on the platform of our tree house.

From on top of my world, I could see it all. Not at once, but as a collection of viewpoints gathered in my mind's eye while hugging, shedding a tear, waving, and raising a glass. Thinking about the ducks we first oriented by keeping them confined within the radar installation and then setting free to fly into the sunset and back, I compared them to the geese we tempted with secure and open space between two ponds but kept driving away when they wanted to nest here. The two experiences have provided me with an abundance of metaphors and similes to view and review the process of being raised and partnered, then nurturing William, and finally welcoming his partner—who didn't hatch here.

The comparisons would also give us a perspective on America.

When dusk fell, Chinese lanterns glowed on land while candles on the bridge flickered over PondB. Inside the white tent, George Gee led his swing band with music from his *Buddha Boogie* repertoire while guests and the bridal party sat down to dinner. As salads were served and the "fork" people admired its spare aesthetics while "chopsticks" elders worried that the gods might notice there wouldn't be enough leftovers for another feast, I toasted the bride and groom.

William,

When I was in high school, I learned about Hybrid Vigor in Biology class. The idea was that when two different strains of corn were crossed, the result was better than was normal for either type of parent.

When you were born, we figured we had the physical makings for a variation on the principle. So we spent the next two decades making you into a cultural hybrid as well.

Intellectually, it was easy to form your prospects from the wealth of your Bao and Bean heritage. But practically, we worried just how much difference it would make that you weren't an ear of corn.

Now you are 27 and I am pleased to tell you that, except for a brief period of your adolescence, you have more than fulfilled our most optimistic expectations. Indeed, you have brought us Lisa—for whom we are very grateful.

Lisa ,

After 12 months of planning this occasion—you are here. William is here. I am here. And most of our family and friends are here. All smiling. This alone is testimony to our relationship and how solid our future as a family will be.

However, if you need even more evidence of how very special this occasion is in the history of the Bao Bean clan, please note that this is the first time since William's father and I were married—almost 35 years ago—that Bennett has been both clean-shaven AND in a suit. This is auspicious indeed.

Thank you for being—for us and for William.

POSTSCRIPT: COMING AROUND

That October, Bennett came up to my study. "Come with me."

"Outside?"

"Yes."

"Do I have to?"

"Yes."

On the deck, we paused. It was a different kind of beautiful now than in June. With just the right combination of warm and cool, wet and dry, the giant maples surrounding our pale house were a glorious profusion of red, orange and yellow gold, made alive by the sun. Walking toward the hillock, I realized that my memories—literal and figurative building up to the wedding and the event itself—were no longer tinted with anxiety and I could look at the past as "done" though not finished, and the future as more mine though no less connected to people and circumstances beyond my control.

From afar, I could see that the large stoneware pot that had held the red roses was still on the altar. In contrast to the flowers, this dark smoky vessel was hardened in a primitive, wood-fired, *anagama* kiln. Without glaze or ornamentation, it looked as sturdy as it was. Looking up at the tree house, I smiled to see that our indomitable willow was still growing and would have to be pruned.

Mounting the stairs as William and Lisa had done five months before, I could see why Bennett insisted I venture out of the house. The heavy vase, still holding the block of green "oasis" into which was stuck the browned remnants of a deep red wedding display, was now also the home of new growth—young leaves yielding a single tall rose from its midst. In pink.

Walking back to the house, I looked at our first pond. After an especially dry autumn, all the water had, once again, seeped through the Federal Springs Thrust Fault to China. It occurred to me that now was the time I could walk the bottom and find all those marbles I had lost. My effort yielded two white marbles and one golf ball. In pink.

Hybrids appear in the most surprising and delightful ways.

REFERENCES

PART ONE

Chapter 1: The Customs Exchange: Coming In, Going Out

Coming In:

Stephen *Birnbaum Travel Guide* series. edited by Stephen Birnbaum, Alexandra Mayes B. Birnbaum et al. New York: Harper Perennial, 1992. [Birnbaum's Rome, p. 67]

Sansan as told to Bette Lord. *Eighth Moon.* New York: Harper & Row, 1964.

Going Out:

Robert Storey. *Lonely Planet Travel Survival Kit, Taiwan.* Australia. Lonely Planet Publications, 1990. [pp 22-23]

The Random House Dictionary of the English Language. New York: Random House, 1966. [p. 895]

Grimm's Fairy Tales (Specially adapted and arranged for young people). Translated by Mrs. H. B. Paull. New York: Grosset & Dunlap. [p. 93]

Francis L. K Hsu. *Americans and Chinese, Reflections on two cultures and their people.* New York: Doubleday Natural History Press, 1970. [p. 77]

Dr. Benjamin Spock. *Baby and Child Care.* New York: Pocket Books, 1946. [p. 250, 256]

J. L. Austin. *Philosophical Papers.* Oxford: The Clarendon Press, 1961.

Chapter 2: Commonwealth, Common Touch

Commonwealth:

Lewis Thomas. *The Lives of a Cell, Notes of a Biology Watcher.* New York: Bantam Books, Inc., 1974. [p. 6]

Common Touch

Hans Zinsser. *Rats, Lice and History.* Boston: The Atlantic Monthly Press by Little, Brown, and Company, 1935. [pp. 176-7]

Chapter 3: MAMA-HUHU

MAMA:
Richard J. Barnet and Ronald E. Müller. *Global Reach, The Power of the Multinational Corporations.* New York: Simon and Schuster, 1974. [p. 71]

HUHU:
Wang, L. Ling-chi. "Roots and Changing Identity of the Chinese in the United States," *Daedalus*, Vol. 120, No. 2 (Spring 1991), pp 181-206. [p. 205]

Theodora Lau. *The Handbook of Chinese Horoscopes.* New York: Harper & Row, Publishers, 1979.

Craig Claiborne with Pierre Franey. *The New York Times Cookbook.* New York: Times Books, 1975. [p. 553 and p. 573]

Chapter 4: How Do You Say "I Love You" In English? In Chinese? In America?

In English?
Hsiao-Tung Fei. *China's Gentry/Essays in Rural-Urban Relations.* Chicago & London: The University of Chicago Press, 1953. [p. 74]

In Chinese?
Edward T. Hall. *The Silent Language.* Greenwich, Connecticut: Fawcett Publications, 1959. [p. 39]

Chapter 5: Judge And Jury

Judge
Jiqing Hua. "The Story of Tragic Love," *Women in Chinese Folklore.* Beijing: Women of China, 1983. [p. 91]

Mark Elvin. "The Inner World of 1830," *Daedalus*, Vol. 120, No. 2 (Spring 1991), pp. 33-61. [p. 54]

Jury
John Rawls. *A Theory of Justice.* Cambridge, Massachusetts: The Belknap Press of Harvard University, 1971. [p. 55]

Laszlo Matulay. *Bible Stories for Jewish Children*. New York City: Ktav Publishing House,1954.

Chapter 6: Between Past And Future

Hannah Arendt. *Between Past and Future: Six Exercises in Political Thought*. Cleveland and New York: The World Publishing Company, 1954.

Past
Making Connections. Edited by Carol Gilligan, Nona P. Lyons, and Trudy J. Hammer. Cambridge, Massachusetts: Harvard University Press, 1990. [pp. 6, 9-10]

Future
Edwin Way Teale. *A Book About Bees*. Bloomington: Indiana University Press,1940. [p. 20]
Abigail S. Bean. *A Coral Tree*. Coralville, Iowa: Privately Printed, 1981. [p. 39]

PART TWO

General Henry M. Robert. *Robert's Rules of Order Revised*. New York: Morrow Quill Paperbacks, 1979. [pp. 242-3]
Judith Martin. *Miss Manners' Guide to Excruciatingly Correct Behavior*. New York: Warner Books, 1979. [p. 119-20]

Chapter 7: Exercise #1

Jack Kornfield. "Difficult Problems & Insistent Visitors," *Shambhala Sun*, (June 1993).

Chapter 8: Exercise #2

Carol Gilligan. *In A Different Voice*. Cambridge & London: Harvard University Press, 1982.
Carol Gilligan. Conference "On *In A Different Voice*" at the State University of New York at Stony Brook, March 22-4, 1985.
John Gillis. *A World of Their Own Making: Myth, Ritual, and the*

Quest for Family Values. New York: Basic Books, 1996. [p. xv]
   The Sayings of Confucius. Translated by James R. Ware. New York:
The New American Library, 1955. [p. 66]

Chapter 11: Exercise No. 5

Geroge Leonard Herter and Berthe E. Herter. *Bull Cook and
Authentic Historical Recipes and Practices.* Waseca, Minnesota, U.S.A:
Herter's, Inc., 1960. [p. 148]

> Marvin Minsky by email to Cathy Bao Bean, 11/14/01,
> prefaced his remarks, "In my introduction to 'Semantic
> Information Processing' I made some offhand estimates of
> the size of a typical person's body of 'commonsense
> knowledge and suggested that it might be the order of a
> few tens of millions of 'knowledge-units'. Herbert Simon
> once made some estimates about the 'size' of each well-
> developed human skill, such as chess-playing, and con-
> cluded that such a person might know the order of
> 20,000-50,000 (or fewer) 'patterns' to recognize.
> Somewhere else, perhaps in "Society of Mind," I observed
> that human prodigies like Mozart appear to learn never
> more at than just twice the usual speed. (Mozart started
> around age 4, but approached mastery around 12, so that
> took 8 years; other good composers did not take much
> longer, but only Mozart and a few others continued to
> advance much after that.)"

Cathy Bao Bean (www.cathybaobean.com), author of
The Chopsticks-Fork Principle, A Memoir and Manual
and co-author of *The Chopsticks-Fork Principle x 2, A
Bilingual Reader* for ESL and CFL learners, is a daughter,
mother, wife, friend, sister, aerobics instructor, business
manager and President of the Society for Values in Higher
Education (www.svhe.org). In a previous incarnation, she
was a philosophy teacher, cook, student, carpool driver,
and on the Board of Advisors of the Claremont Graduate
University School of the Humanities, on the New Jersey
Council for the Humanities, as well as a founding member
of the Ridge and Valley Conservancy. In the process, she
has been learning how to make the "foreign" more familiar
and the ordinary and extraordinary into each other. None
of it has been painless. All of it has been fun -- except
the cooking.